Humanitarian Intervention and the Responsibility to Protect

This book explores attempts to develop a more acceptable account of the principles and mechanisms associated with humanitarian intervention, which has become known as the "responsibility to protect" (R2P).

Cases of genocide and mass violence have raised endless debates about the theory and practice of humanitarian intervention to save innocent lives. Since the humanitarian tragedies in Rwanda, Burundi, Bosnia, Kosovo and elsewhere, states have begun advocating a right to undertake interventions to stop mass violations of human rights from occurring. Their central concern rests with whether the UN's current regulations on the use of force meet the challenges of the post-Cold War world, and in particular the demands of addressing humanitarian emergencies. International actors tend to agree that killing civilians as a necessary part of state formation is no longer acceptable, nor is standing by idly in the face of massive violations of human rights. And yet, respect for the sovereign rights of states remains central among the ordering principles of the international community. How can populations affected by egregious human rights violations be protected? How can the legal constraints on the use of force and respect for state sovereignty be reconciled with the international community's willingness and readiness to take action in such instances? And more importantly, how can protection be offered when the Security Council, which is responsible for authorizing the use of force when threats to international peace and security occur, is paralyzed? The author addresses these issues, arguing that R2P is the best framework available at present to move the humanitarian intervention debate forward.

This book will be of interest to students of peace and conflict studies, human security, international organizations, security studies and international relations in general.

Cristina Gabriela Badescu teaches peace and conflict studies at the University of Toronto, Canada. Her research interests include international relations, human security, transitional justice, and the responsibility to protect.

Global Politics and the Responsibility to Protect

Series Editors: Alex J. Bellamy
Griffith University
Sara E. Davies
Griffith University
and
Monica Serrano
The City University New York

The aim of this book series is to gather the best new thinking about the responsibility to protect into a core set of volumes that provides a definitive account of the principle, its implementation, and role in crises, that reflects a plurality of views and regional perspectives.

Global Politics and the Responsibility to Protect
From words to deeds
Alex J. Bellamy

The Responsibility to Protect
Norms, laws and international politics
Ramesh Thakur

Humanitarian Intervention and the Responsibility to Protect
Security and human rights
Cristina Gabriela Badescu

Humanitarian Intervention and the Responsibility to Protect

Security and human rights

Cristina Gabriela Badescu

Routledge
Taylor & Francis Group
LONDON AND NEW YORK

First published 2011
by Routledge
2 Park Square, Milton Park, Abingdon, Oxon OX14 4RN

Simultaneously published in the USA and Canada
by Routledge
711 Third Avenue, New York, NY 10017

Routledge is an imprint of the Taylor & Francis Group, an informa business

First issued in paperback 2012

Typeset in Times by Wearset Ltd, Boldon, Tyne and Wear

British Library Cataloguing in Publication Data
A catalogue record for this book is available from the British Library

Library of Congress Cataloging-in-Publication Data
A catalog record has been requested for this book

ISBN13: 978-0-415-58627-6 (hbk)
ISBN13: 978-0-203-83454-1 (ebk)
ISBN13: 978-0-415-53244-0 (pbk)

Contents

Acknowledgments

Attention to the responsibility to protect topic increased exponentially after its UN endorsement in September 2005. In light of the large – and incessantly growing – market on R2P, and especially because of the demand for conceptual clarification regarding its framework, a book on the topic that would go back to basics and consider why the responsibility to protect emerged in the first place seemed necessary. The seed for this book was my Ph.D. dissertation, which focused on the search to develop a more acceptable account of the principles and mechanisms associated with humanitarian intervention. In the past three years, however, I have significantly altered and updated the initial chapters to incorporate the key developments on R2P that occurred since I received my Ph.D. in February 2007.

I am indebted to my colleagues, former supervisors, family, friends, scholars working on the topic, and sponsors for making this study possible. First of all, I am very thankful to my Ph.D. co-supervisors, Elizabeth Riddell-Dixon and Richard Vernon, for their feedback, invariable support, and guidance through a different version of this project. I am also grateful to my post-doctoral supervisors, Janice Stein and Robert Matthews, for their encouraging words, thoughtful comments, and helpful discussions while I was revising the book manuscript. I am indebted for the opportunities and funding that have been provided to me during my Ph.D. and post-doctoral years, which funded my trips to conduct interviews in Ottawa, New York, and Washington, DC. The Canadian Consortium on Human Security doctoral fellowship, and the Social Sciences and Humanities Research Council of Canada doctoral and post-doctoral fellowships have been particularly helpful in this context. The interviews with representatives from civil society groups, the United Nations, US and Canadian government officials, individual country missions at the UN, and discussions with scholars working on the topic provided me with a variety of perspectives on the political dynamics surrounding R2P. I owe special thanks to the UN officials from the Department of Political Affairs, the UNHCR, Legal Affairs, DPKO, and OCHA, who kindly made time for confidential interviews, which comprised many discussions on the various implications R2P might have for the work of their respective departments and agencies. Such conversations have helped me grasp the complexities of humanitarian endeavors in general, and more specifically, of the calls to protect civilians and implement the R2P agenda. Also, I am especially appreciative of the suggestions and conversations with Victoria Holt, Heidi Hulan, Elissa Golberg, and Bruce Jones, who were very generous in taking the time to answer my questions in the incipient stages of this project.

I was privileged to obtain feedback, information, and advice from several key people actively involved in the emergence and advancement of the R2P framework. Thomas G. Weiss shared his deep knowledge of R2P, and provided helpful guidance on this book project during the academic year 2008–2009, which I spent as a visiting research fellow at the Ralph Bunche Institute for International Studies at the City University of New York's Graduate Center. Tom read some of my work and offered very helpful suggestions on how to improve it. It was actually his writing on humanitarian intervention, together with Nicholas Wheeler's *Saving Strangers*, that first made me interested in the topic, and so I felt honoured to work with Tom on a collaborative journal article during my stay in New York. I have also benefited from Ramesh Thakur's valuable comments, guidance and extremely useful suggestions that forced me to refine many issues, particularly at two key stages of reorganizing my book chapters. Furthermore, I am very grateful to Gareth Evans for taking the time from his very busy schedule to cover the many questions I had on the various facets of R2P, and for sharing his vision, insightfulness and R2P-related expertise with me. Similarly, Edward Luck has been extremely accommodating in taking the time to meet with me and discuss the various efforts to build consensus on R2P at the UN and among member states, especially in preparation of the July 2009 UN debate on the topic. I am also thankful to Don Hubert for sharing valuable knowledge and advice at earlier stages of this study, which were reflected in my Ph.D. dissertation, but also in regards to subsequent refinements and changes I presented during our ISA panels in 2008 and 2009. Allan Rock also generously took the time earlier this year to answer in detail my questions on R2P with respect to the period when he was Canada's Permanent Representative to the UN.

I am very grateful to Alex Bellamy, who has offered suggestions to make the manuscript better and provided encouragement for such a book project from our very first chat on the topic at the 2007 conference of the Peace and Conflict Studies Program at the University of Toronto. Paul Williams has also provided helpful comments on several arguments in the book, which were introduced, among others, in two papers presented at the 2008 and 2009 ISA conferences. During the academic year spent at the Ralph Bunche Institute for International Studies updating and refining the key arguments of this book, I have benefited greatly from the many conversations with the Global Centre for the Responsibility to Protect (GCR2P) team: Mónica Serrano, Nicole Deller, Diego Dewar, Naomi Kikoler, Nicola Reindorp, and James Traub. I am grateful to all, but especially to Mónica for our discussions providing helpful suggestions and comments that pushed me to think through the implications of some of my central arguments. Also, I am much indebted to Naomi who patiently read several of this book's chapters and provided me with constructive comments. Sapna Chhatpar from the International Coalition for the Responsibility to Protect (ICRtoP) has kindly shared information on the ICRtoP's efforts to consolidate support for R2P. I have also benefited from the comments and insights of academic colleagues, such as Linnea Bergholm, with whom I have collaborated on several projects. Furthermore, I am grateful to the small but wonderful administrative team from the Ralph Bunche Institute who made my stay there as visiting research fellow so pleasant. Once I returned to the University of Toronto, Jutta Brunnée patiently answered my questions on the legal dimensions of R2P, and I am thankful for her time. All these people have influenced the views expressed in this book, and the discussion of R2P's prospects for implementation.

At Routledge, I am thankful to Andrew Humphrys for finding the proposal of this book interesting in the first place, and to Rebecca Brennan for her patience throughout our communications until this book moved to the production stage. I would also like to thank the reviewers for their insightful suggestions and very helpful comments.

Some of the material in this book was revised from pieces that I had published elsewhere. Chapter 2 is a revised version of "'The Responsibility to Protect': Embracing Sovereignty *and* Human Rights," in Noha Shawki and Michaelene Cox (eds), *Negotiating Sovereignty and Human Rights: Actors and Issues in Contemporary Human Rights Politics* (Farnham: Ashgate, 2009). I would like to thank Ashgate for granting me permission to reprint portions of this chapter. Chapter 3 is a refined version of "Authorizing Humanitarian Intervention: Hard Choices in Saving Strangers," *Canadian Journal of Political Science*, vol. 40, no. 1 (2007). I am thankful to Cambridge for allowing the reprint of this earlier version of what is now Chapter 3. One section in Chapter 6, namely "Cases where R2P was considered," includes some elements from an article co-authored with Thomas Weiss: "Misrepresenting R2P and Advancing Norms: An Alternative Spiral?," *International Studies Perspectives*, vol. 11, no. 4 (2010).

Finally, I want to thank my family for their support. To my parents, Sabina and Puiu, I owe everything. They are wonderful human beings, who have constantly provided encouragement and a comforting source of listening ears all the way through. And the utmost gratitude goes to my husband, Andrei. Andrei is a brilliant science scholar, who somehow tolerated a neverending series of late nights and weekends I have spent exclusively "working on the book." He put up with my withdrawal from any residue of normal domestic life and accepted that complete isolation with my laptop and chapters – for a long time – was what I needed to finish this book. He also showed tremendous patience in the face of the grumpiness that comes with undertaking such an exercise. And all these, for a topic he jokingly referred to as the little droid R2-D2 from *Star Wars*. It is with great appreciation that I dedicate this book to Andrei.

Abbreviations

AMIB	African Mission in Burundi
AMIS	African Union Mission in the Sudan
AMISOM	African Union Mission to Somalia
ASEAN	Association of South East Asian Nations
ASF	African Standby Force (AU)
AU	African Union
CFR	Council on Foreign Relations
DPKO	Department of Peacekeeping Operations (UN)
DRC	Democratic Republic of the Congo
ECHR	European Convention for the Protection of Human Rights and Fundamental Freedoms
ECOMOG	ECOWAS Monitoring Group
ECOWAS	Economic Community of West African States
ESF	ECOWAS Standby Force
EU	European Union
EUFOR RD	European Union Reserve Deployment (DRC)
GCR2P	Global Centre for the Responsibility to Protect
G77	Group of 77
HLP	High-Level Panel on Threats, Challenges and Change (UN)
HRC	Human Rights Council
ICC	International Criminal Court
ICCPR	International Covenant on Civil and Political Rights
ICESCR	International Covenant on Economic, Social and Cultural Rights
ICG	International Crisis Group
ICISS	International Commission on Intervention and State Sovereignty
ICRC	International Committee of the Red Cross
ICRtoP	International Coalition for the Responsibility to Protect
IDP	Internally Displaced Person
IFOR	Implementation Force (in Bosnia and Herzegovina)
KFOR	Kosovo Force (NATO Mission in Kosovo)
MINURCAT	United Nations Mission in Central African Republic and Chad

MONUC	United Nations Organization Mission in the Democratic Republic of the Congo (Mission des Nations Unies en République Démocratique du Congo)
MSF	Médecins sans Frontières (Doctors without Borders)
NAM	Non-Aligned Movement
NATO	North Atlantic Treaty Organization
NGO	Non-Governmental Organization
NRF	NATO Response Force
OAS	Organization of American States
OAU	Organization of African Unity
OCHA	Office for the Coordination of Humanitarian Affairs (UN)
OHCHR	Office of the High Commissioner for Human Rights (UN)
ONUB	United Nations Operation in Burundi (Opération des Nations Unies au Burundi)
OSCE	Organization of Security and Cooperation in Europe
P5	Permanent Five Members of the UN Security Council
R2P	Responsibility to Protect
SADC	Southern African Development Community
SFOR	Stabilization Force (in Bosnia and Herzegovina)
SHIRBRIG	Stand-by High Readiness Brigade
UDHR	Universal Declaration of Human Rights
UK	United Kingdom
UN	United Nations
UNAMID	United Nations/African Union Mission in Darfur
UNAMIR	United Nations Assistance Mission for Rwanda
UNAMSIL	United Nations Mission in Sierra Leone
UNMIS	United Nations Mission in Sudan
UNOCI	United Nations Operation in Côte d'Ivoire
US	United States
WFM–IGP	World Federalist Movement – Institute for Global Policy

1 Introduction

Humanitarian intervention and the responsibility to protect

Beginning in April 1994 and lasting for ninety days, Tutsis and moderate Hutus became the victims of a systematic genocidal campaign that resulted in 800,000 deaths in Rwanda. In July 1995, with United Nations (UN) peacekeepers present, 8,000 Bosnian men and boys were massacred in the safe haven of Srebrenica over a few days. In March 1999, the North Atlantic Treaty Organization (NATO) started a bombing campaign against the former Federal Republic of Yugoslavia to protect the Albanian population in Kosovo from being ethnically cleansed. While the first two examples epitomize the lack of reaction in the face of atrocities, NATO's military action in Kosovo was portrayed as illegal. NATO's actions were morally justified yet violated international law, as the UN Security Council had not authorized the military intervention. The above examples of intra-state violence illustrate unimaginable humanitarian consequences resulting from conflicts brought by the end of the Cold War. The horrors of the twentieth century, however, go beyond the mass killings of the 1990s, as suggested by the Holocaust during World War II, and the killing fields of Cambodia during the tyrannical Khmer Rouge rule, when up to two million people were slaughtered between 1975 and 1979. These horrors were not confined to the less developed parts of the world, but affected both North and South. However, an agreed normative foundation for dealing with such crises seemed to be missing.

The humanitarian intervention conundrum

Cases of genocide and mass violence have raised endless debates about the theory and practice of humanitarian intervention to save innocent lives. Since the UN proved itself unable to react in an appropriate and prompt manner to halt the humanitarian tragedies in Rwanda, Burundi, Bosnia, Kosovo and elsewhere, states have begun advocating a right to undertake interventions to stop mass violations of human rights from occurring. Their central concern rests with whether the UN's current regulations on the use of force meet the challenges of the post-Cold War world, and in particular the demands of addressing humanitarian emergencies. International actors tend to agree that killing civilians as a necessary part of state formation is no longer acceptable, nor is standing by idly in the face of massive violations of human rights. And yet, respect for the sovereign rights of states remains central among the ordering principles of the international community. How can populations affected by egregious human rights violations be protected? How can the legal constraints on the use of force and respect for state sovereignty be reconciled with the international community's willingness and readiness to take action in such instances? And more importantly, how can protection be offered when the Security Council, which is responsible for authorizing the use of force when threats to international peace and security occur, is paralyzed? Despite many competing proposals and contentious debates, can a prescriptive framework be developed to tackle such concerns? These questions are addressed in this book.

Although humanitarian intervention is believed to be a rather recent phenomenon, its earlier manifestations date back to the nineteenth century. The changes of the international system have impacted the practice of humanitarian intervention over the course of history, with distinctive patterns characterizing interventions in the nineteenth century, the post-UN Charter era, and the more recent post-Cold War period.[1] Until recently, the topic of humanitarian intervention occupied center stage in academic discussions. The concept of military intervention for humanitarian purposes has been one of the most divisive topics in international relations, especially in the post-9/11 environment and even more so in the aftermath of the 2003 invasion of Iraq. The language of morality, law and politics framed its contentious dimensions. Lawyers, international relations theorists, philosophers, and policy makers alike have addressed the dilemmas of humanitarian intervention[2] from a variety of approaches. Discussions on whether there is a legal right of humanitarian intervention, on how to address ethical considerations and what morality requires, and on the practical dilemmas related to the politics of intervention abound in the relevant literature.

Despite extensive consideration, no consensus was reached on the principles governing humanitarian intervention. To its proponents, intervention simply signals the imperative of action in the face of mass violence and is intertwined with a perception of sovereignty as conditional to a state's respect for the human rights of its citizens. To its detractors, humanitarian intervention is an oxymoron that serves as a pretext for selective military intervention without legal sanctioning, and an exercise that only achieves uncertain results. Throughout the 1990s controversy reigned – particularly over Rwanda, Somalia, Bosnia and Kosovo – between supporters of a right of humanitarian intervention and those who argued that state sovereignty precluded any intervention in the internal matters of a state where egregious human rights violations took place.

At the 54th session of the UN General Assembly in 1999, Kofi Annan, then UN Secretary-General, challenged member states to prevent "another Rwanda" and to reach consensus on the issue of humanitarian intervention. This moment was soon dubbed by commentators as the trigger for the search to produce a new prescriptive framework for the contentious humanitarian intervention debate. The response to this question was the creation of the responsibility to protect, hereafter referred to by its acronym, R2P.[3] This innovation signals a potential breakthrough to the age-old debate. This book focuses on the contributions made by R2P to the debate on intervention.

In response to Kofi Annan's challenge, the Canadian government established the International Commission on Intervention and State Sovereignty (ICISS) in 2000 to address the quest of solving the humanitarian intervention conundrum. The Commission was launched in September 2000, and was chaired by the former Australian foreign minister, Gareth Evans, and one of the UN Secretary-General's special advisers at the time, Mohamed Sahnoun. The ICISS issued its ninety-page report, "The Responsibility to Protect," in December 2001, together with a 400-page supplementary volume under the same title, by Thomas Weiss and Don Hubert, detailing the background research on the topic. Despite being established by the Canadian government, the ICISS was an independent commission, whose report reflected its balance in composition, its innovative character, comprehensiveness, and outreach.[4] The concept of R2P was then endorsed in the 2004 report of the UN High-Level Panel entitled "A More Secure World: Our Shared Responsibility," and in the 2005 report of the former UN Secretary-General, "In Larger Freedom." Its most significant normative advance came in September 2005, when heads of state and government supported R2P in paragraphs 138 and 139 of the World Summit Outcome Document. The UN Security Council made specific references to R2P on three occasions: in two resolutions on the protection of civilians in armed conflict, namely resolution 1674 of April 2006 and resolution 1894 of November 2009, and in the August 2006 resolution 1706 on Darfur, which was the first to link R2P to a particular conflict. UN Secretary-General Ban Ki-moon appointed a special adviser tasked with promoting R2P, Edward Luck, and released his own report in January 2009 suggestively entitled "Implementing the Responsibility to Protect."

The responsibility to protect framework

R2P provides a prescriptive framework to further the discourse beyond the controversial use of force for humanitarian purposes, to addressing the protection of mass atrocity victims. As R2P emerged from the quest to solve the intervention conundrum, its recommendations address many of the contentious issues raised by the concept of humanitarian intervention. This book will assess the extent to which such recommendations bring consensus to some of the most controversial questions on intervention. Equally important, R2P has been described as "the most dramatic normative development of our time" (Thakur and Weiss 2009: 22). The attention to the topic among academics and practitioners increased exponentially after the world leaders' endorsement of R2P at the UN in September 2005, which had a genuine impact on the humanitarian intervention debate.

The political evolution of R2P deserves a brief description to pinpoint the key steps in its normative trajectory and also the elements that capture its transformation from the framework proposed in the 2001 ICISS report to its representation in 2009, in the report of the UN Secretary-General and the General Assembly debate on the topic. As expected, however, its central normative tenet has remained a constant throughout its progression: state sovereignty entails responsibility and, therefore, each state has a responsibility to protect its citizens from mass killings and other gross violations of their rights. If that state is unable or unwilling to carry out that function, the state abrogates its sovereignty, and the responsibility to protect falls to the international community. Two aspects of the R2P framework are, thus, key: state sovereignty as responsibility, and international responsibility in egregious circumstances. The 2001 report put forward three components of the broader responsibility to protect umbrella, namely the responsibility to prevent, the responsibility to react and the responsibility to rebuild. The report includes separate chapters on the need to prevent gross violations of human rights from arising, the responsibility to react to them when they occur, and the responsibility to rebuild after any military intervention.

Given the goal of this study to assess R2P's contributions to the humanitarian intervention debate, the responsibility to react is the focus in subsequent analysis. It is this component that has come to be broadly equated with R2P, especially since its endorsement under "the international responsibility to take collective action" format in the UN Summit Outcome Document of September 2005. This is not to say that the other two elements identified by the ICISS report as essential components of the R2P agenda – prevention and post-conflict rebuilding – are less attainable or valuable; they are equally important, as recently acknowledged in UN and regional forums. Rather, the recommendations regarding the reaction component of R2P provide the material to assess this norm's theoretical potential to solve the contentiousness of the humanitarian intervention debate.

One of the major contributions of R2P to the intervention debate is conceptual. The novelty came from the way in which the ICISS posed the underlying question of the report to the countries opposing the basic tenets of the humanitarian intervention model: If humanitarian intervention was not an acceptable answer, then what would such countries envision if the international community was faced with another Rwanda? R2P shaped itself as the answer to this question. The ICISS report changed the language of "humanitarian intervention" with "responsibility to protect," in order to move away from the impasse reached by the "right to intervene" debate. In correlation, the focus also moved from the prospective interveners to the civilians in need of protection. This occurred in a context in which broader security concepts were shifting from national to human security. The ICISS report tackled the widening gap between the codified practice of international behavior captured in the UN Charter by the explicit emphasis on the need to respect state sovereignty, on the one hand, and actual state practice during the 1990s, which underlined the limits of sovereignty and the need to protect human rights, on the other (2001: 15).

The reinterpretation of sovereignty, portrayed in terms of responsibility rather than control, is another major facet of the ICISS report. The revolutionary formulation of "sovereignty as responsibility" Francis Deng initially proposed in relation to the protection of internally displaced populations served as inspiration for the Commission, although this aspect was not formally acknowledged in the

ICISS report. Deng's own work on internal displacement from the late 1980s, together with Roberta Cohen's emphasis on the internal dimension of protection, while depicting sovereignty as implying "a responsibility on the part of governments to protect their citizens," mark the origins behind the ICISS representation of R2P (e.g. Cohen 1991; Deng and Zartman 1991; Deng 1993, 1995). This formulation also helped to make R2P more acceptable to strong adherents of sovereignty and nonintervention.

The R2P framework addresses the "moral imbalance" between sovereignty and human rights, and suggests that approaching sovereignty as responsibility answers this moral inadequacy. Essentially, the right to interfere in a state where extreme violations of human rights are taking place comes from the failure of that state to meet its responsibilities as a sovereign member of the international community. The conditions to be satisfied before the most coercive form of reaction – military intervention – takes place represent another key element of the ICISS report. The commission sets the bar very high in terms of thresholds for humanitarian intervention:

> A. large scale loss of life, actual or apprehended, with genocidal intent or not, which is the product of either deliberate state action, or state neglect or inability to act, or a failed state situation; or B. large scale 'ethnic cleansing', actual or apprehended, whether carried out by killing, forced expulsion, acts of terror or rape.
>
> (2001: xii)

The report also proposes five criteria of legitimacy, as a set of benchmarks for reaching consensus in any particular case requiring intervention. Although not novel – but molded after Saint Augustine's Just War doctrine of the 400s – the criteria of legitimacy could have been further refined to address modern conflicts and to make it into subsequent R2P formulations at the UN, to prevent abuse.[5] They were not. Evidently, criteria cannot guarantee reaction. Apart from the legitimacy criteria, the sixth condition relates to legality and depicts the right authority for any intervention. The ICISS recommends that UN Security Council authorization needs to be sought prior to the use of force. However, there are two alternatives if authorization fails in a case "crying out for action," namely the UN General Assembly holding an emergency session under the "Uniting for Peace" procedure, and regional organizations opting for Chapter VIII of the UN Charter.

Despite being eclipsed by the events of 11 September 2001 and the war on terror, R2P managed to survive with the help of norm entrepreneurs like the former UN Secretary-General Kofi Annan who played an important role in keeping it on the UN agenda after the release of the ICISS report. One key exercise was the endorsement of R2P in the report of the High-Level Panel on Threats, Challenges and Change (HLP), as "an emerging norm … [establishing] a collective international responsibility to protect" (United Nations 2004a: paras 65–66). Apart from proposing that the UN adopt the emerging norm of R2P, the

HLP also recommended that guidelines governing the use of force be adopted by the UN General Assembly and the Security Council, closely paralleling those proposed in the ICISS report. The HLP report departed from the R2P recommendations in its omission to discuss what happens in instances where the Security Council is unable or unwilling to act. Still, the proposition that the Security Council has the authority and also the responsibility to use force preventively to maintain international peace and security was an innovation in the HLP report. The High-Level Panel report informed the work of the former UN Secretary-General, Kofi Annan, who was asked to submit to the General Assembly his recommendations for the agenda of the 2005 Summit.

Annan's report talked about the need to "embrace the responsibility to protect, and, when necessary, [to] ... act on it" (2005a: para. 135). If a state fails to protect its citizens, the international community must apply a range of peaceful diplomatic and humanitarian measures, with force to be employed only as a last resort. The report of the UN Secretary-General departed in one significant way from the HLP recommendations. This departure had an important impact on governmental acceptance of R2P later on. The HLP considered R2P a subset of its discussion of "Collective Security and the Use of Force," including it under "Using Force: Rules and Guidelines" (United Nations 2004a: paras 183–209). As such, many governments viewed the HLP's recommendations on R2P as resuscitating the humanitarian intervention debate and reconfirming an unlawful interference in the internal affairs of sovereign states. In contrast, the former UN Secretary-General's report, "In Larger Freedom," separated the normative aspects of R2P (the assertion of the responsibility to protect as a basis for collective action) from the discussion of the use of force.

Few expected R2P to be among the issues discussed in the 2005 Summit Outcome Document, in spite of Annan's support for it. And yet, R2P made it into the final Outcome Document. In relation to key landmarks of the twentieth century, R2P inclusion occurred approximately ten years after the failures to react to the horrors of Rwanda and Srebrenica, thirty years after the Cambodian killing fields, and sixty years after the liberation of the Holocaust Nazi death camps, when the "never again" dictum was born. September 2005 was a defining moment in the normative evolution of the responsibility to protect. It marked the first time R2P was endorsed in a universal forum, with all UN member states unanimously accepting their responsibility to protect their own populations from genocide, war crimes, ethnic cleansing and crimes against humanity. As a result of a compromise to obtain the consent of concerned states, the final text of the Summit Outcome Document was weaker than the text of the ICISS report and those of the High-Level Panel (2004a) and the former UN Secretary-General (Annan 2005a). However, the language was sufficiently strong to express endorsement for a new set of principles on national and international responsibility.

The two paragraphs referring to R2P in the Summit Outcome Document, namely paragraphs 138 and 139, explicitly state that there is not only a state responsibility to protect its population but also a subsidiary responsibility for the international community. These paragraphs express a willingness to act when agreed thresholds take place, however, the "sovereignty as responsibility" argument could have been more clearly stated. The responsibility to protect framework as adopted by the General Assembly is different from that originally envisioned by the ICISS. As expected in this format, the references to R2P neither reintroduce criteria for the use of force into the UN regime nor recognize legality for armed humanitarian intervention outside the use of force regime established by the UN Charter. However, there is no doubt that the adoption of R2P represents an ideological and normative shift which affects the way in which states' responsibilities, as set forth in the UN Charter, are implemented. Given the history of the debates on humanitarian intervention, R2P's inclusion in the Summit's Outcome Document is significant. Indeed, this marked R2P's most important normative advance to date.

The UN Security Council has referred to R2P in three resolutions since then. On 28 April 2006, resolution 1674 on the protection of civilians in armed conflict "reaffirms the provisions of paragraphs 138 and 139 of the World Summit Outcome Document regarding the responsibility to protect populations from genocide, war crimes, ethnic cleansing and crimes against humanity." This is the first official Security Council reference to the responsibility to protect. For the normative development of R2P, the significance is that this is legally binding, unlike all its previous incarnations. R2P was further promoted by its reference in relation to specific conflicts. On 31 August 2006, the Security Council passed resolution 1706 that demanded a rapid deployment of UN peacekeepers in Sudan. This resolution made explicit reference to R2P, by reaffirming the provisions on R2P from resolution 1674 and from paragraphs 138 and 139 of the 2005 World Summit Outcome Document. Resolution 1894 passed in November 2009 was the last one, to date, to reaffirm the provisions on R2P included in the 2005 Outcome Document.

The next highlight that brought fresh momentum to R2P occurred in 2008, when the UN Secretary-General, Ban Ki-moon, declared his personal commitment to turning R2P into reality in a July 2008 speech in Berlin. It was in this speech that he first exposed the new portrayal of R2P as "a three-pillar approach." Also in 2008, Ban Ki-moon appointed his special adviser on issues related to R2P, Edward Luck, whom he tasked with the conceptual development of R2P and a report on the topic, in addition to building consensus on R2P among UN member states. The report of the UN Secretary-General, "Implementing the Responsibility to Protect," was released in January 2009. It details the representation of R2P along three pillars: the protection responsibilities of the state; the responsibility of the international community to assist states in fulfilling their national obligations; and the commitment to timely and decisive collective action consistent with the UN Charter. The three pillars are equal in terms of size, strength and viability. Equally significant, the report argues that there is no sequence for implementation to be followed from one pillar to another (United Nations 2009a: 2).

The report's view on R2P is narrow by maintaining the focus of its application to the four crimes identified in the Summit Outcome Document, namely genocide, war crimes, ethnic cleansing, and crimes against humanity. In light of arguments made in the Security Council to oppose intervention in Darfur, some expressed concern that the "primary responsibility" of the state to protect its population may be used as a pretext to discourage military intervention (e.g. Stahn 2007: 116–117). While the General Assembly did not include the criteria on the use of force previously suggested in the reports by the ICISS, the High-Level Panel and the former Secretary-General, the 2009 report "Implementing the Responsibility to Protect" restated Ban Ki-moon's recommendation that such criteria be considered (United Nations 2009a: para. 62).

The three-pillar approach to the responsibility to protect drew from its previous representations starting with the ICISS report, but was fundamentally defined by the provisions of paragraphs 138 and 139 of the 2005 Summit Outcome Document. The premise of this report was that in order to make R2P a reality it was paramount not to reinterpret or renegotiate the conclusions of the World Summit Document on R2P. Instead, finding ways to implement consistently the provisions of paragraphs 138 and 139 was needed, since they "are firmly anchored in well-established principles of international law" (ibid.: para. 3). The importance of this portrayal of R2P emanates from the fact that the 2009 report does not retreat from the principles adopted in September 2005. Instead, it constructively elaborates on what states need in order to offer protection, what other actors could do to assist them, and on the prevention, reaction and rebuilding measures that could be employed if a state is unwilling or unable to offer protection or receive assistance in this sense. Specifically with respect to the use of force, the focus of the discourse changed significantly from that in the ICISS report. That is, for political reasons, the report downplayed intervention, which moved from the headlines in the ICISS report to an afterthought in the Secretary-General's report, namely a "possibility … in extreme cases" (ibid.: para. 56).

Between January 2009, when the UN Secretary-General's report on R2P was released, and July 2009, when the General Assembly debate on R2P took place, fears of a potentially negative outcome of the debate loomed. The reasons had to do with the strong resistance from the President of the UN General Assembly at the time, Father Miguel D'Escoto Brockman from Nicaragua, and a few very vocal skeptical states, including Venezuela, Egypt, Sudan, Pakistan, and Syria, trying to mobilize disagreement with R2P principles among other members of the Non-Aligned Movement. However, a close reading of the remarks of the 92 countries and 2 observers who addressed the plenary showed faint support for undermining R2P. Only Venezuela, Cuba, Sudan and Nicaragua directly questioned the 2005 World Summit agreement and attempted to roll back R2P. Of special relevance were remarks from major regional powers that had previously been reticent or hostile to R2P, including India, Brazil, Nigeria, and Japan. Despite disagreement and contestation, the General Assembly debate over three days in late July 2009 showed governmental support for implementing the September 2005 consensus. There was broad consensus among member states that R2P was not open for renegotiation. The plenary debate on R2P represents the latest significant step to date in R2P's normative trajectory. It allowed for constructive dialogue among UN member states that helped refine R2P. It also confirmed that states felt bound by their previous political commitments to R2P. The General Assembly adopted a procedural resolution in September 2009 calling for continued consideration of the issue, which validates the fact that R2P is at the beginning of a slow-moving normative process.

Conceptual concerns

Agreeing on a definition of humanitarian intervention is in itself a challenge. There is usually disagreement over whether the action is limited to instances without consent from the host state, or when authorization comes solely from the UN Security Council. More recently, interventions that initially began as military operations with political goals and later developed into humanitarian emergencies have blurred the clarity of the concept. There is a tendency to regard today's emergencies as a blend of humanitarian impulses coupled with more complex political objectives, which, by comparison, make interventions in the 1990s appear as "nostalgic reminders of a simpler, gentler age" (Urquhart in Weiss 2005a: xix). Conflicts nowadays are progressively more deadly and require rapidly deployable forces with the authority, political will and capacity to act to stop the violence. Traditional peacekeeping operations have become less prevalent, as the UN is increasingly facing complex humanitarian crises in which there is no peace to keep.

The definition of humanitarian intervention used in this study is the use of armed force[6] by either a state, a group of states, or an international organization to address widespread suffering or death among civilians in another state affected by grave violations of human rights. The literature on humanitarian intervention has been primarily concerned with the legal and ethical debates associated with the topic (e.g. Walzer 1977, 2000; Laberge 1995; Welsh 2002; Chatterjee and Scheid 2003; Lang 2003a). Others have acknowledged, however, that political dilemmas deserve the same level of attention, given the deep connection between law and politics, and especially since most questions related to intervention involve a political decision (e.g. Abbott and Snidal 2000; Farer 2003; Weiss 2003; Rochester 2006; Thakur 2006; Heinze 2009).

Three themes in particular seem to reoccur in all debates on humanitarian intervention, each combining moral, legal, and political considerations. They shape the focus of the first part of the book, which looks at the theoretical contribution of R2P to the humanitarian intervention debate. These themes emerge as the most contentious, but also the most relevant ones for the state of the debate on intervention: How can the alleged conflict between the norms of sovereignty and nonintervention, and the norms demanding respect for human rights be reconciled so that humanitarian intervention becomes permissible? What is the right authorization for humanitarian intervention? Who has the military capacity required to actually translate an authorized humanitarian intervention into practice? The broader theoretical question in this context becomes: What would be the best approach to move the debate on intervention out of the impasse it has reached, within a framework that integrates legal, ethical and political perspectives?

Before proceeding with answering this question, an important distinction relates to clarifying the relationship between R2P and humanitarian intervention. Misunderstandings about the association of the two are not only evident at the level of scholarly exchanges on the topic, but also among governments and policy makers. Failures to comprehend this relationship correctly – either disingenuous and geopolitically driven, or disinterested but wrong – often make the news. The 2003 invasion of Iraq and the Russian–Georgian war in August 2008 over South Ossetia are examples in point. Indeed, the ICISS report was interested mainly in reconciling sovereignty and the need to protect from gross human rights violations with an emphasis on humanitarian intervention versus the prevention and rebuilding aspects of R2P. The report dedicated thirty-two pages to the question of intervention versus 16 pages to both the responsibility to prevent and rebuilding.

Despite the obvious initial emphasis on intervention, R2P does propose a continuum of measures to respond to conflicts responsible for mass killings, which includes prevention, reaction and post-conflict rebuilding. The Commission itself described prevention as "the single most important dimension" of R2P (ICISS 2001: xi), with subsequent analyses from scholars and representations at the UN emphasizing the same dimension (e.g. Bellamy 2009; United Nations 2009a). The development of early warning mechanisms to respond to conflicts in a decisive and timely manner is an important component of R2P. The humanitarian intervention approach can only be discussed in relation to one of the three key forms R2P takes, namely reaction. Even within the reaction aspect, humanitarian intervention speaks only to the most extreme measures to address conflict situations, implying the use of force in extremis. The format in which R2P was institutionalized in the 2005 UN Summit Outcome Document portrays the commitment UN member states made to protect their own citizens from genocide, crimes against humanity, war crimes, and ethnic cleansing, and, as members of the international community, to assist other states in providing protection. Military intervention is thus solely a last resort option, and only in regard to the latter commitment. The distinction between R2P and humanitarian intervention has been emphasized in all R2P formulations between 2001 and 2009. And yet, some scholars writing on the topic treat humanitarian intervention and R2P as synonymous (e.g. Kuperman 2008).

Confusion in academic literature furthers the negative effect of portraying R2P as a more sophisticated legitimization mechanism for intervention. The practical reverberations of such scholarly confusions were witnessed in the language used by governments to defend their actions in recent crises, emphasizing the importance of achieving conceptual clarity on the topic. The election-related crisis in Zimbabwe and the distribution of humanitarian assistance in Burma in the wake of Cyclone Nargis – both occurring in 2008 – illustrate the misunderstanding about what R2P entails. The need for a state to justify its actions by employing the R2P language, as was the case with the Russian misuse of terminology to explain its military endeavor in Georgia, demonstrates the importance of R2P as a new normative framework to address humanitarian crises. Once this framework was embraced in international fora, the unresolved debate over *whether* to act, which used to dominate the intervention approach, was soon replaced by a conversation about *how* and *when* to act to protect.

Any fundamental question on a unified theory of humanitarian intervention necessitates a systematical assessment of the normative development of R2P to determine its potential to change state practice and influence civilian protection. It is in this context that R2P can make a positive contribution to the humanitarian intervention debate. Clarifying the status R2P reached after passing through the stages of concept, principle, and finally emerging norm also influences the discourse. Moreover, the importance of this conceptual distinction springs from determining whether R2P alters the meaning of sovereignty or works with the existing parameters of nonintervention norms. The language of nascent norm, rather than concept or principle, is used throughout this book, as it best captures the stage R2P has reached and how it is currently portrayed in the international discourse.

R2P started as an idea in the ICISS report, and was perceived as a concept in the immediate aftermath of the report's release. It quickly moved to the status of principle close to its adoption at the 2005 World Summit, once states accepted its content and pledged to act in accordance with its recommendations. For a concept originating in a report its normative progress was very impressive. No idea has moved faster in the international arena (e.g. Thakur and Weiss 2009: 23). September 2005 was the defining moment in R2P's normative trajectory, described by some as a "profound shift in international law" (Tuner cited in Pace and Deller 2005: 27) that carried the potential for significant change in the notoriously difficult area of the law on the use of force (Brunnée and Toope 2006: 3). The subsequent references to R2P in Security Council resolutions also propelled it from the status of a principle to that of an emerging norm. To gain universal respect, as in the case of the norm prohibiting torture, a long normative process is expected. The consolidation of R2P through practice versus rhetorical reference is of course needed at this point, but the *opinio juris* necessary for customary law to be formed already acknowledges that innocent civilians cannot be left to die in the four types of crimes R2P addresses.

Another important distinction is between R2P and the protection of civilians. While R2P is broadly about protecting civilians and is explicitly invoked in relation to calls for protection in such conflicts as Darfur and Sri Lanka, there are important differences between the two agendas.

Since R2P was embraced at the UN level, diplomats and policy makers have warned against the dangers of intertwining R2P with the "protection of civilians" agenda, mainly because this might translate into an unnecessary politicization of the concept of civilian protection (Security Council Report 2008: 4). The protection agenda is more broadly defined than the R2P framework. It covers measures meant to protect the dignity and safety of individuals under threats of violence, while R2P refers to the need to protect civilians facing mass atrocities, such as genocide, war crimes, ethnic cleansing and crimes against humanity.

R2P and the protection of civilians agenda are based on international humanitarian law and human rights law, and they are both focused on the protection of individuals. Both the R2P and the civilian protection frameworks recognize the primary responsibility of states to protect their own populations. Furthermore, neither of the two agendas should be understood as tantamount to the use of military force. Indeed, only in the most extreme cases is the use of force with a Chapter VII mandate envisaged. Also, the successful implementation of R2P towards civilian protection is contingent upon several conditions occurring at the same time. These include the existence of one of the four types of mass atrocities triggering R2P, a willingness on the part of contributing states to risk their soldiers' lives to "protect strangers," appropriate training and doctrine to address the specific requirements of non-permissive conflict environments, and sufficient and reliable capabilities to react.

A related source of confusion involves operations launched specifically to halt mass atrocities and genocide, as might be required under the R2P framework, and peacekeeping missions. Most contemporary peacekeeping operations are placed under the UN flag, presume conditions such as a pre-existing "peace to keep" and the consent of the parties for the deployment of forces, anticipate the enforcement of a political agreement, and expect a functional government or a transition to one. While blue helmets are not engaged in armed conflict as agents of humanitarian intervention can be, peace operations with mandates to protect populations physically may face significant violence growing to extreme levels. Civilians usually come under direct attack in such instances, and using deadly force might be required. Enforcement operations are most often carried out by individual states under the authorization of the UN Security Council. An intervention to prevent or stop mass atrocities falls between peacekeeping operations, which might include more robust Chapter VII UN missions, and traditional military operations. Using force to stop the conflict and provide physical protection to the targeted population can thus pose conceptual, operational, and political challenges distinct from the requirements and characteristics of the more traditional peacekeeping operations.

Overview and organization

This book is about the search to develop a more acceptable account of the principles and mechanisms associated with humanitarian intervention. It provides an in-depth analysis of the responsibility to protect approach, which emerged from the quest to solve the humanitarian intervention conundrum. The book focuses on the contributions made by R2P to the debate on intervention. Its premise is that a study on the topic that goes back to basics and considers why R2P emerged in the first place is required. I incorporate legal, ethical and political insights throughout my argumentation, but also historical and contemporary examples of humanitarian intervention. As such, this book has two dimensions: it is normative in its examination of how the R2P framework, as first envisaged in the ICISS report and later taken on board in the UN setting, addresses the major debates on humanitarian intervention; and it also applies the normative findings to real-world situations to reveal how R2P might operate in practice. The investigation is, then, global in focus, and does not concentrate on one state or region or a single case study, but rather uses several examples to identify trends in state practice to verify the theoretical findings.

My starting point is the assumption that there is a real protection gap in the world today, which the humanitarian intervention approach was not able to address. Framing the intervention discourse in relation to an existing "right" to intervene in order to protect explains this failure, which only emphasized the need for new language that would permit finding new solutions to the civilian protection problem. R2P emerged because of the necessity to fill this obvious normative gap regarding ways to address the needs of the victims in instances of genocide, ethnic cleansing, mass crimes, and crimes against humanity. R2P's relevance is explained by the fact that it proposes a more viable way of engaging with protection issues than the humanitarian intervention framework.

The first part of the book provides the theoretical foundations and clarifies the scope and boundaries of the R2P framework. It addresses three of the most contentious, but also most relevant questions in the humanitarian intervention debate: How to address the alleged conflict between norms of sovereignty and nonintervention, on the one hand, and norms demanding respect for human rights, on the other, to make humanitarian intervention permissible? Who is the right authority for humanitarian intervention? Who has the military capacity required to actually translate an authorized intervention into practice? The goal of the first part of the book is to assess whether the R2P recommendations in regard to each of these three questions are well founded. In doing so, the focus is on R2P's contribution to the humanitarian intervention debate. The latter had proven conceptually unhelpful and politically unfeasible, hence the need for a novel approach to move beyond the impasse. R2P introduces new principles and concepts to reconcile sovereignty with the need to protect, which was previously unachievable given the focus on the "right" to intervene. Its theoretical framework is also evidence of changing security trends in the international system and the focus on those in need of help rather than the interveners' perceptions. R2P's practical relevance is shown by its depiction of intervention as part of a wider spectrum of measures designed to protect civilians from mass atrocities, short of the use of force.

The second part of the book takes the topic away from the theoretical realm and follows the normative development of the R2P doctrine up to the support it has attracted in principle in the political realm. A significant gap is scrutinized in this section, namely the one between R2P's rapid evolution on the normative side and the enduring and serious problems on the operational side, in terms of the ability of the international community, be it the UN or regional organizations, to implement effectively the responsibility to protect civilians. By drawing together the theoretical concepts and closely examining several recent examples dubbed as "test cases" for R2P, this section proposes a new approach to the challenge of implementing R2P that more critically engages with international and regional organizations, and individual states. As such, these chapters focus on the practical dimensions of the responsibility to protect civilians and propose policy-relevant means to address the challenges of implementing R2P on the ground.

Overview of chapters

This study begins by situating R2P within the broader search for a consensus on the humanitarian intervention dilemma. I then assess the extent to which the R2P report and the shorter references to R2P in subsequent UN documents and resolutions have proposed feasible recommendations to some of the most contentious issues of humanitarian intervention. In order to investigate this question, I look at three major controversies related to the intervention debate. Chapter 2 focuses on the dilemma regarded as being at the heart of the humanitarian intervention debate, namely the alleged opposition between sovereignty and human rights. A shift from sovereignty as a feature of governments to sovereignty as something functional for societies is identified as having taken place at the level of international law, political theory, and practice. The workable relationship between sovereignty and human rights proposed in the R2P report and adopted in its subsequent representations is discussed here. I argue that the R2P framework respects what is important in sovereignty, while first acknowledging the changes in how sovereignty is accepted and perceived on the international stage, and second accommodating universal respect for human rights, especially in extreme humanitarian emergencies.

Chapter 3 discusses another problematic aspect of the intervention debate, namely the question of authority. This chapter introduces the two major opposing positions in the debate, namely those rejecting any exception to the requirement for UN Security Council authorization and the proponents of considering alternative sources of authority in cases of exceptional humanitarian emergencies. I look at state practice and I base my arguments on trends of legitimacy found in the cases of intervention occurring since the 1990s to identify the likely directions in which the debate is going. I argue that the two alternative mechanisms to authorize the use of force recommended in the R2P report for instances when the UN Security Council fails to agree on collective action are well founded, as long as the "authority pyramid" criterion is followed. However, the fact that the ICISS report's recommendations in such instances were not taken on board in the subsequent endorsements of R2P at the UN, for obvious reasons, is problematic.

The question of capacity, which is closely related to that of authorization, is the third controversial issue in the humanitarian intervention debate addressed in this study. Even if an intervention is authorized, there is still a need to find those available, willing and capable to carry out the intervention. While the ICISS report clearly states its recommendations on the question of authority, it only broadly considers operational issues, without embarking upon answering the specific question of who actually has the capacity to put R2P into practice. Thus,

Chapter 4 suggests that the ICISS report does not consider operational principles in depth, mainly because it was designed as a political solution to the intervention debate, rather than as an instrument to address military concerns. While the ICISS report offers workable recommendations in regard to the previous two questions, it fails to give the same specific answers in regard to the question of capability. Similarly, subsequent formulations of R2P in the UN setting avoid discussing capabilities for the use of force and focus instead on the need to enhance early warning.

After assessing the theoretical weight of the R2P recommendations, I examine the practical relevance of the R2P framework in the following two chapters. Chapter 5 follows R2P's normative progress, tracing its evolution from the expression of the responsibility to protect in the ICISS report to the representation advanced in the 2009 report of the UN Secretary-General, "Implementing the Responsibility to Protect," and the General Assembly's plenary debate on R2P. I highlight the most important steps along the progressive route that propelled R2P's status from an "idea" in the ICISS report to a nascent norm. I then discuss the stage R2P reached on its normative trajectory, and explain the factors that contributed to this progress. The last section of the chapter explores whether this normative development provides R2P with any legal force, that is, whether it brings R2P closer to a binding norm of international law. In line with this study's focus on the contributions made by the responsibility to protect framework to the debate on humanitarian intervention, I refer in this context to R2P's potential for the collective use of authorized force.

Chapter 6 establishes the correlation between the normative and the operational dimensions of R2P, by focusing on the ways in which practice and politics could catch up with the framework's normative development. An array of cases representing four distinct categories[7] of R2P-type interventions is discussed in order to illustrate the stage R2P has reached on its normative path toward implementation. This examination exposes the limitations faced when dealing with complex humanitarian emergencies, which are divided into five major challenges related to the implementation of R2P, namely conceptual, political, institutional, operational, and a serious gap between expectations and capacity. Various mechanisms to address these challenges are then considered, that could translate into effective reaction in cases triggering R2P-type responses.

The concluding chapter summarizes the findings of the study as a whole and discusses the theoretical and policy implications. While considering the potential utility of R2P in regard to instances of mass killings, the conclusion also highlights its limitations, as shown by the significant gaps between its normative and operational dimensions. Despite such shortcomings, R2P is at the beginning of a long normative trajectory that usually characterizes emerging human rights paradigms. Further opposition to the issue is to be expected in the future, despite its encouraging normative developments so far. As Darfur has gloomily suggested, there is evidently no guarantee that the endorsement of R2P at the UN level would automatically translate into action when the thresholds for intervention are reached. After all, R2P's dimension that regards the use of force cannot substitute for political will and military capacity, two requirements that ultimately are to be fulfilled by states. Implementation is still pending on states matching their agreement, in principle, with a willingness to help strangers elsewhere when the time comes to put principle into practice. It ultimately requires intervening agents to move beyond the conscious recognition that a responsibility to protect exists, into acting in line with their conscience.

Part I

R2P's theoretical weight

2 The responsibility to protect

Sovereignty *and* human rights

> If humanitarian intervention is, indeed, an unacceptable assault on sovereignty, how should we respond to Rwanda, to Srebrenica – to gross and systematic violations of human rights that offend every precept of our common humanity?
>
> (Annan 2000: 48)

Annan's much cited quotation encompasses the central dilemma of the humanitarian intervention debate, namely the challenge of reconciling two competing norms in international law: sovereignty and human rights. On the one hand, sovereignty inhibits intervention into the internal affairs of states, and on the other hand, there is a growing concern that the international community should react to massive and systematic violations of human rights by any state. The tension between these two sets of norms rests at the heart of the humanitarian intervention debate. In finding ways to resolve this contention, I discuss first sovereignty as a legal principle that predates the human rights regime, and second, the emergence of the human rights discourse. Both aspects are considered in relation to the movement toward a broader understanding of the term sovereignty and greater concern for human rights. I then discuss the extent to which R2P proposes a workable relationship between sovereignty and human rights.

The core of the dilemma: sovereignty versus human rights

Chris Brown argued that "the status of international law is a topic in jurisprudence that the wise avoid if they can" (1999: 115). And yet, one cannot consider international law without acknowledging its complexity, especially with respect to the alleged opposition between state sovereignty and protection of human rights. As Fernando Teson puts it, the basic dilemma of humanitarian intervention is that either we intervene to end massacres and so we are liable to violate the prohibition of war and respect for sovereignty, or we do not intervene, which means we tolerate the violation of the prohibition of gross human rights abuses (2003: 110).

It has long been argued that the concept of state sovereignty is a fundamental pillar of the international system: the "basic norm" upon which the society of states rests, the "cardinal principle" of international law, the "cornerstone" of the UN Charter, and "the global covenant" (e.g. Brown 1999; Jackson 2000; Ayoob 2002). According to such views, international law, international organizations, and other rules and institutions governing international society share the fundamental premise that international order can be maintained only if states respect each other's sovereignty (Ayoob 2002: 81). But views of this kind, while far from obsolete, now share center stage with others: arguments that present the defense of human rights as a basic norm or cardinal principle, and thus pose a question for theories of sovereignty; for, necessarily, they make the respect due to sovereignty something less than absolute. Each of these views will be addressed in separate sections, which will provide a basis for analyzing the recommendations of the ICISS report with respect to moving beyond the sovereignty–intervention dichotomy[1] through a reinterpretation of sovereignty and human rights.

Sovereignty

The notion of sovereignty has been much criticized. It has been described as "problematic" (Philpott 1995; Krasner 2001) and as generating "genuine intellectual difficulties" (Thompson 2006: 253). Sovereignty is also very broad and highly contested. For the most part, the disputes question whether the concept is absolute or not, whether it implies solely a legitimate authority, or if it also requires the power to perform that authority, and discuss the extent to which existing norms on sovereignty hinder the solution to key pressing issues today. Such disagreements also involve debating the interplay and the various degrees of importance assigned to the two major aspects of sovereignty, internal and external, and assess the current relevance or the so-called "demise" of the state. In light of the difficulty of setting out *one* definition of sovereignty, scholars have attempted to communicate how it works and how it might change or transform under new conditions, instead of delineating exactly what it comprises (e.g. Nagan and Hammer 2003). Many seem to agree that since it was introduced into political science, sovereignty has never had a meaning which was universally agreed upon.

Legal approaches to sovereignty

There are various approaches to sovereignty, ranging from "conventional sovereignty," "sovereignty as authority," "shared sovereignty," and "sovereignty as responsibility." Stephen Krasner identified at least four different meanings for the term sovereignty: Westphalian sovereignty, understood as excluding external actors from domestic authority; domestic sovereignty, understood as the organization of public authority within a state and the level of control exercised by those holding authority; international legal sovereignty, meaning the reciprocal recognition of states; and, interdependence sovereignty, referring to the ability of public authorities to control movements over the borders (1999, 2001).

Despite disagreements, sovereignty is taken to be a combination of two elements, external and internal. The traditional meaning of sovereignty can be reduced to internal control and external autonomy, which are encompassed under a different terminology, namely sovereignty "as authority." This interpretation implies both an internal and external dimension, emphasizing mainly the capacity of state sovereignty to act as a barrier to unwanted external intervention (Ayoob 2002: 82–83).

In the "Westphalian" system that has governed international relations since the seventeenth century, sovereignty signifies "the legal identity of a state in international law" (ICISS 2001: 12). The state is the sole repository of sovereign authority, understood as the capacity to make authoritative decisions with regard to the people and resources within the territory of the state. Legal scholars have argued that a state possesses sovereignty when it is able to act independently of the consent or control of another state (e.g. Slomanson 2007: 234). The principle of the sovereign equality of states is enshrined in the UN Charter, in Article 2.1. Its corollary, the norm of nonintervention, is enshrined in Article 2.4. and Article 2.7 of the Charter. According to the UN Charter, which is the most important source of legal authority on the use of force, a sovereign state is empowered to exercise exclusive and total jurisdiction within its territorial borders, and other states have the corresponding duty not to intervene in its internal affairs. After World War II, membership of the UN became the final symbol of independent sovereign statehood and thus the seal of acceptance into the community of nations. As stated in the UN Charter, the UN is dedicated to the maintenance of international peace and security on the basis of protecting the territorial integrity, political independence and *national sovereignty* of its members.

The key assumption in this context used to be that international order can be maintained only if states respect each other's sovereignty. Some speculated that the one value all world leaders would agree on relates to their government presiding over a sovereign state (Rochester 2006: 56). The best illustration of this argument is seen in the common position of developing states with respect to intervention, which they often interpret as an erosion of the principle of sovereignty: "We remain extremely sensitive to any undermining of our sovereignty … because sovereignty is our final defense against the rules of an unequal world…"[2]

Sovereignty has been understood to belong to the category of *jus cogens*[3] or peremptory norms. The problem, however, relates to the lack of agreement on the clarity, content, impact and source of *jus cogens* (Shelton 2006: 299). Despite its unclear scope and applicability as well as disagreement over which principles of international law have a peremptory effect there is general agreement that the following are examples of it: the prohibition on the use of force, slavery, genocide, and torture. Sovereignty has thus been described as "hard law," meaning that it encompasses legally binding obligations that are precise. And so, many scholars argue that respect for the sovereignty of other states is the universal standard of international conduct (e.g. Jackson 2004).

Sovereignty is frequently connected with the norm of nonintervention. This has been regarded as a basis for the well functioning of international society, implying the principle of states' equality of protection against outside interference. As a crucial corollary of the concept of sovereignty, nonintervention has been reiterated since the foundation of the UN, in various resolutions and declarations throughout the years.[4] As seen in the UN Charter, states have freely consented to refrain from the use of force against another state, among other commitments deemed basic by the international community, such as the peaceful settlement of disputes, respect for human rights and fundamental freedoms, and self-determination. It is no secret, however, that the main problem with international law is ensuring compliance by states that have consented to such obligations. Under these circumstances, the value of labeling norms as peremptory is open to question (Shelton 2006: 305).

Despite the fact that nonintervention is one of the most basic international law norms, states have intervened in the affairs of other states in the past, for various reasons, including strategic interests, security of their territory, and humanitarian motives. The norm of nonintervention was never absolute in practice. As early as the thirteenth century, European rulers declared their right to protect Christians within the Ottoman Empire (Krasner 1999: 76). Rulers have not always had autonomy over their populations, and the protection of minority rights is one area where the Westphalian model has been persistently violated. As one of the first jurists to articulate the principle of nonintervention, Vattel argued, "if the unjust rule of a sovereign led to internal revolt, external powers would have the right to intervene on the side of the just party when disorder reached the stage of civil war" (1852, cited in Krasner 1999: 74).

Over the last two centuries, several humanitarian interventions have taken place in the Balkans and Central America. During the nineteenth century, there were at least three instances of military intervention based on humanitarian claims and one instance when the threat of intervention was used to protect people other than the intervener's own nationals. The following are examples in point: the intervention by European powers, particularly Russia and France, against the Turks, partly for humanitarian considerations (blended with religion considerations) related to atrocities committed against Orthodox Christians during the Greek War of Independence (1821–1827); the intervention by the six great European powers (Austria, France, Britain, Prussia, Russia and Turkey) to save Christians under Ottoman rule in what is now Lebanon, but at that time was Syria, in 1860–1861; Russia's unilateral intervention in the wake of the Ottoman troops' massacres of unarmed and unorganized agitators in Bulgaria in 1876–1878, which ended with the defeat of the Ottoman troops and the creation of the independent state of Bulgaria; and the threat of the major European powers to use force in response to the wave of massacres against the Armenians (1894–1917), based on humanitarian justifications.

Interventions were not that numerous during the Cold War, and took place for reasons related to strategic security. The Soviet Union interventions in the former Czechoslovakia in 1968 and in Afghanistan in 1971, US interventions in the Dominican Republic in 1965 and Grenada in 1983, India's intervention in Bangladesh in 1971, Tanzania's in Uganda in 1979, and Vietnam's resort to force in Cambodia in 1979 are a few examples. The number of interventions for humanitarian purposes has increased considerably in the post-Cold War period. This has occurred primarily because of new actors emerging on the world stage and new challenges to international peace and security resulting from an increase in internal conflicts and failed states. This is the context in which some have suggested that nonintervention is a doctrine of the past (e.g. Teson 2003: 128).

Indeed, the nonintervention principle has been weakened in recent thinking, as suggested by the shift from sovereignty as a feature of governments to sovereignty as a functional concept for societies. This has taken place at the level of political theory, international law, and practice. It seems necessary then to look at all three approaches to assess whether this shift has amounted to a weakening of state sovereignty.

Evolving interpretations of sovereignty

An extensive literature on changing norms of sovereignty reflects the substantial evolution of the conditions under which sovereignty is exercised. This literature covers the emerging challenges to the traditional interpretation of sovereignty, such as the broadened concept of threats to international peace and security, the collapse of state authority, the importance placed on popular sovereignty, and new demands for self-determination (Weiss and Hubert 2001: 6–12). In line with these transformations, human rights also cease to be a purely domestic matter (Badescu 2009). The interventions from the 1990s brought new attention to the concept of sovereignty, and a switch in the international discourse from "sovereignty as authority" to "sovereignty as responsibility" occurred.

Francis Deng (1993, 1995) was the first to articulate the approach of "sovereignty as responsibility" to protect the people of a given territory, which explicitly challenged the key principle of nonintervention. The terminology has since been embraced by many in the field (e.g. Teson 1997; Barkin 1998), and described as a "new normative principle of international order" (Etzioni 2006). It was the 2001 ICISS report, however, that produced the loudest resonance of the principle after its adoption as a key element of the R2P framework.

In terms of political theory, various attempts have been made to show that sovereignty and humanitarian intervention rest upon the same footing: both are justified only to the extent that they diminish the vulnerability of populations. Domestic political institutions produce a network of relations that protect and advance their members' interests. They also bring into being a system of power that can turn against those whom it is assumed to protect: and in such cases, external intervention simply takes on the role that justified domestic political institutions in the first place (Vernon 2006). This is the moment when sovereignty ceases to be solely a feature of governments. Others, however, rest the argument on an appeal to the "natural duty" of justice, defined specifically as the protection of basic human rights (Buchanan 2004). Along the same lines are arguments based on common morality or the tradition of natural law, which regard humanitarian intervention as a basic moral duty to protect the innocent from violence (Nardin 2003). Yet others develop a case built on the provision of basic needs. If one starts from the premise of global justice, the tension between sovereignty – that is, respecting governments' authority and desire for nonintervention – and responding to the plight of those in need – that is, respecting and protecting the individuals who suffer under their government's control – should be resolved in favor of the latter (Brock 2006). According to such models of global justice, consensus about the nature of sovereignty is building slowly, and the above tension subsides in certain cases, warranting humanitarian intervention to protect fundamental human rights for vulnerable populations (ibid.: 278).

For Henry Shue, a scholar who offers one of the most enthusiastic and convincing contributions in favor of a limited notion of state sovereignty, sovereign states also have duties, apart from rights (rights which may include a state's right to do some wrongs). Such duties constrain states' behavior by making their sovereignty conditional on a minimal level of respect for the human rights of their own citizens (Shue 2004). And so, sovereignty is not, as it used to be, a natural feature of political societies, but a status conferring membership of the international system: that it should not be unconditionally conferred reflects simple moral intuitions as well as recent trends in international law. In the twentieth century, sovereignty came to be justified increasingly in terms of the state's role as guarantor of certain basic human rights, replacing the politically ineffective legitimating principle of absolute right (e.g. Reus-Smit 2001).

Most scholars now seem to agree that sovereignty is not absolute, and that any defense of state sovereignty cannot be made by claiming that a state can do what it wants to its own people (ICISS 2001: 8). Even so, according to Hedley Bull, Robert Jackson, and Henry Kissinger for example, states can legitimately disagree about the right way to organize their political systems, which means that domestic conditions should not be linked to the maintenance of international order. Others have argued that recent interpretations of sovereignty as conditional have been translated into a new interventionism where intervening states portray themselves as agents of the "international community," while in fact being proponents of Western interests (Ayoob 2002; Chandler 2002, 2006). The present debate in international politics on whether we are witnessing the demise, the renaissance, or the transformation of state sovereignty is an eloquent illustration of the contentiousness of the topic. While some argue that the power of national governments is eroding irremediably (e.g. Mills 1998), others engage in a defense of the traditional concept of the powerful sovereign state (e.g. Ayoob 2002; Chandler 2002).

Despite all these debates, there seems to be agreement on the changed meaning of sovereignty in response to transformations that have affected the international community and international institutions.[5] A significant number of scholars, especially liberal international lawyers, have persuasively argued that sovereignty is vested in the people and not in the state (e.g. Makinda 2002; Franck 2003; Teson 2003). Such interpretations of state sovereignty are not centered on a primary need to respect territorial borders, but on a key requirement to protect the citizens of a state caught up in internal strife. States that have failed or collapsed, however, may represent a distinct category, as in these instances sovereignty ceases to exist and therefore international norms that privilege state sovereignty are no longer relevant. Examples of countries where state authority collapsed altogether as a result of internal conflict are: Afghanistan in the early 1990s; Liberia in the 1990s; Congo and Sierra Leone in the late 1990s; to name just a few. This illustration refers to internal conflicts and leaves aside cases where state authority has collapsed as a result of external interventions, such as the more recent examples of Afghanistan and Iraq. As for instances when sovereignty is no longer relevant, the answer resides in what Krasner (2004) calls shared sovereignty. This refers to various arrangements where individuals chosen by international organizations or coalitions of the willing share authority with nationals over some aspects of domestic sovereignty. Even so, developing an alternative to conventional sovereignty – one in which external actors control many aspects of domestic sovereignty in failed states, for an indefinite period of time – can be a very difficult exercise.

There is now a growing acceptance that humanitarian objectives advanced in extreme cases of human rights violations are permissible in accordance with international law and cannot be held hostage to the norm of state sovereignty, classically understood. While some argue that the norm of sovereignty "is no longer sacrosanct" (Chopra and Weiss 1992), others phrase it differently but launch the same critical message, namely that state sovereignty is becoming less than absolute (Philpott 1995; Mills 1998: 3). Even some of the strongest supporters of the traditional concept of sovereignty suggest there is a certain hierarchy with respect to each sovereign state's responsibilities, which ultimately includes humanitarian objectives. Robert Jackson (2004) argues that the first-tier responsibility of a state is focused on national and international responsibility, and so humanitarian responsibility is simply subordinated to these two types of responsibilities that a state has on the international stage, and thus plays a secondary role.

Apart from becoming a topic of scholarly debate, the concept of conditional sovereignty has also reached the realm of practice. Policy makers from around the world ponder the sovereignty versus responsibility dilemma, which may become even more central to the international order since the endorsement of R2P by the General Assembly in September 2005. Three Secretaries-General of the UN, Boutros Boutros-Ghali, Kofi Annan, and Ban Ki-moon, declared that sovereignty is no longer absolute and that it can be overridden in exceptional circumstances. Annan, in particular, has achieved significant progress in advancing his argument that there are "two concepts of sovereignty," and that the international community should embrace the one that encompasses the responsibilities, along with the rights, of statehood (1999; 2005a).

Concrete examples of the modern decline of the traditional state-centric concept of "absolute" sovereignty add further weight. They include norms of customary international law, to the extent that they bind rogue states, such as Libya in its dispute with the international community in the aftermath of bombing a passenger jet over Lockerbie, Scotland, in 1988. Other examples refer to the watering down of sovereign immunity, from the absolute to the "restrictive" approach in the aftermath of World War II. The limitations on absolute immunity for heads of state, which culminated with the 1998 Rome Statute of the International Criminal Court (ICC) is another example in point. This is notable because state immunity is derived from the independence and sovereign equality of states, and yet only parties to the ICC Statute have waived the international law immunities of their senior officials (Akande 2006: 75–76). Another good example is the willingness of the twenty-seven member states of the European Union (EU) to yield their sovereignty status to the EU requests to refrain from acting in accordance to their sovereign preferences. The willingness of certain states to voluntarily embrace international agreements, such as the Kyoto treaty against global warming, is another example of this decrease.

Such examples of reinterpretations of sovereignty – at the level of political theory, international law and practice – advance one question: Does this amount to a weakening of state sovereignty? I argue that no, the shift away from the traditional meaning of sovereignty does not translate into a diminution of the concept's *relevance*. First, sovereignty has had a complex historical evolution since the thirteenth century and it is a concept that has always evolved (Philpott 1995). This continuous development started with the first modern revolution in sovereignty – the 1648 Peace of Westphalia – followed by the two different kinds of norms of sovereignty demanded in the nineteenth century, namely minority rights and self-determination.[6] More recent defining moments in the evolution of sovereignty include the creation and expansion of what is now the EU and the emergence of norms allowing UN-sanctioned interventions for humanitarian purposes.

A second reason why the present shift, from sovereignty as a feature of governments to a functional interpretation for societies, does not translate into sovereignty's weakening relates to the reality that the nonintervention principle has never been rigorously observed. Westphalian sovereignty, defined as the exclusion of external actors from authority structures within given territorial boundaries, has been widely recognized but constantly violated since the Treaty of Westphalia itself, either through coercion or voluntary agreements. Krasner's famous "organized hypocrisy" assessment best captures the decoupling between the norm of autonomy and actual state practice, with rulers consistently vowing their commitment to nonintervention but not respecting it in practice (1999: 8–9).

A third reason why the redefinition of sovereignty does not weaken the relevance of sovereign statehood relates to the fact that the shifts described so far only affect the internal aspect of state sovereignty, leaving statehood intact. Even if the content of states' obligations changes, the basic authorities that agree to such obligations and enforce them do not change. That is, the locus where legitimate authority resides remains the same (Philpott 1995). And so, reinterpreting the classical concept of sovereignty does not translate into what has been described in the literature as "the retreat of the state."[7]

Approaching sovereignty as a link between a status and a bundle of rights, responsibilities, and norms is one way to clarify this point. The first component of this relation refers to the international recognition of a state, its juridical sovereignty, its external rights,[8] while the second element covers a state's ability to enforce authority internally, by its government. The latter is generally associated with the empirical description of sovereign statehood in terms of effective control of territories. In line with the "descriptive fallacy" addressed by several prominent scholars,[9] one can persuasively argue that state sovereignty cannot be perceived exclusively as an empirical concept, relating only to internal control. Instead, if one perceives sovereignty as both a status and a collection of norms, powers and responsibilities, it becomes clear why changing a state's responsibilities does not translate into a weakening of sovereignty. The final form of legitimizing the endurance of sovereignty in legal and political practice comes from its widespread acceptance and usage (Werner and de Wilde 2001).

Another argument against the retreat of the sovereign state theory is offered by the two instances in which the end of sovereignty is often proclaimed: quasi-states and European integration.[10] Even in these two instances, states maintain their sovereign status, and they still enjoy juridical statehood. Of course, certain powers and rights are either lost to various extents, or handed over to other states or international organizations. Despite the move away from the classical conception of external sovereignty, these states still enjoy their sovereign status.

The reinterpretation of sovereignty shows the deep connection between law and politics. Moreover, it illustrates how law is also linked to ethics, and as a result of this relationship, how law becomes a means "to achieve the fundamental values of an international society" (Shelton 2006: 323). The linkages between international law and both politics and ethics are also present in the assessment of the evolution of human rights. The international human rights regime, the second component of the dilemma central to humanitarian intervention, deserves a closer examination to assess the transformation of the balance between the two. This discussion will consider the key norms of the international human rights regime and their legal weight, in the context of an evolving "humanization" of international law.

The human rights regime

Philosophers, political theorists and legal scholars have conceptualized and updated the meaning of human rights for centuries. Key historic documents, such as the English Magna Carta (1215), the French Declaration of the Rights of Man (1789), and the US Constitution's Bill of Rights (1791) – all drafted at a time when human beings were far from equal – describe human rights as inalienable individual rights. Similarly, natural law theory suggests that human beings retain at any time their fundamental prerogatives that relate to human dignity and property (Tuck 1979). Starting in the mid-twentieth century, leading human rights advocates examined the need for new interpretations of sovereignty to ensure respect for human rights. Human rights cover the protection of individuals and groups against governments' violations of their internationally guaranteed rights. There are three generations of human rights: first-generation rights described as the heart of the international human rights regime, which include political rights and liberty; second-generation rights, which include economic and social rights; and, third-generation rights, which comprise the rights of peoples, among which the human right to peace. There is a certain prioritization of basic human rights, and the most basic one is, evidently, the right to life. Security rights and subsistence rights are among the basic rights of peoples, and since they are essential for the enjoyment of all other rights they are in need of most protection (Shue 1996, 2004).

The regime's key international legal norms

Human rights are part of a universal set of normative standards. The international human rights regime has emerged in the last sixty years as an articulation of norms and standards of behavior, and a codification of these standards into treaties, practices and legal decisions. The first two key international legal norms of the regime are the UN Charter and the 1948 Universal Declaration of Human Rights (UDHR). Over time, a series of legally binding international treaties have complemented the latter, which served as foundation for these treaties.[11] Furthermore, two legally binding UN human rights treaties, which develop the more general principles identified in the UDHR, are: the 1966 International Covenant on Civil and Political Rights (ICCPR) and the International Covenant on Economic, Social and Cultural Rights (ICESCR). Other key human rights treaties include: the 1965 International Convention on the Elimination of All Forms of Racial Discrimination, which predated the two Covenants, and three treaties of the utmost importance following the two Covenants: the 1979 Convention on the Elimination of All Forms of Discrimination against Women, the 1984 Convention against Torture and Other Cruel, Inhuman or Degrading Treatment or Punishment, and the 1989 Convention on the Rights of the Child.

The repeated references in the UN Charter to the phrase "without distinction as to race, sex, language and religion" suggest that non-discrimination and equality for all human beings lie at the center of the UN approach to human rights. The Charter makes seven references to human rights,[12] including the oath that members "pledge themselves to take joint and separate action in cooperation with the Organization" to achieve the human rights goals specified in the Charter (Article 56). The UN Charter requires "universal respect for … human rights and fundamental freedoms for all" (Article 55c), but its human rights provisions lack specificity. For instance, no state was obliged to act immediately on the UN Charter's "Article 56 pledge." The Charter allowed member states to defer the decisions on "how" and "when" to achieve the human rights goals specified in the Charter until implementation would be economically and politically feasible. The UN Charter provides only a skeletal backbone for the global and regional human rights regime, which have evolved continuously since the mid-twentieth century.

The Universal Declaration of Human Rights (UDHR) was the most significant step in the effort to universalize human rights, for it was the first comprehensive international human rights document. It was adopted on 10 December 1948, as a non-binding instrument to interpret the obligations contained in treaty provisions. While not elaborate, its specificity "readily eclipsed the UN Charter's minimal references to human rights" (Slomanson 2007: 541). The UDHR promotes two general categories of rights, namely civil and political rights, and economic, social and cultural rights.

Although declarations, just like principles and recommendations, have no binding legal effect, they provide practical guidance for the conduct of states. The value of instruments such as the UDHR rests on their recognition and acceptance by a large number of states. There is still no consensus as to the legal status of the UDHR. The UDHR is important, however, because it is the first UN document to state that individuals have a right to protection by the *international community*, as opposed to being protected by their own states.

The same message that evil affecting a group or population is of concern not only for that group but also for the entire international community appears in the 1948 Convention on the Prevention and Punishment of the Crime of Genocide, which emerged one day before the UDHR. It outlines states' obligations toward genocide prevention and makes the gravest violation of human rights – the international crime of genocide – punishable by law. Article 8 in particular advances a message that is extremely relevant for the central question of this chapter: it calls for international action when genocide occurs.

The Genocide Convention deals solely with one type of human rights violations. This is why an international treaty further elaborating on the rights expressed in the UDHR was required. In 1966, two separate treaties were added to the human rights regime, namely the International Covenant on Civil and Political Rights (ICCPR) and the International Covenant on Economic, Social and Cultural Rights (ICESCR), known as the "two Covenants." The UDHR together with these two Covenants provide the main legal foundation in human rights law. The two Covenants were expressly designed as multilateral treaties, with legally binding provisions. Taken together, they constitute a comprehensive codification of human rights and fundamental freedoms, and they are often referred to as the International Bill of Human Rights. They both restate the human rights provisions expressed in the 1948 UDHR. The most notable distinction from the UDHR, however, is that they compel ratifying States to establish effective mechanisms for filing charges and then for dealing with alleged violations of human rights. Out of the two, the ICCPR has been the more influential one, for it addresses the "harder" individual rights expressed in the UDHR and it has a monitoring mechanism, the Human Rights Committee (Aust 2005: 236). The most fundamental of these rights is the inherent right to life, which is protected by law. Conversely, after the decolonization movement of the 1960s, most of the new UN member states regarded economic rights as a more pressing goal than the political rights expressed in the ICCPR.[13]

Despite the variety of such UN instruments, addressing specific rights and formulating more detailed obligations remained a pressing need. This was addressed in the remaining key human rights treaties: the Convention on the

Elimination of All Forms of Discrimination Against Women (1979) covering rights relevant for women, such as education and family rights; the Convention Against Torture and Other Cruel, Inhuman or Degrading Treatment (1984) on the right not to be subjected to torture; and the Convention on the Rights of the Child (1989), which details the obligations for protecting children.

Apart from the UN global regime, there are also several regional human rights programs, whose degrees of success depend on the political cohesion of their respective region. The European regime has been the most successful one so far, with the 1950 European Convention for the Protection of Human Rights and Fundamental Freedoms (ECHR), and especially with its enforcement mechanism, the European Court of Human Rights. The Court is the most successful tool in Europe's human rights arsenal and a very useful force for preserving human rights in Europe. This is partly explained by the right to individual application to the Court: unlike other international venues, individuals themselves, and not just states, can be parties. Enforcement has been a significant achievement, especially in light of this institution's authoritative decision-making powers. Nonetheless, the European human rights regime is the exception in terms of regional enforcement.

In Latin America, human rights norms are expressed in the 1948 Charter of the Organization of American States (OAS), the 1948 American Declaration of the Rights and Duties of Man,[14] and the 1969 American Convention on Human Rights. All these norms are monitored by the Inter-American Commission on Human Rights. However, Latin America in general is extremely deferential to state sovereignty, while few countries have effectively independent judiciaries committed the enforcement of human rights. Nonetheless, the OAS decision to amend its Charter, in 1997, to permit suspension of a member whose democratic government is overthrown by force is a notable example of agreement among sovereign states to link recognition of state sovereignty to the protection of internal popular sovereignty (Cohen 2004: 21).

On the African continent, the former Organization of African Unity (OAU) made an important contribution to the human rights regime through its focus on collective or peoples' rights, as suggested by the African Charter on Human and People's Rights, the youngest of the regional human rights treaties, adopted in 1981. Nonetheless, the OAU was also regarded as extremely deferential to sovereignty, and was replaced by the African Union (AU), in 2002, which presently lacks resources to take serious action against gross human rights violations. There is also an African Court of Justice for Human Rights, designed after the European model, but far behind it in terms of achievements. If the African human rights regime is weak, the regimes in Asia and the Middle East are even less developed (Donnelly 2003: 144). In Asia there are no regional norms and no decision-making procedures. The League of Arab States, known as the Arab League, is another largely inactive organism on the world stage, which could hardly be regarded as forming a regional regime.

The mere existence of key international human rights instruments does not, of course, guarantee the protection and promotion of human rights. There is an important distinction between international law as "law" and its enforcement mechanisms. One big problem with the international human rights regime is that, despite being very elaborate, it is not very powerful in terms of enforcement. The actual conduct of some states in the treatment of their own nationals provides endless illustrations. Overall, the existing monitoring procedures and programs developed to ensure states' compliance under international law have been weak. "Embryonic" is a word used to describe the capacity to enforce the requirements of human rights law (Beitz 2002). Given space limitations, it is impossible to cover in detail the key mechanisms to supervise the implementation of human rights and their mandates. For this analysis, it is enough to mention that the international system of human rights supervision includes procedures known as Charter-based, and mechanisms established in relation to specific human rights treaties, known as treaty-based procedures.

The most notable components of the former have included the now-defunct UN Commission on Human Rights, which was replaced by the Human Rights Council (HRC), and the Office of the UN High Commissioner for Human Rights (OHCHR). One of the most important UN human rights organs, the OHCHR has an explicit mandate to deal with governments to increase their respect for internationally recognized human rights and to review the implementation of human rights treaties. The Human Rights Council was perceived by many as an encouraging attempt to address the serious problems of the former Commission on Human Rights. The HRC is responsible for promoting universal respect for the protection of all human rights and fundamental freedoms and for addressing violations of human rights – including gross and systematic violations – and making recommendations thereon (United Nations 2005a: paras 157–159).

The latter category of supervision procedures, developed in relation to specific human rights treaties, is more advanced. A mandatory reporting procedure is an integral part of the six best known human rights treaties. But in order to be effective, a human rights treaty ultimately needs not only international machinery, such as an international court or tribunal where individuals can complain, but especially domestic legal mechanisms to implement the judgments of the international court. Presently, there is a huge discrepancy between the acceptance of human rights treaties and of supervisory mechanisms and the actual enforcement of human rights.

Although examining the serious problems related to compliance and implementation of the human rights regime is beyond the scope of this chapter, a quick look at the influence of ratifications and accessions on the level of compliance is necessary before concluding this review. The numbers of state parties look encouraging, with 193 state parties for the Convention on the Rights of the Child (CRC) for instance, and 140 for the Genocide Convention. Ratifications and accessions, however, are quite different from the effective enforcement of treaties. On the one hand, the proliferation of the human rights regime and the increased number of ratifications could suggest an increase in the number of countries formally committed to respecting human rights. On the other hand, the mere codification of international human rights norms does not necessarily make any difference to some states that are following their own national interest. How can one then measure the connection between ratification and compliance, and, especially, what factors count for the latter?

One notable problem with assessing the human rights regime is that the analysis seeks to compare "is" with "ought." Attempts to measure human rights quantitatively usually employ a standardized reporting framework for all countries, which can be problematic given the serious differences among countries' levels of development (Carr Center Project Report 2005: 30). Human rights analyses also make a distinction between qualitative and quantitative data. Nonetheless, both methods are the results of human judgment and interpretation, and they both come from human accounts. The quantitative assessments of ratifications and accessions can be relative. China, for example, has declared, in principle, its compliance with important human rights treaties such as ICCPR and the ICESCR, but its compliance has been much more procedural than substantive. Despite signing these two international covenants in an attempt to diminish international embarrassment, China's record of continued abuse of fundamental freedoms demonstrates only a superficial compliance with international norms.

Conversely, non-ratification does not translate into a bad record of respect for human rights. The UK provides a good example of the relative value of numbers for ratification: the UK is party to the European Convention for the Protection of Human Rights and Fundamental Freedoms (ECHR) but is not a party to the ICCPR Optional Protocol. The rationale for countries like UK is that the protection given by ECHR seems effective enough that there is no need to ratify an alternative procedure (Aust 2005: 250). The US is another example in point. When the US ratifies international human rights conventions, it typically does so with a stipulation that the provisions cannot supersede US domestic law. The US has not ratified some of the treaties with most states parties, such as the Convention on the Rights of the Child and the Convention on Elimination of Discrimination against Women. But this does not mean that the standards of child protection in the US are as poor as those of the only other state that has not ratified it, Somalia. Also, it took the US forty years to ratify the Genocide Convention, after initially signing it in 1948.

And so, the failure to ratify does not necessarily translate into a failure to comply and to respect human rights; and vice versa, ratification does not automatically translate into respect and compliance. Ultimately, the implications of non-ratification or non-accession depend on the difference between state standards and international norms. Where this distinction is significant, citizens of states that have not ratified international treaties might lack rights available to citizens belonging to other states. Moreover, some states ratify human rights treaties without intending to respect their provisions or to put in place the domestic mechanisms required for such rights to be properly protected. Human rights performance remains difficult to measure. This is why the answer to the question of whether international human rights treaties improve respect for human rights is not a straightforward one. While some scholars argue that the proliferation of human rights norms has had a limited effect on the protection of human rights (Landman 2005: 147–157), most agree that treaty ratification usually affects human rights compliance (e.g. Goodman and Jinks 2003; Neumayer 2005).

There is agreement on trends though. Evidently, there is a better chance for increased respect for human rights if the citizens participate in international non-governmental organizations and the country is democratic. Also, wealthy democratic states are more likely to ratify human rights treaties and to protect civil and political rights (Landman 2005: 166). In the absence of civil society or in authoritarian states, human rights treaty ratification may make no difference or even worsen the record of respect for human rights (Hathaway 2002; Neumayer 2005). If powerful states are not interested in having effective human rights regimes, states with poor human rights records ratify treaties with very few costs, while actually maintaining their poor record, precisely because monitoring and enforcement are usually weak.

The international human rights regime has grown in width and depth in the last decades, and so did the protection of human rights, in aggregate terms. And yet, international human rights treaties do not offer solid guidance regarding assistance when faced with insufficient compliance. When states violate treaties' provisions on human rights, NGOs and the broader international community usually employ a "naming and shaming" approach in order to pressure repressive governments to reform and to change the behavior of state parties responsible for human rights violations. But there is a serious case of time lag between undertaking and performance in this context. The intention of this brief discussion on ratification and compliance was to pinpoint one notable trend, namely that the key instruments of the human rights regime reveal a process of universalization of human rights. This point is particularly relevant when discussing the delicate balance between state sovereignty and human rights.

The acceptance and universality of human rights norms

Just as the meaning of sovereignty as an international legal concept evolved, the human rights regime evolved as well. Human rights are not developed within a static system, precisely because their codification is ongoing and ever changing, both nationally and internationally. Human rights have now penetrated all policy areas; they are an important aspect of the work of the UN Security Council when dealing with threats to international peace and security. In the 1990s, when faced with situations that did not directly threaten the security of a particular state, but rather involved large-scale violations of human rights, the Security Council authorized enforcement action. Legal scholars have argued that respect for human rights gradually became one of the main concerns of the international community in the post-Cold War era, and that obligations to respect human rights have started to imply the right to take action to enforce such respect (e.g. Cassese 1999: 26).

The acceptance of individual criminal responsibility for gross violations of human rights was another major development of the 1990s, together with the adoption of the Statute of the International Criminal Court in 1998. Human security also underlines ongoing developments in international law, further contributing to the "humanization" of international law (Meron 2006). Humanitarian law now addresses the most significant challenge for human security today, namely the regulation of internal armed conflicts. The affirmation that crimes against humanity are punishable not only when committed in armed conflicts but also during internal disturbances or peaceful times was a defining moment in the evolution of international humanitarian law. As some argued, the goal of the UN founders to add a human dimension to international law and international relations has become a reality (Flinterman and Gutter 2000: 24).

And yet, the debate over universal human rights versus cultural relativism is a constant challenge when discussing the allegedly opposed concepts of sovereignty and human rights. In Chris Brown's words, "...rights discourse is a minefield, where each conceptual step risks a detonation and self-destruction; moreover, this is so even without introducing complications allegedly generated by cultural relativism" (1999: 111–112). Critics of the universal approach to human rights typically describe it as a liberal concept, attempting to reshape the world according to a Western pattern. Most arguments against humanitarian intervention make reference to the selective application of human rights principles, reflecting particular interests of Western states. Others argue that the UDHR is itself a Western product, for in 1948 when the UDHR was adopted, the number of states participating in the drafting process was limited; both because the UN numbered fifty-eight member states at the time and also limited geographically and culturally, since many African and Asian states were still colonies and not directly represented.

The central criticism against the universality of human rights, then, depicts the major human rights documents as representing Western values, which liberal countries have imposed on Asian and Islamic states in an attempt to interfere in their internal affairs. However, Asian traditions, for example, also focus on tolerance and freedom (e.g. Sen 1997: 27, 30). Moreover, there seems to be consensus between Western and Asian traditions on a core of international law regarding genocide, torture, and slavery.[15] And yet, the dominant literature on cultural relativism emphasizes how the various Asian, Islamic, and African traditions each have their own characteristics that cannot be brought to a common denominator. Even within one regional human rights regime, such as the Asian one, it is difficult to define a single, coherent set of rules encompassing the different traditions from East and Southeast Asia, such as Islamic, Buddhist, Hindu, and Confucian (Kausikan 1993). The contentiousness of this debate stems from sensitive issues, such as respect for religion, culture, family, and women's status, with gender equality and religious liberty at the forefront of the clashes between Western and Islamic concepts of human rights.[16] Western commentators, too, have argued that human rights are embedded in Western liberal individualism (Huntington 1996), which explains why universal human rights represent a manifestation of Western domination (Brown 1999). An important approach suggests that it is *still* possible to examine and criticize existing practices regarding human rights without reference to universal norms (e.g. Walzer 1993). The idea behind this is that we can employ an analysis of violations of human rights based on the context in which life is lived in particular societies, instead of considering general moral standards.

But such views risk eliminating the very point of the idea, that is, its critical point. If human rights are simply equated with local standards, they add nothing to them. This does not necessarily translate into a uniform application of human rights, regardless of the variety of cultures and religions, or potentially differing interpretations by different states. From the outset, human rights are not compatible with all religious, philosophical and cultural doctrines (Kausikan 1993; Bielefeldt 2000). This does not mean, however, that states are entitled to ignore the international human rights regime either, based simply on diversity justifications. The "universality" of human rights clearly does not refer to "that which is done in every region or country," but rather means the protection that people in *all* parts of the world are entitled to, regardless of race, religion, colour and sex (e.g. Higgins 1999: 20). That is, universal human rights have the normative force to lead to a political and legal order based on equal freedom and participation (Bielefeldt 2000: 115). Universality does not entail an elimination of regional or national characteristics and differences. Instead, the universality of human rights implies inalienable rights based on the dignity of human beings, which are *minimum* standards established by international law. By the very act of becoming a member of the UN, which means subscribing to such principles included in the UDHR and the UN Charter, states commit themselves to observing the universal character of human rights.

The international human rights regime, despite not being very effective in terms of ensuring compliance, does offer a standard for analysis for what happens at the international level. As some of the strongest supporters of the universality of human rights argue, when in doubt, one should question whether people in the non-Western, developing world would not appreciate such basic human rights as political freedom for instance (see Booth 1999; Wheeler 2000; Donnelly 2003; Teson 2003). For the best way to test true universalism is to listen to *the victims* of human rights abuses. Not accounting for this may translate into defending repressive regimes that deny civil and political rights to their citizens.

Even if oppressive regimes are uncomfortable with universal human rights, the notion itself is sought by the victims of these regimes (Baehr cited in Booth 1999: 54, 56). In describing cultural relativism as "the tolerance of diversity," one needs to consider also the extent to which "diversity" should be tolerated, especially when toleration translates into abuses of human rights. Ultimately, the strongest case in defense of the universality of human rights comes from examining the number of state parties to the key human rights treaties. In this context, one can easily reject the arguments in favor of a Northern bias, based on observations that the majority of Southern countries have ratified or acceded to the major human rights treaties.[17]

The case for the universality of human rights has been keenly made. Examining the level of acceptance of human rights in relation to sovereignty is at the forefront now. I exemplified the variations across continents in terms of general acceptance of human rights principles. Contemporary international human rights law has not been adopted by all social and political systems. Some states, especially Southern developing countries, emphasize the conflict between two UN Charter goals: sovereignty, which precludes UN interfering in matters that "are essentially within the domestic jurisdiction of any state" (Article 2.7) and "universal respect for ... human rights and fundamental freedoms for all" (Article 55c). According to such views, human rights are to reflect local rather than internationally defined conditions.

If sovereignty is an overwhelmingly accepted norm, human rights, on the other hand, do not thrive in countries where the rights of the state take priority over the rights of the individual. An interesting approach in this context introduces the idea that human rights tend to spread worldwide by the "leapfrogging" of human rights norms toward the developing world. Globalization increases respect for the international human rights regime in the developing world, particularly in newly industrialized countries, through such various means as the evolution of the global communication network, the growing importance of international civil society, and the unprecedented level of global governance that assists the international human rights movement. It thus becomes increasingly difficult for those suffering from serious human rights abuses not to hear the arguments of human rights defenders (Howard-Hassmann 2005).

I have suggested that canvassing a general approach to human rights as "hard" or "soft" law[18] is also problematic since there is no agreement among legal scholars on such issues. While some argue that it is wrong to assume that all provisions of human rights treaties are *jus cogens* or even rules of customary international law (Aust 2005: 11), others emphasize the importance of legally non-binding, "soft" laws, such as the UDHR, which has been the source of many universal and regional human rights treaties (Shelton 2006; Slomanson 2007). Apart from such diverse perspectives, even if universal agreement is reached with respect to certain core human rights, an innate subjectivity remains when assessing whether human rights are threatened and must be protected in any given situation (Slomanson 2007: 490). Even so, subjectivity is plainly unsatisfactory when discussing the most obvious violations of human rights, those that might trigger humanitarian intervention. It then becomes important to consider briefly the question of thresholds triggering the use of force for humanitarian purposes.

Thresholds for humanitarian intervention

The use of force becomes morally permissible when thresholds for human rights violations are crossed. Generally, such thresholds are set very high, allowing interventions to take place only to halt or avert widespread, systematic, and gross violations of human rights, of the type of the genocidal killings in Rwanda, and the ethnic cleansing in Bosnia and Kosovo.

There seems to be agreement in the literature that the use of force is justified only when ethnic cleansing, genocide, intentional starvation or mass expulsion takes place. Some, however, argue that the phenomenon of "failed states" also qualifies as a just cause for humanitarian intervention (e.g. Hehir 1998: 43). Although it is evident that any form of human rights violations within a state should produce a reaction from the international community, this does not mean that it must automatically trigger humanitarian intervention. Indeed, genocide and ethnic cleansing are gross human rights violations, but the same language can and is sometimes used to describe attacks on the freedom of religion, speech, press and so on. Clearly the latter category should not – and cannot – be a justification for military intervention.

Associating mere numbers with breaches of human rights that trigger intervention has always been a contentious and unpleasant task; however, there seems to be agreement on the criterion of loss of life of hundreds or thousands of innocent people, carried out on the territory of a sovereign state, either as a result of total collapse of state authorities, or at the orders of governmental authorities or with their support (e.g. Cassese 1999: 27). In the original R2P report, the threshold for international action is set as large-scale loss of life or ethnic cleansing, either "actual or apprehended." The 2005 Outcome Document restricted the application of R2P to four crimes that are already part of international legal instruments, namely genocide, war crimes, crimes against humanity, and ethnic cleansing. As will be discussed in more detail below, the R2P report itself does not provide any figures in terms of large-scale casualties. However, this cannot be regarded as a failure of the report, since mentioning any figures in real life would be extremely difficult, especially in more complex situations involving mixed motives behind decisions to intervene. There is, nonetheless, agreement among scholars that only the most terrible violations of human rights involving significant loss of lives trigger military intervention for humanitarian purposes. As such, the threshold for the reaction component of the responsibility to protect is activated when faced with exceptional situations in regard to the seriousness of the violations of human rights and humanitarian law.

The need to "strike a balance" between sovereignty and human rights

Basic assumptions intrinsic to the two contrasting legal concepts of sovereignty and human rights make military intervention for human protection purposes a challenging concern each time serious violations requiring such action occur. The tension between the two – sometimes described as overplayed (e.g. Chesterman 2001; Acharya 2002) – is a constant in any discussion on humanitarian intervention and in all debates on finding ways to react to gross violations of human rights. This tension is also the foundation for the majority of arguments put forward by most critics of actions to protect civilians from egregious crimes occurring in other parts of the world. The obvious resolution would be to find a workable balance between the two norms.

For the most part, the sovereignty debates question whether the concept is absolute or not, whether it implies solely a legitimate authority or if it also requires the power to perform that authority, and whether sovereignty norms hinder the solution to today's key pressing issues. Disagreements over the norm of state sovereignty also involve debating the interplay and the various degrees of importance assigned to the two major aspects of sovereignty, internal and external, and assess the current relevance of the so-called "demise" of the state. Sovereignty is frequently connected with the nonintervention principle. And yet, despite the fact that nonintervention is one of the most basic norms of international law, states have intervened in the affairs of other states in the past, for various reasons, including strategic interests, security of their territory, and humanitarian motives. As a result of the substantial evolution of the conditions under which sovereignty is exercised, an extensive literature on changing norms of sovereignty has appeared. This literature covers the emerging challenges to the traditional interpretation of sovereignty, such as the broadened concept of threats to international peace and security, the collapse of state authority, the importance of popular sovereignty, and new demands for self-determination (Weiss and Hubert 2001: 6–12).

Just as the meaning of sovereignty as an international legal concept has evolved, the human rights regime has evolved as well. The focus on individual human rights – itself a phenomenon of the twentieth century – has materialized into a proliferation of human rights agreements after World War II. The last six decades show an increased recognition of the importance of adopting a human rights perspective in all policy areas, at all levels, along with the gradual acceptance of individual criminal responsibility for gross violations of human rights. Such developments encourage some legal scholars to argue that the respect for human rights has gradually become one of the main concerns of the international community, and so obligations to respect human rights have started to imply the right to take action to enforce it (e.g. Cassese 1999: 26). And yet, the debate over universal human rights versus cultural relativism remains a constant challenge for all efforts to find the balance between sovereignty and human rights.

Being a member of the international society does imply that a state has to respect human rights. When a state fails to do so, the international community has the responsibility to take action to protect the rights of those affected by internal strife, and this includes, as last resort, military intervention for humanitarian purposes. The language of human rights that has been used to justify the increased number of humanitarian interventions in the 1990s comes to support the norm of sovereignty as responsibility. It is also illustrative of how the old rules of international legal sovereignty do not suffice (Cohen 2004: 24) and of the consequential need to rethink them.

During the consultations that helped shape the R2P report, the ICISS reached broad agreement among participating countries from both North and South that the responsibility to protect people from atrocity crimes "was the most basic and fundamental of all the responsibilities that sovereignty imposes – and if a state cannot or will not protect its people … then coercive intervention for human protection purposes … may be warranted" (ICISS 2001: 69). Thus, contrary to popular misconception, the Commission did not find widespread support for an unlimited, absolute view of sovereignty. Instead, both developed and developing countries agreed during consultations that sovereignty implies a dual responsibility: externally, toward respecting the sovereignty of other states, and internally, in terms of respecting the basic rights of a state's population. They also concluded that "the defence of state sovereignty, by even its strongest supporters, does not include any claim of the unlimited power of a state to do what it wants to its own people" (ibid.: 8).

The ICISS report found grounding for intervention under existing international law. As the report explains, R2P is grounded in a variety of legal foundations, such as the Genocide Convention, the Geneva Conventions, human rights treaty provisions, the International Criminal Court statute, in growing state practice, and the Security Council's own practice (2001: 50). The erosion of the absolute principle of national sovereignty is rooted in today's reality of global interdependence. In line with such transformations, human rights cease to be a purely domestic matter.[19]

Even so, reaction to large-scale violations of human rights remains obstructed by the explicit language of the UN Charter highlighting the respect owed to state sovereignty. Most criticisms of the current legal system governing intervention regard it as morally inadequate, for privileging the principle of sovereignty. The UN itself faces a major difficulty, namely finding ways to reconcile its foundational principle of member states' sovereignty and the primary mandate to maintain international peace and security "to save succeeding generations from the scourge of war," with the equally compelling mission to promote the rights and welfare of people within those states. This quandary was described in the relevant literature as an unacceptable gap (Makinda 1996, 2002; Buchanan 2003, 2004; Teson 2003; Franck 2003). And so, it becomes necessary to examine whether R2P, in the format expressed in the 2001 ICISS report, properly addresses this gap, and how it meets the main objections to humanitarian intervention. Such analysis will also assess the extent to which R2P strikes a workable balance between the two norms of state sovereignty and respect for human rights.

The R2P balance: addressing the main objections to humanitarian intervention

R2P's response to relativism

The ICISS was designed to reconcile both the tension, in principle, between sovereignty and humanitarian intervention, and the opposing perspectives on intervention in the policy world. The composition of the commission was a reflection of these goals. The commission was inclusive and balanced, as suggested by the commissioners' different backgrounds and positions on the sovereignty–intervention debate. It represented both industrialized and developing countries' perspectives, and it was also diverse as per continent inclusions and civilizations (Thakur 2006: 248). Furthermore, the ICISS was an independent body, and produced its report after extensive consultations and round tables held on all continents and in the major capitals around the world, as explained in the supplementary research volume of the R2P report. The ICISS report's deference to both norms is a reflection of this consultation process.

This was the context in which military intervention for humanitarian purposes was canvassed by the ICISS, and only in respect to extreme cases (ICISS 2001: 32), where issues of cultural relativism *do not* arise. The R2P's insistence that humanitarian intervention is to be "an exceptional and extraordinary measure" represents a key feature of the ICISS report. It was designed to address the main objections vis-à-vis the potential for abuse of humanitarian intervention justifications. That is, the R2P report describes the use of force to protect human rights as an extreme measure, justified only in egregious circumstances. As such, some scholars have praised the report for advancing "standards and benchmarks with admirable caution" (e.g. Malone 2003: 1001). R2P emphasizes that the rights described in humanitarian law and human rights law apply to all human beings, because they are universal. As opposed to rights such as freedom of expression or assembly, which might be more controversial and less clear cut, the rights to freedom from arbitrary killing, genocide and torture apply equally to all people (Weiss and Hubert 2001: 145).

Genocide and ethnic cleansing of the type seen in Rwanda and Bosnia are the most egregious violations of human rights that cause large enough losses of life to trigger humanitarian intervention. In the words of the R2P report, the two key triggers are:

> A. large scale loss of life, actual or apprehended, with genocidal intent or not,... the product either of deliberate state action, or state neglect or inability to act, or a failed state situation; or B. large scale "ethnic cleansing", actual or apprehended, whether carried out by killing, forced expulsion, acts of terror or rape.
>
> (2001: xii)

Such thresholds reveal the exaggeration of the claim according to which sovereignty – understood as the sole defense the weak states have against the more powerful ones – is negatively affected by the reconceptualization of "sovereignty as responsibility." The ICISS report specifically emphasizes these two thresholds for intervention, whose primary purpose should be halting or averting human suffering (ICISS 2001: 35). Thus, the commission discards any other triggers for military intervention that might, potentially, be used abusively to support the national interests of the interveners, while disguised as "humanitarian" endeavors. The subsequent representations of R2P have maintained this focus. Accordingly, using force for the alteration of borders, the overthrow of regimes, or for supporting a particular group's claim to self-determination is not considered a genuine aim for humanitarian interventions (ICISS 2001: 35).

Independent statehood

While some have criticized the R2P approach for being too state centered (e.g. Makinda 2004),[20] the "sovereignty as responsibility" thesis generally encourages others to announce the demise of the state,[21] given its acceptance of outside intervention in the internal affairs of a state. The R2P approach to sovereignty does pose important challenges to the traditional concept of sovereignty; however, it does not announce its demise. That is, the challenges covered in the R2P report are not tantamount to an abandonment of the discourse of state sovereignty. R2P actually reinforces the importance of state sovereignty, while acknowledging the changes in how sovereignty is accepted and perceived on the international stage and in evolving customary law. The Commission's focus on state sovereignty is in line with the relevant scholarly literature, which argues that the sovereignty discourse remains the dominant one in international politics and international law (e.g. Werner and de Wilde 2001; Cohen 2004). The discourse has evolved significantly from the imperial concept of sovereignty to that of popular sovereignty, according to which sovereignty now resides in the political will of a population, rather than in the will of its ruler or government.

R2P reaffirms the nonintervention principle as default through its focus on independent statehood, and this is the primary way in which it meets any objection to humanitarian intervention. According to the report, "nonintervention ... is the norm from which any departure must be justified ... [and] exceptions to the principle of nonintervention should be limited" (ICISS 2001: 31–32). The responsibility to intervene in a state where extreme violations of human rights are taking place comes from the failure of that state to meet its responsibilities as a sovereign member of the international community. As such, the ICISS report encapsulates the shift in the culture of sovereignty from one of impunity to one of accountability and responsibility of states in light of their obligation to protect. The essence of this shift, however, entails reformulating, not abandoning, the default position of sovereignty and its correlate, the principle of nonintervention. The Commission's proposals respect what is important in sovereignty, namely the nonintervention principle as a basis for the international society to protect against outside interference. As Thakur has aptly noted, "the continuing validity of the nonintervention norm needed restatement and got it in R2P" (2006: 257).

The R2P report emphasizes that the main responsibility to protect lies with the state, which is illustrative of the role of the state as the primary level of action (ICISS 2001: xi, 17, 69). The focus of the ICISS on the prerogatives of the sovereign state rightly mirror the continuing relevance of the sovereignty norm. R2P is based on "the principles inherent in the concept of sovereignty ... the impact of emerging principles of human rights and human security, and the changing state and intergovernmental practice" (2001: 12). After all, for the foreseeable future, nation states will continue to be the main providers of security and welfare for their populations.

According to R2P, it is *only* when states fail to prevent or put an end to the gross human rights violations taking place within their borders that the responsibility to protect falls on the international community, as a second tier of responsibility (ICISS 2001: 69). Henry Shue best captures this in a suggestive synopsis:

> ...to claim, on the one hand, that one believes that Hutu and Tutsi alike, like all persons, have a basic right not to be killed arbitrarily (genocidally or otherwise), but to claim, on the other hand, that it is the job of "their" state to protect them, in accord with the customary international division of labour – each state, its own police – is not to be serious about implementing rights in the real world. If we do not believe that anyone beyond their own state can reasonably be asked to bear the responsibility of protecting these people against the single most serious threat to their lives – their own state – we do not believe in any practically meaningful way that they have a basic right not to be killed.
>
> (2004: 21)

To highlight further the enduring importance of states, the expectation to pick up the responsibility to protect innocent civilians elsewhere falls on *other states*; the international community, however, is not an abstract concept, but one that depends on its members, the society of states. In addition, if the UN is at a deadlock, which makes a Security Council authorization for intervention in instances "crying out for action" impossible, the responsibility to react falls, ultimately – and again – on states, which are part of the so-called coalitions of the willing, or sub-regional, regional and international organizations.

Equality of states

Apart from emphasizing independent statehood, another way in which the R2P report meets the main objections to humanitarian intervention is by focusing on the equality of states. And yet, critics of R2P have suggested that the "sovereignty as responsibility" thesis has negative consequences for sovereign equality. The most common objection portrays sovereignty as the only shield that weak states have against the intrusive powerful ones, and suggests that undermining state sovereignty results in generalized world disorder (Ayoob 2002; Chandler 2002). Critics of the approach to sovereignty as responsibility argue that a shift towards human rights replaces sovereign equality "with an abstract universality that can never be realized within the confines of contemporary society ... [since] human rights can be nothing more than an empty concept" (Chandler 2002: 137). Others suggest that if we presume that a cosmopolitan legal order already exists, one that replaces core international law principles of sovereign equality and nonintervention with cosmopolitan rights, and regards intervention as the enforcement of such rights, "we risk becoming apologists for imperial projects" (Cohen 2004: 3).

Such critics are correct to suggest that states relate to each other as equals through international law, and that sovereign equality is essential for the application of international law. However, the reconceptualization of sovereignty as responsibility does not translate, as some wrongly imply, into a "redistribution of sovereign power; or [to put it differently, into] an acceptance of sovereign inequality" (Chandler 2002: 122). According to the R2P report, the redefinition of sovereignty does not imply a dismissal of sovereign equality – states continue to remain equal (ICISS 2001: 7). The principle of sovereign equality has constantly been updated as a result of key transformative developments in international relations. These include sovereign states giving up their "sovereign" right to go to war, aggressive war becoming illegal, colonialism being deemed a violation of the principle of self-determination, sovereign states beginning to cooperate in a multiplicity of international institutions, and states accepting to be limited by human rights principles, renouncing thus their impermeability to international law in this domain (see Cohen 2004: 20).

As such, sovereignty is not an untouchable concept, but one which also encompasses responsibilities, in both internal functions and external duties (ICISS 2001: 13), including responsibilities towards one state's own citizens. This affects a failed state, for instance, where the government is lacking authority and, therefore, the state lacks capacity to protect its citizens and needs help from outside. The fact that the sovereign status of this state is claimed and recognized by the international community, even under these circumstances, suggests that sovereignty, as a status, is never lost and therefore is not "less equal" in this particular instance than in others. States that are involved in gross violations of their citizens' rights do, indeed, lose some of their "sovereign" attributes, but not in regard to their status as sovereign states; rather, they lose some of the rights and powers that come with it. While this is in agreement with the new rules of state sovereignty, it is not an indication of the abolition of sovereign equality.

Scholars have long argued that sovereignty is best tested in moments of crisis and in exceptional circumstances (e.g. Morgenthau 1948). More recently, Werner and de Wilde suggested that the most fervent defenses of state sovereignty occur in times when states' freedom and independence are at stake (2001: 284). Such arguments reinforce the idea that instances when a state's ability to rule and its autonomy are threatened, strengthen, rather than weaken, the claims to sovereignty. In light of the central question of this chapter, one can easily take up this argument and move it one step further. If one embarks on a theoretical exercise, the next level is represented by instances when gross violations of human rights are taking place, as a result of internal strife. This particular context is one clear example of sovereignty being at stake. Nonetheless, it is also an instance when state sovereignty is a claimed status, which is accepted and perceived as such by the international community. The very fact that the sovereign state represents the first tier of responsibility to stop gross human rights violations is the first indicator of the continuing importance of sovereignty, particularly in moments of crisis. It also illustrates that states are treated as equal, since the broad assessment regarding the first-tier responsibility of sovereign states applies to *all* states.

Another major criticism against the practice of humanitarian intervention relates to some states being "more equal than others." This argument emerged from the syllogism that no major intervention is likely to occur, for instance, against the most powerful states, such as the five permanent members of the Security Council. This raises the important question of double standards, which, unfortunately, cannot be overridden since it is a matter of political reality. The R2P report acknowledges that the regime will be applied selectively: "the reality that interventions may not be able to be mounted in every case where there is justification for doing so is no reason for them not to be mounted in any case" (ICISS 2001: 37). Nonetheless, such selectivity is just a realistic characteristic of today's world, and it signals no departure from the past when nonintervention was allegedly sacred, but never treated as such.

The emphasis R2P places on the sovereign state is accurately justified by considerations of risk of abuse with regard to humanitarian intervention, but also by practicalities regarding enforcement mechanisms for the human rights regime. It is precisely the prominence of sovereign states in enforcing human rights that deserves further consideration.

Enforcement of the human rights regime

The R2P report placed considerable emphasis on states because it correctly assessed that the most problematic of the various governance tasks in human rights is enforcement, and therefore, states' compliance is key in a context in which international institutions, such as the UN, have limited capacity to compel enforcement. The same focus on states was later on reflected by the embracement of R2P in the 2005 General Assembly resolution, and also present in subsequent Security Council resolutions of 2006 and 2009 referencing the principle. Ultimately, states are the only actors capable of ensuring respect for international law and compliance with the human rights regime. That is, international law cannot be put into practice without states' consent. And yet, the enforcement of the human rights regime remains a critical problem, and the mechanisms in place appear insufficient and weak, as suggested by the gross human rights violations that are presently taking place in various parts of the world, and by the lack of mobilization and political will to address them.

Despite the many controversial dimensions of the international human rights regime, one conclusion on which all opposing parties seem to agree is that international legislation is effective only if the law-making parties also consider provisions for enforcement and compliance. This generally occurs either by involving existing institutions, such as the International Court of Justice, or by generating treaty-specific bodies. So far, however, the international human rights regime has not forced the creation of effective enforcement mechanisms for compliance. The reason for this is a very obvious one: state sovereignty. The international legal system is founded on the concept of sovereignty and international obligation depends, after all, on the will of particular sovereign states. Indeed, individual states have to be willing to enforce international human rights norms.

In most cases, states are not willing to accept international supervision, and this applies not only to the obvious category of states with a bad record of respect for human rights, but also to states with a positive record, such as the United Kingdom and the United States. The enforcement of human rights by the international community relies on the sovereign will and the foreign policy goals of states, which tend to give a relatively low priority to issues of human rights. Furthermore, as Robert Jackson (2004) argues with respect to the responsibilities of statecraft, great power brings greater privilege, but also greater responsibility on the world stage. According to this view, states such as the US and the UK, for instance, have heavier responsibilities than others. This is an appealing argument, especially given the need for states to play a leading role in the enforcement of the human rights regime. However, as suggested above, it might well be the case that the very same states with "greater responsibilities" lack the political will to react.

Focusing on the role of individual states is important, given that sovereign states decide whether to ratify international human rights treaties in the first place, and whether they go through with implementation afterward. While some of the powers that used to be performed by states have moved upward to regional and international organizations, others have shifted toward NGOs, and even individuals. Even so, while international organizations and NGOs push for compliance, it is *individual states* that have to put human rights norms into practice. Indeed, if one examines the success of the European human rights regime as compared to the modest accomplishments of the other regional regimes, it is clear that the first owes its achievements, to a great extent, to the voluntary acceptance of the regime by its member states. European states are nationally committed to respecting human rights, and are, thus, very supportive of international procedures vis-à-vis human rights. Undoubtedly, the European regime has strong enforcement mechanisms; however, the power of the European states' deliberate compliance to the human rights regime is also critical.

Having rules about the responsibility to protect and using the R2P language in diplomatic circles are hardly enough. What matters most is to get the necessary political commitment right, in order to implement the R2P guidelines. It is in regard to such issues that another merit of the R2P report emerges; one chapter – Chapter 8 – deals exclusively with key considerations regarding implementation. This chapter warns that without mobilizing the political will when action is needed, the debate about intervention for humanitarian purposes will largely remain academic (ICISS 2001: 70). Paper rights are meaningless for victims of atrocities, without ways to impose compliance; the problem, however, is that human rights and humanitarian law "say little about the role of other states in insuring compliance" (Weiss and Hubert 2001: 146).

The R2P report emphasizes that *national* commitment to respect human rights is both an essential component of a strong human rights regime, and the source of the political will that lies behind strong regimes. The most important steps of the human rights regime, namely the move toward implementation and enforcement, require a significant qualitative increase in states' commitments to human rights. R2P rejects the views advanced by some opponents of the "sovereignty as responsibility" principle, according to which human rights treaties and conventions fundamentally violate the essential sovereign attributes of a state. As Krasner (1999) aptly points out, states voluntarily enter into conventions on human rights, as equal actors on the world stage, and therefore willingly authorize external monitoring procedures that might come with signing such conventions. This is in itself a validation of a state's international legal sovereignty, and therefore contradicts the criticism according to which human rights are in direct opposition to state sovereignty.

Conclusion

The 2001 ICISS report provides the most convincing rejection of the argument that human rights and sovereignty are essentially irreconcilable concepts. The level of detail in the ICISS analysis explains my focus on the report's recommendations, as compared to other representations of R2P in the UN setting. Some UN documents adopted this terminology, despite not elaborating on the alleged human rights–sovereignty contradiction in detail. The reinterpretation of sovereignty as responsibility, which focuses on what sovereignty obliges versus what it endows, is one of the key values of R2P, both in the report and its subsequent formulations of R2P at the UN. It was clearly embraced in paragraph 138 of the 2005 World Summit Outcome Document. Also, it was forcefully advanced in the Secretary-General's report on "Implementing the Responsibility to Protect," which argued that R2P "is an ally of sovereignty, not an adversary" (United Nations 2009a: 7).

More importantly, most UN member states accepted the principle of sovereignty as responsibility during the General Assembly debate on R2P at the end of July 2009. Also, states agreed that internal conflicts can become threats to international peace and security. Accordingly, some member states that took the floor during the General Assembly debate on R2P, such as Qatar for instance, suggested that the notion of international security should be expanded to include the responsibility to protect. There was also agreement that R2P applies only to the four types of human rights violations that the ICISS proposed, namely genocide, ethnic cleansing, war crimes and crimes against humanity. This was included in paragraph 139 of the 2005 Summit Outcome Document, and in the 2009 report of the UN Secretary-General. The same agreement that R2P is confined to these four crimes was reached during the General Assembly debate on the topic.[22] However, one area where disagreement persists relates to the lack of clarity on triggers for intervention. The R2P report does not provide much detail beyond suggesting the two thresholds of genocide and ethnic cleansing, and subsequent references to R2P in UN documents do not elaborate either. As such, the General Assembly debate on R2P concluded that the issue of thresholds triggering R2P action needs to be addressed.

The essence of approaching sovereignty not so much as control but rather as responsibility has been a constant throughout the normative evolution of R2P. Such responsibility is owed by the state to its citizens, to the international community, and to the institutions representing it. The ICISS report suggests that sovereignty and intervention should be viewed as complementary, rather than at odds. It proposes to solve the frustrating, traditional conflict of placing human rights and state sovereignty in permanent opposition to each other by arguing that human rights and state sovereignty can be intertwined. The report contradicts the assumption that respect for human rights runs counter to sovereignty practice, mainly in developing countries, explaining instead how the two components are actually interrelated.

I have dubbed the relationship between sovereignty and human rights put forward by R2P as balanced, because it expresses deference to both state sovereignty and protection of human rights. The ICISS report identified the problems related to the traditional meaning of sovereignty and made recommendations accordingly, in a successful effort to accommodate universal respect for human rights in regard to extreme humanitarian emergencies. Should it have placed more emphasis on sovereignty at the expense of human rights, the balance would have inclined toward a no longer morally sustainable, absolutist, state-focused approach. Instead, R2P's depiction of sovereignty implies a very clear-cut dual responsibility: internally, toward a state's population, and externally, toward other states, as a member of the society of states. The focus of the R2P report on relativism, independent statehood, and the equality of states had the double purpose of putting forward a workable balance between sovereignty and human rights, and of addressing the main objections to humanitarian intervention.

The envisaged relationship between the two norms appears apposite from human rights considerations as well. Should the R2P report have focused more on the human rights module in light of the constantly increasing public discourse emphasizing human rights and human security, the balance would not have remained a workable one. More importantly, it would not have been politically achievable. Limiting the sovereignty emphasis would have given rise to selectivity and abuse vis-à-vis intervention for humanitarian purposes, and it would have clearly failed to capture the endurance of the sovereignty norm. More emphasis on human rights would have given more leverage and fed the worries of those convinced that "[h]e who invokes humanity wants to cheat" (Schmitt cited in Cohen 2004: 4). Also, the latter scenario would have never been accepted by developing countries and by some of the permanent members of the Security Council that are still deeply committed to the traditional meaning of sovereignty, such as Russia and China.

In sum, the most important characteristic of the balance between sovereignty and human rights advanced by the R2P framework results from the focus on the durability of state sovereignty. The ICISS report's initial emphasis on the state and its reinterpretation of sovereignty as responsibility were justified by two key motives: the need to appease the claims regarding the potential for abuse of humanitarian intervention, and the practicalities related to the enforcement mechanisms of the human rights regime. Without doubt, the meaning of the responsibility to protect, as expressed in the ICISS report and in subsequent formulations of R2P at the UN, encompasses deference to both sovereignty *and* human rights.

3 Who authorizes interventions?

> To those for whom the greatest threat to the future of international order is the use of force in the absence of a Security Council mandate, one might say: leave Kosovo aside for a moment, and think about Rwanda. Imagine for one moment that, in those dark days and hours leading up to the genocide, there had been a coalition of states ready and willing to act in defense of the Tutsi population, but the Council had refused or delayed giving the green light. Should such a coalition then have stood idly by while the horror unfolded?
>
> (Annan 1999)

The question of authorization for the use of force is another controversial component of the humanitarian intervention debate. The query has recently become more contentious than ever. Participants on both sides of the debate, namely those rejecting any exception to the requirement for UN Security Council authorization and the proponents of surpassing the Council in instances of exceptional humanitarian emergencies, do not seem to reach any consensus. One of the eight sections of the ICISS report deals with the issue of authority; overall, however, authority is one of the two key questions[1] addressed in the 2001 report in regard to intervention. I discuss whether the ICISS recommendations on authorization are well founded and then I briefly look at what subsequent reformulations of R2P in the UN setting say about who should authorize interventions.

To assess the problematic debates on authority within the humanitarian intervention framework, the major opposing arguments on this question and their legal interpretations are exposed first. I observe how both developed and developing countries approach the issue of authorization and the role played by the Security Council in this context. The theoretical assumptions are then tested against state practice, through a review of several major humanitarian interventions since the 1990s, and the authorization patterns they illustrate. The emphasis is placed on institutional questions, with the normative goal of identifying the most authoritative actors to undertake interventions when humanitarian emergencies arise.

The ICISS approach to the question of authority

The question of authorization for the use of force has become central to recent debates on military intervention for humanitarian purposes. Although not a humanitarian intervention, the 2003 Iraq War brought new interpretations to the topic; "proper authority" was debated fiercely prior to the invasion, during the diplomatic efforts to produce a resolution authorizing the use of force against Iraq. The failure to generate one, combined with the US decision to go to war without UN authorization, made both scholars and practitioners question the purpose, procedure and relevance of the UN. While some asserted the Security Council's irrelevance in maintaining international peace and security (e.g. Perle cited in Thakur 2006: 224), others argued that the UN served its purpose by refusing to endorse recourse to military action that could not be reconciled with its Charter and with international law (Price 2004; Meron 2006).

The R2P report covered all sources of authority under the UN Charter. It argued that the general provisions of Chapter VII and Chapter VIII, including the specific authorization for self-defense action in Article 51, represented a "formidable source of authority to deal with security threats of all types" (ICISS 2001: 48). The R2P report suggested that, undoubtedly, the Security Council was the most appropriate body to deal with military intervention issues for humanitarian purposes. If this does not bring much novelty, the key recommendations are those discussing the question of authority when the Security Council *fails to agree* on collective action. It is to the report's merit that it recognized the significance of this matter.

In fact, the main motivations to set up the ICISS revolved around developing a normative framework to ensure that no more Kosovos and Rwandas would result from the Security Council's own failure to act. In view of the Security Council's past inability or unwillingness to fulfill the role expected of it, the ICISS report considered alternative mechanisms to discharge the responsibility to protect. In the Commission's words, "the Security Council has the 'primary' but not the sole or exclusive responsibility under the Charter for peace and security matters" (2001: 48). The report suggests two sources of authorization for collective action when the Council fails to act: the General Assembly, and regional organizations. They are both referred to in the UN Charter.[2] In regard to the former, the Commission received significant support for the idea during the consultations conducted on the topic, in various parts of the world (2001: 53). In practical terms, the first alternative implies seeking support for military action from the General Assembly meeting in an Emergency Special Session under the established "Uniting for Peace" procedure. However, the report noted the practical difficulties in reaching the two-thirds majority required for this option to work. In regard to the latter, the ICISS report aptly highlighted the strong collective interest regional and sub-regional organizations have in quickly addressing humanitarian catastrophes within their defined boundaries (2001: 53).

Three ICISS recommendations are particularly helpful: first, the Commission proposed the two alternatives *only* when calls for the Security Council authorization had been left unanswered. This can occur either in instances when the Security Council expressly rejects a proposal for intervention where humanitarian issues are notably at stake, or when the Council fails to deal with such a proposal within a reasonable time frame. While outlining the significant implications of inaction, the ICISS report emphasized the importance of having Council authorization, and of states always requesting it before acting. Second, the report suggests the permanent five members of the Security Council refrain from exercising their veto when their vital interests are not at stake, and when a resolution in favor of military intervention has majority support. The use of veto by the permanent five members (P5) of the Council can be the principal obstacle to effective intervention in instances when quick action is needed. Accordingly, the ICISS report suggested the P5 concurred to a code of conduct for the use of veto, or to a mutually agreed practice to govern these situations, referred to as "constructive abstention." Third, an important caveat made its way into the report, which argued that in conscience-shocking situations, when faced with the failure of the Security Council to discharge its responsibility to act, concerned states would not rule out action. If organizations fail to authorize collective interventions, the pressures for action from ad hoc coalitions or individual states intensify. This translates into the "...risk that such interventions, without the discipline and constraints of UN authorization, will not be conducted for the right reasons or with the right commitment to the necessary precautionary principles." Apart from such negative consequences, Security Council inaction can also diminish the credibility of the UN significantly when such interventions *are* successful and are carried out properly (ICISS 2001: 51–55).[3]

Authorizing the use of force

This section explores the two main positions in the debate on authorization for the use of force, and briefly looks at a related facet, namely the politics behind authorization.

The two main positions

For decades, the question of authorization has been controversial. The main positions in this debate are clear: on the one hand, there is no exception to the requirement for UN Security Council authorization; on the other hand, this obligation is not absolute in cases of exceptional humanitarian emergencies. The latter is based on interpretations of customary international law, and, since 1990, on the impact changing state practice has had on previous requirements for authorization.

According to the first position, if prior approval is not forthcoming from the UN, then any intervention is illegal. I stress the "prior" condition because the opposing camp in the debate includes examples of *ex post facto* UN authorization to support their arguments. Within this position, the most common criticisms revolve around the disturbing effects of such interventions on international order (Bull 1977) and the serious consequences of weakening the constraints on the use of force (Chesterman 2001). Since this side of the debate is very straightforward, I focus on the opposing position.

The interventions of the 1990s have led some to oppose the absolute requirement of Security Council authorization. The reasons vary, and encompass deep moral dilemmas in the literature on intervention. They range from criticizing the UN for its lack of authority, and pressing for various reforms of the legal framework governing intervention, to considering the role regional arrangements played in interventions which either lacked prior Security Council authorization or received *ex post facto* authorization. Scholars who offer the harshest criticisms of the relevance and purpose of the UN, and consequently see no need for UN authorization, are at the farthest end of this range of positions. After all, if there is an obligation to react to human tragedy with the approval of the Security Council, this obligation remains even without the Council's blessing (Weiss and Hubert 2001: 162). While some scholars disagree with the generally held view that the UN represents the proper body to authorize humanitarian intervention, others even doubt an appropriate authorizing body exists. For the latter, the UN is neither democratic nor impartial, as the Security Council's vetoes are permanently assigned to the same five states (Shue 1998: 73). It is indeed hard to regard the Security Council as representative, given the lack of permanent members from the South.

An increased consensus emerged among proponents of such positions that the requirement for UN authorization could obstruct the protection of basic human rights in internal conflicts. And so, several alternatives for authorizing the use of force have made their way into the relevant scholarly literature (e.g. Hoffman 1992; Farer 1993; Shue 1998; Buchanan 2004; Pattison 2008). Some emphasize the need for a new legal framework and suggest changing the requirement for UN authorization altogether. Within this category, reform proposals suggest creating a treaty-based, rule-governed liberal-democratic regime for intervention that bypasses the requirement of Security Council authorization.[4] Others recommend that instead of consideration by the Security Council, an arrangement for intervention among several states should be pursued.[5] The Security Council is assigned various roles in such proposals, ranging from no say at all in proceeding interventions, to the requirement that interventions are explained to the Security Council, even if its consent is not required.[6] Despite their variety, such suggestions for alternatives to the UN authorization focus explicitly on collective intervention. Others, however, argue that a group of states writing their own treaty could include a provision for unilateral intervention by an acceptable party, after all the other attempts to halt the humanitarian disasters had failed (e.g. Shue 1998: 75). An important point here relates to how international lawyers use the term "unilateral" to suggest non-authorized intervention, and therefore an intervention with dubious authority, even if more states have approved it. Conversely, social scientists use it to describe a decision or action taken by a single state.

The present context of the debate on authorization was framed in the 1990s, when the UN was in "strategic overstretch" (Weiss 1998: xi). This was the time when calls for a larger role for regional organizations in peace operations surfaced. The record of interventions involving regional actors, culminating with NATO's intervention in Kosovo, heated up the authorization debate, and made some argue in favor of a new trend toward regionalization. Apart from interventions authorized by the Security Council and some authorized by regional organizations, there were also interventions authorized by ad hoc coalitions of the willing, acting without UN endorsement. Given the latter's dubious legal status and the eroding effect it has on sources of legitimacy in international society, in this chapter I am only discussing the regional arrangements' potential of authoritativeness, as an alternative source to the Security Council.

When used in relation to military interventions, "regionalization" refers to operations carried out by regional actors, either alongside the UN or autonomously. The trend toward regionalization started with the 1990 intervention in Liberia, undertaken by the Economic Community of West African States (ECOWAS) and its Ceasefire Monitoring Group (ECOMOG). The ECOWAS interventions in Liberia and Sierra Leone triggered extensive debates on *subsequent*, rather than prior UN authorization. Following the 1999 NATO intervention in Kosovo, which also proceeded without Security Council authorization, more arguments emerged in favor of regional organizations as alternative mechanisms to the Council's authorization. They seemed important when time was essential and the criteria for just intervention were met. It is in this context that the argument that regional arrangements do not necessarily need the Security Council to authorize the use of force started to gain momentum. To further support this position, the UN has developed a practice of retroactive authorization.[7]

The politics behind authorization

The politics behind the authorization of an intervention are essential in understanding how everyday decision-making occurs. It seems then necessary to observe how various actors approach the issue of authorization and the Security Council's role in this context. One distinct category includes developing countries. They openly reject the idea that there is no absolute requirement for UN authorization. Because non-democratic states and Southern states are the most likely targets of humanitarian interventions, they are really keen about their sovereignty and usually claim to have priority in expressing their right of consent (Jackson 1993: 584). Given their colonial experiences, many African and Asian countries are skeptical about Northern countries' justifications for intervention. As such, these states are less inclined to view interventions as legitimate, even if they are undertaken to stop serious human rights abuses. They regard UN authorization as a prerequisite for intervention. Official declarations of developing countries, from the 1999 meeting of the 113 members of the Non-Aligned Movement and the 2000 G-77 summit involving 133 countries, rejected the "so-called right of humanitarian intervention." Two main concerns explain this position. First, developing countries argue that the UN is expanding its peace and security agenda at the expense of its economic and social agenda, the latter being a priority for them. Second, developing countries generally fear that the humanitarian language masks a new round of imperialism. The skepticism regarding Northern humanitarian interventionism increased significantly in the aftermath of the 2003 invasion of Iraq.

China's own stance on various interventions – proceeding either with or without Security Council approval – also illustrates the politics of authorization. China strongly opposed NATO's 1999 intervention in Kosovo. It joined Russia in its efforts to pass a resolution criticizing this intervention, because it perceived it as an attempt to impose US domination and to internationalize "domestic issues."[8] On the other hand, China supported the Australian-led intervention in East Timor, which proceeded *with* the authorization of the Security Council. In this case, however, Indonesia's consent to the Australian-led intervention defused the issue of state sovereignty. A more recent example of the politics game is the Security Council response to the crisis in Darfur. As one of Sudan's allies, China has supported the position of the government in Khartoum during Security Council debates, which rejected the presence of non-African troops on Sudanese territory, even after the Council voted in favor of the hybrid UN–African Union Mission in Darfur (UNAMID).[9]

Even if the opposition of developing countries to using force without UN authorization seems absolute, it actually is not. The way in which the General Assembly reacted to the resolution on Kosovo, which condemned the NATO bombing campaign and called for respect for the principles of nonintervention, offers strong evidence in this sense: fifty-two states opposed the resolution and thirty-three abstained or did not vote at all (Weiss and Hubert 2001: 163). Several developing countries also non-permanent members of the Security Council, such as Malaysia, Gabon, Gambia, Argentina and Brazil, played an important role in the defeat of the Russian draft resolution that criticized NATO's intervention in Kosovo. Furthermore, two of the four interventions that took place without UN authorization in the 1990s,[10] namely those in Liberia (1990) and Sierra Leone (1997), were carried out by the African sub-regional organization ECOWAS. Developing countries were aware of the consequences of state failure, and their support for ECOWAS' intervention in Liberia and Sierra Leone is a good example in point. During the intervention in Liberia, Zimbabwe, for instance, argued in favor of imposing peace from outside in instances when "there is no government in being and there is just chaos in the country" (Karns and Mingst 2004: 287). Such examples undermine the idea of a simple dichotomy between Northern and developing world attitudes.

The Northern stance on the need for Security Council authorization is also divided. According to one view, represented mainly by the UK and the US governments, humanitarian interventions can proceed without UN authorization in instances when the Security Council is paralyzed by dissension among its permanent five members (P5). In such occasions, the Just War argument is invoked together with new readings of international law to support bypassing the UN process (Welsh 2004a: 188). Such was the position of the British government in regard to the interventions in Kosovo, in 1999, and in Iraq, in 2003. Even if the central rationale behind the war in Iraq was not humanitarian, and thus different from the other cases of intervention in the 1990s, Iraq remains suggestive of the present state of the debate.

Frequently, the US is an indispensible mechanism for the effective use of force. Its decreased interest in committing political and military resources to humanitarian protection then becomes problematic, as has been the case since the inception of the "war on terror." Despite taking the same view on authorization as the UK with respect to the interventions in Kosovo and Iraq, the US showed less interest in ensuring UN backing. The US stance reflects its perception of the legitimacy of international institutions. For the US, the legitimacy of the Council depends on its ability to advance the American notion of what best ensures international peace and security (ibid.: 189). This can prove to be rather thorny. That is, the US' recent preferences for unilateral action, coalitions of the willing, and interventions without UN authorization could seriously damage the role of the UN in the future. No wonder many envisage the future of the UN as "clouded," and regard "the multilateralism within the UN framework [as being] on the ropes" (Job 2004: 228; Welsh 2004a: 190). Given such considerations, Allen Buchanan suggests minimizing the dependency on the US for humanitarian interventions, and, instead, increasing the rich European states' involvement and investment in military capacities (2004: 452–453). However, this is not an easy task, as the US pays the largest percentage of all UN peacekeeping costs, currently around 25 percent.

International and domestic politics play a big role in the decision-making process of the most powerful governments. Generally, calls for humanitarian intervention are channeled toward public opinion in Northern countries, rather than urging African, Asian or Latin American governments to intervene. Interventions aimed at preventing or stopping genocide usually have large public and moral support. However, at the domestic level, the costs and risk of lives for personnel involved in any intervention makes it politically imperative for the intervening state to claim a certain degree of self-interest to convince its citizenry about the appropriateness of such operations (ICISS 2001: 36).

The different reactions of the above state actors to the ICISS report best reflect the politics of authorizing the use of force. In this context, Russia supported the rhetoric of the responsibility to protect but shared China's position that no military intervention should take place without Security Council authorization. Russia argued that the UN was already able to deal with humanitarian crises, and that the R2P risked undermining the UN Charter by opening the door to interventions unauthorized by the Council.[11] Even if the UK and France – the strongest R2P supporters among the permanent five members of the Council – stoutly rejected the Russian and Chinese position on unauthorized intervention, they too worried that agreeing on criteria for the use of force might prevent intervention from taking place in due time. The US and the UK have continuously argued that the need to prevent "future Rwandas" implied that unauthorized interventions were not to be entirely overlooked (Bellamy 2006: 152, 164).

Apart from the divisions among Security Council member states, developing countries were also ambivalent. As such, while the Non-Aligned Movement (NAM) members rejected the concept, the Group of 77 did not offer a joint position.

According to the suggestion the ICISS offered to the problem of politicization, mentioned above, the P5 should refrain from using their veto in cases where their vital interests are not at stake. Despite its obvious desirability in theory, this remains difficult to achieve in practice. As expected, the proposition was left out of the September 2005 UN Summit Outcome Document, which endorsed R2P. The most serious drawback in this regard relates to the different interpretations of vital interest among the P5. For instance, China used its veto to refuse extending the peacekeeping operations in Macedonia and Guatemala because these two countries had previously established diplomatic relations with Taiwan. Another example is the US threat to use its veto in regard to the continuation of the operation in Bosnia because of concerns related to the potential subjection of American peacekeepers to the jurisdiction of the ICC (MacFarlane, Welsh and Thielking 2002).

In addition to the divisions in perception and the politics of authorization, there are also different legal interpretations of the "proper authority" question, which tend to emphasize emerging customary law. It is important to discuss these perspectives in relation to the increased reliance on legitimacy, which is an essential element of the authority question.

Legal interpretations

As T. J. Lawrence wrote, "only a few issues [in international law] are as complicated as those concerning the legality of interventions" (cited in Zajadlo 2005: 665). This section looks at what the UN Charter suggests in regard to the use of force and what customary international law implies, while also discussing recent legitimacy trends.

The UN Charter

The UN Charter provides the most important source of legal and constitutional authority regarding the use of force. The Charter is noninterventionist. It restricts states' right to use force internationally, first, to instances of individual or collective self-defense (UN Charter Art. 51), and, second, to cases in which states have to assist in UN-authorized or UN-controlled military endeavors (UN Charter Chapter VII). The UN Charter does not directly address the question of humanitarian intervention, either under UN backing or by states acting independently. Nonetheless, some of its principles are relevant to humanitarian intervention, and thus to R2P. I will therefore briefly review the Charter's provisions regarding the use of force to highlight the conditions under which intervention is legal.

Two distinct elements in the UN Charter appear to pertain to humanitarian intervention. The first is rooted in the Preamble and Article 1 provisions regarding fundamental human rights. These provisions raise but do not address the question of what should happen once fundamental human rights are violated.[12] The second relates to the possibility of using force under UN patronage. The final phrase of Article 2(7) of the UN Charter allows for the use of force within states under Chapter VII.[13] These two aspects of the Charter, which at the time of its drafting were seen as important but not as controversial, turned into significant points of reference for humanitarian intervention (Roberts 2004: 74). Even so, the legal authority of the UN Charter can be ambiguous given the uneasy tensions between some of its norms and provisions, most notably between the promotion of human rights and the respect for domestic jurisdiction. This tension is further complicated by the evolution of state practice.

The Security Council's legal capacity to settle humanitarian crises is set out in Chapter VI and Chapter VII of the UN Charter. Despite being designed for international disputes, the evolving practice of the UN suggests that the provisions in these two chapters empower the Security Council to regard internal situations with broad security reverberations as legitimate subjects for UN response. Article 24 of the UN Charter confers upon the Security Council the "primary responsibility" to deal with security threats of all types. Thus, the Council is empowered to "decide what measures shall be taken … to maintain or restore international peace and security" (Article 39). The Council appears to be at liberty to determine its modes of operation and even its mandate, irrespective of what the Charter states. Accordingly, Security Council actions related to the use of force for humanitarian purposes can become precedents, even if they are not compatible with the UN Charter provisions. As the supplementary volume to the ICISS report observed in regard to Security Council-authorized interventions, "there appears to be no theoretical limits to the ever-widening interpretation of international peace and security" (Weiss and Hubert 2001: 159). The meaning of "threats to peace and security" has been expanded to encompass humanitarian crises.[14]

In addition to the Security Council, the UN Charter refers to two other sources of authority. Despite being subordinated to the Security Council, the General Assembly can also address matters of peace and security. As noted earlier, however, the politics paralyzing any decision within the Council would tend to have similar or worse effects on the General Assembly's "Uniting for Peace" procedure. "Regional arrangements or agencies" are the second potential source of authorization for humanitarian interventions. They lack an explicit definition in the literature on humanitarian intervention, but are usually perceived as cooperation among regional states to enhance their national well-being through collective action. Neither the UN Charter nor the political organs of the UN or the International Law Commission have attempted to define "region" for the purpose of explaining Chapter VIII. There are, however, some distinctions in the "regional actors" or "regional arrangements" category; the purpose and scope of a multipurpose regional organization like the Organization of American States (OAS) or the African Union (AU) differ from those of sub-regional ones, like The Economic Community of West African States (ECOWAS) or the Association of South East Asian Nations (ASEAN), which in turn differ from specific task-oriented institutions like NATO.

Regional arrangements started to assume a larger role in peace operations in the 1990s. According to Article 53(1) of the UN Charter, the Security Council has the power to utilize regional arrangements under its authority, but these organizations lack independent authority with respect to enforcing peace processes. Chapter VIII of the UN Charter requires regional organizations to keep the Security Council fully informed of activities undertaken or contemplated with respect to the maintenance of international peace and security (Article 54). The only exception is the provision for collective defense, which states that the Security Council has to be informed, but military action by regional arrangements is allowed *until* the Council takes action (Article 51).

Consequently, on the one hand the UN Charter assigns responsibility for maintaining peace and security and authorizing the use of force to the Security Council (Article 24). On the other hand, however, it allows regional organizations to use force to defend member states without *prior* UN authorization, by guaranteeing states' rights to act in self-defense or in collective self-defense (Article 51). The hierarchy, though, is clear, as the Security Council takes precedence. However, Article 52 also supports the responsibilities of regional arrangements with respect to security by stating that "nothing in the Charter should preclude the existence of regional arrangements or agencies for dealing with such matters relating to the maintenance of international peace and security as are appropriate for regional action." The Charter left unanswered important concerns about the relationship between regional actors and the UN. Thus, their rapport, as described in the Charter, is not that apparent. The UN Charter does not establish a context for consultations between the two, and it does not even offer a definition of regional organizations in Chapter VIII, which initiated the term.

Some have described the Charter's vagueness regarding the requirement of securing UN approval for the regional use of force as purposeful (e.g. Job 2004: 229). This ambiguity resulted from the tensions between states' requests to respect their individual sovereignty and to protect themselves, and their aspiration to establish an institution able to prevent aggression. In practice, regional organizations at times avoided invoking Article 53, which requires *prior* UN authorization. Instead, they chose to invoke Article 51, which recognizes the legitimacy of collective self-defense, and is subject only to *subsequent* controlling action by the UN, whose intervention can ultimately be prevented by the use of the veto.[15] As Inis Claude noted in 1971, "regional arrangements *may* place themselves at the service of the UN and voluntarily accept its restraining influence, but they have escaped the subordinate status which was intended for them by the drafters of the Charter" (117). And so, in spite of the expected straightforward answers, the range of legal interpretations in the UN Charter appears very broad and ambiguous at times. Since such inconsistencies make clear-cut conclusions on authorizing the use of force difficult, I also look at customary international law for a more complete outline of the legal interpretations.

Customary international law

Changing state practice alters international law. Apart from the codified international law, custom can also dictate what is legal, illegal and legitimate. "Changing experiences shape principles and norms, just as principles and norms influence policies, decisions and operations" (Weiss and Hubert 2001: 156). Those opposing an absolute requirement for UN authorization turn to customary international law to support their stance. They argue in favor of the potential legality of interventions proceeding outside the framework of the UN Charter. However, while many scholars point to the advantages of the gradual emergence of normative consensus based on recent practice (e.g. Stromseth 2003), others emphasize the limits of this route toward legal reform (e.g. Buchanan 2004). The latter suggest that international law allows states to opt out of the practice of the new customary norm during its "crystallization." It is also difficult both to determine the existence of any new pattern of state behavior and to assess its prevalence before it becomes crystallized. As such, satisfying the *opinio juris* requirement becomes more debatable (Buchanan 2004: 447).

The post-Cold War record of interventions, however, made many scholars argue that a basis to support interventions without UN authorization, in response to large-scale threats to life, already exists in customary international law. The debates on the changing nature of state practice and its impact on codified law represent the core of the disputes over whether humanitarian intervention can proceed in the absence of prior UN authorization. The most cited example in support of an emerging customary law is the rejection of the Security Council resolution proposed by Russia, condemning NATO's intervention in Kosovo by a vote of twelve (encompassing both developed and developing nations) to three (China, Russia, and Namibia). NATO's intervention in Kosovo was described as "legitimate but illegal" (Independent International Commission on Kosovo 2000: 4).

The question of legitimacy of interventions without the Security Council stamp of approval was extensively debated after the Kosovo intervention, with scholars portraying it as indicative of a new norm of humanitarian intervention (e.g. Cassese 1999). Most democratic governments and numerous scholars perceived this intervention as legitimate,[16] even if it was deemed "illegal" because it was not authorized by the Security Council. Accordingly, it was used as evidence of state practice toward the creation of a customary legal norm that permits intervention without UN approval. But the distance between law and legitimacy could also, first, undermine the authority of the Security Council and the role the UN plays in peace operations, and second, intensify the difficulties of individual states and regional organizations when asked to intervene (Voon 2004: 47). Even so, given the blurry area in which international custom evolves, the concept of "unauthorized but legitimate" intervention started to be mentioned more often in the literature on intervention. But what does legitimacy entail?

Legitimacy trends

Since international law alone does not seem to establish the legitimacy of various interventions, I consider additional factors that collectively paint a more complete answer. Regardless of whether or not a military operation is authorized by the UN, certain characteristics may enhance its legitimacy, such as the evidence of the scale of the humanitarian disaster, longer-term outcomes, the conduct of the intervening states, and the requests for help. There are instances when factors undermining the legality of an intervention, such as an isolated veto in the Security Council or a majority supporting vote in the General Assembly that does not reach the necessary two-thirds, actually strengthen its legitimacy (ICISS 2001: 156). Also, the effectiveness of an intervention can be sufficient for reaching an adequate degree of legitimacy, in extraordinary circumstances where extremely beneficial consequences are more than likely (Pattison 2008: 402). It becomes apparent why legitimacy is an essential factor in any discussion on who should authorize the use of force: different attributes contribute cumulatively to the legitimacy of an intervener, and can add up to an adequate degree of legitimacy, even if the intervening agent does not fully pass the legality test.

The conflict between legitimacy and legality has been a subject of controversy for lawyers, philosophers, and political scientists alike, long before the International Commission on Kosovo suggested in 2000 the need to bridge the gap between the two (10). At present, this conflict appears more intense than ever. This is due to the conditional sovereignty discourse, which became more prominent after the US-led invasion of Iraq. Even if this intervention was not humanitarian, it did increase the controversy on the "proper authority" question. Recent military enterprises seem to boost the requirement for more legitimacy from powerful international actors in the near future; they also tend to decrease the appetite for controversial interventions (Pattison 2008). Because of the increased importance placed on the legitimacy of an intervention, even superpowers like the US might hesitate before intervening through the so-called coalitions of the willing. What the world regards as legitimate has become of significant concern in the international realm. In this context, even an intervention without UN authorization can become legitimate if others validate either the moral or the legal justifications offered by the interveners (Bellamy and Williams 2005: 174).

In essence, there are many arguments supporting the UN's role in conferring legitimacy to an intervention. There are also objections to perceiving a Security Council authorization as *the* necessary condition for legitimacy. According to the former category, the central source of UN legitimacy derives from the fundamental purpose of the UN to maintain peace and security. Several characteristics of the UN are of concern for the latter position: even if the Security Council is the forum designed to authorize intervention, this certainly does not guarantee that an agreement can be reached in regard to specific cases; there is a need to react to humanitarian emergencies,[17] whether or not the Security Council is seized by a crisis; and the UN has little power to conduct military operations.

The proponents of these positions argue that the protection of civilians from gross violations of human rights plays a significant role in the contemporary human rights regime, and in the UN Charter. Inaction by the Security Council can result in even greater human rights abuses, thus making the UN liable to charges of ineffectiveness (Weiss and Hubert 2001: 163). In such instances, regional organizations appear as the next authoritative alternative in what would resemble a legitimacy pyramid.

Regional organizations taking charge of an intervention are one alternative, even if this means using force without UN authorization (Bellamy and Williams 2005; Badescu 2007). By recognizing regional arrangements and agencies, the Charter may have enhanced their legitimacy even when they act without specific authorization from the Security Council (Smith and Weiss 1998: 235). Regional notions of legitimacy have thus emerged. There is, however, no universal agreement on the topic. To use the controversial example of NATO's intervention in Kosovo, despite being seen as legitimate by the nineteen NATO member states, it was not perceived as such by countries like Russia, China, India, and by most of the rest of the South. Generally, the more endorsements any given intervention receives from respected institutions and states, the greater its legitimacy.

Examining the record of humanitarian interventions since the 1990s is the best method to pinpoint legitimacy trends. Additionally, testing the legal claims introduced so far against state practice yields a better assessment of the relative merits of the two opposing positions on authorization. The review of humanitarian interventions in the post-Cold War era includes both UN and non-UN authorized interventions.

An overview of interventions in the post-Cold War era

The number of peace operations increased significantly in the 1990s. In the last decade of the twentieth century, ten humanitarian interventions took place, both with explicit UN authorization and without it.[18] The rate of initiation of almost seven new peace operations per year in the 1990s decreased slightly after 2000, mainly due to existing commitments, to approximately 4.5 new operations (Diehl 2008: 61–63). The year 1999 can be described both in positive and gloomy terms, because of costly international efforts in East Timor, Sierra Leone, and Kosovo. Between 1999 and 2003 there was a move from UN to non-UN peace operations, with the year 2003 alone witnessing six new non-UN peace operations, and only one new UN mission. Starting with 2004, six new major UN operations commenced, and force contributions to the UN Mission in the Democratic Republic of the Congo (MONUC) increased significantly. No wonder this period was dubbed "the renaissance" of UN peacekeeping (Williams and Bellamy 2005: 43). In 2009 alone, the UN peacekeeping presence in Chad, Darfur and the Democratic Republic of the Congo increased, although some of these missions, especially in Darfur, continue to lack sufficient resources to address all challenges related to protecting civilians on the ground.

Between 2003 and 2004, non-UN actors created eight new peace operations in Africa, Europe, Asia, and the Pacific. This is significant since the UN initiated the same number of peace operations in eight years.[19] The non-UN authorized interventions were undertaken in: Macedonia (2002), under NATO authorization; Central African Republic (2002), under the authority of the Economic and Monetary Union of Central African States (CEMAC); Macedonia (2003), with the EU as the authorizing body; Burundi (2003), under the authority of the African Union (AU); Liberia and Côte d'Ivoire (2003), with ECOWAS as authorizing body; the Solomon Islands (2003), with Australia at the lead, as was also the case in East Timor, under Operation Astute (2006); and Darfur, Sudan (2004), with the African Union (AU) as the authorizing body.

These instances show how various agents have become deeply involved with humanitarian intervention. The increasing role of regional actors is an evident pattern. In addition to humanitarian considerations, authorizing agents have also invoked international peace and security-related concerns for taking action. The increased number of military operations that took place in this period should not conceal the failures of the UN to act effectively in instances like 1994 Rwanda, and in 1995 in Srebrenica, Bosnia – the two most cited examples of UN failures. It was because of these instances that the ICISS report placed so much emphasis on the "right authority" question. To be fair, however, the frequency of UN-authorized peace operations has not decreased. Rather, regional and sub-regional actors have increasingly taken initiative in humanitarian emergencies, filling in the gaps left by the UN.[20]

The non-UN interventions undertaken since 1990 can be divided into three categories: those conducted by individual states, those undertaken by coalitions of the willing, and interventions authorized by regional arrangements. Coalitions of the willing began intervening to stop gross human rights violations in their neighborhoods or in former colonies, as was the case in Sierra Leone, Côte d'Ivoire, Albania, and the Democratic Republic of the Congo (DRC). UN or EU peacekeeping missions usually followed up such interventions. Many of these operations heralded the trend of using coalitions of willing states as "first responders," as opposed to waiting for UN-mandated operations (Taft and Ladnier 2006: 11). Because of authoritativeness and legitimacy concerns, I pay less attention to these agents and focus instead on examining the record of interventions authorized by regional actors, perceived as more valid alternatives to the Security Council. Moreover, the increased role regional agents play in interventions justifies this choice.

The Security Council authorized six out of the ten humanitarian interventions of the 1990s, in Bosnia, Somalia, Rwanda, Haiti, Albania, and East Timor. The UN received the consent of the host government in four of these instances, which made intervention unproblematic at least from the legal point of view.[21] Generally, UN members did not contest the two remaining interventions without host state consent, in Somalia and Haiti. This confirms something which was never questioned in the first place, namely that the UN is perceived as the appropriate body to authorize humanitarian interventions.

I am interested instead in the question of institutional alternatives. For this, I look at the remaining four interventions of the 1990s, which proceeded without Security Council authorization: the ECOWAS intervention in Liberia (1990), the enforcement of no-fly zones in northern Iraq (1991), the ECOWAS intervention in Sierra Leone (1997), and NATO's military operation in Kosovo (1999). They provide useful material for testing the theoretical assumptions introduced above. Several interventions undertaken by regional actors since 2000, without prior Security Council authorization, are also relevant: the ECOWAS interventions in Côte d'Ivoire (2003) and Liberia (2003), and the AU interventions in Burundi (2003) and Darfur (2004). The Security Council has subsequently welcomed the last three. Such examples can be used to verify the trends announcing the end of the absolute requirement for *prior* UN authorization in instances of grave humanitarian emergencies. The details of these interventions are too multifaceted to be covered here; they are potently offered elsewhere.[22] Discussing the points relevant to the authorization question is more helpful.

In 1990, ECOWAS Ceasefire Monitoring Group (ECOMOG) took action to stop the killings of civilians in Liberia and restore peace and democracy. In 1997, the same ECOWAS mandated the ECOMOG to restore order and protect human rights in Sierra Leone, where Nigeria had also intervened in the same year, for similar purposes. These two operations were undertaken without prior UN authorization and without the consent of the host government. In general, the international response to these interventions was positive, and the UN issued statements supporting both of them, retroactively.

Northern Iraq, in 1991, is another example of an intervention undertaken without specific Security Council authorization. In this case, the US, France, and the UK created "safe-havens" to help refugees and displaced civilians to return to their homes. Even if the UN had condemned the Iraqi repression of civilians as a threat to international peace and security before the intervention took place, it did not explicitly authorize the application of military force. Despite the fact that the intervening states justified their action as being in support of UN resolution 688, this resolution did not specifically authorize intervention. The three intervening states further justified their action as an exceptional right to intervene on humanitarian grounds.

NATO's action in Kosovo is by far the most controversial intervention of the 1990s. Undertaken in 1999, it heated up the debate on authority, especially in the context of evolving state practice. In this particular instance, the Security Council did not authorize the use of force. Since such an authorization seemed improbable because of the opposition of China and Russia, it was in fact not formally requested. NATO governments bypassed the Council, and used "humanitarian necessity" as their legal justification. As mentioned above, this intervention was subsequently referred to as "illegal but legitimate."[23]

In 2003, ECOWAS authorized two more missions, without UN approval, in Côte d'Ivoire and Liberia. In February 2003, the AU heads of state approved the first armed peace operation of this regional organization, in Burundi (AMIB), which was undertaken without UN Security Council authorization. Despite a serious lack of resources necessary for such an operation and severe financial difficulties, AMIB managed to improve the security situation on the ground by the end of 2003. Additionally, the operation was widely seen as legitimate, mainly because the UN had refused to deploy troops in Burundi for more than a decade, but it supported AMIB *ex post facto*, and later mandated the UN mission in Burundi. The Darfur region of Sudan was the focus of another operation initiated by the AU. In 2004, the AU authorized its second peacekeeping enterprise, the African Union Mission in Sudan (AMIS), which started as an observer mission. It later expanded its mandate to include election monitoring and deployment of forces to protect civilians. Even without initial Security Council authorization, AMIS was regarded as legitimate because of the severity of the conflict in the area.[24]

Apart from regional actors, coalitions of the willing and individual states have also initiated interventions. For the last two categories of agents, however, the interventions proceeded with the consent of the host state. This is one first reason why they are excluded from the present discussion, as the legitimacy of such operations is unquestionable. Instances of individual states intervening unilaterally at the invitation of the host state are consistent with Article 2 of the UN Charter, and thus not controversial. In fact, the UN itself has yet to authorize an intervention against a functioning state without its consent (Bellamy 2005: 38).[25]

From the typology of non-UN authorized interventions, either by individual states, coalitions of the willing, or regional arrangements, regional actors' initiatives also seem more legitimate. Regional agents are certainly located higher than the other two options on an imaginary legitimacy ladder, whose base is occupied by individual states and coalitions of the willing. Obtaining the Security Council stamp of approval for any humanitarian intervention evidently remains the first choice, at the top of the legitimacy hierarchy; however, regional arrangements seem to come next to the Security Council on the legitimacy ladder, lastly followed by individual states and coalitions of the willing, whose authorization is the easiest to get, which also makes it the least legitimate. Not only are regional actors more legitimate than these last two agents, but they have also been more active, as the record of interventions since the early 1990s shows. In terms of authorization, regional arrangements thus appear as the most promising – and also appropriate – alternative to the UN in cases of supreme humanitarian emergencies. Accordingly, the search for patterns and the discussion below of the merits and drawbacks of authorizing agents will focus primarily on the UN and regional alternatives.

A synopsis of trends

A quick overview of the record of humanitarian interventions since the early 1990s suggests a growing acceptance of military operations undertaken without explicit UN authorization. Not only have such interventions been tolerated, but they have also been embraced in most of the humanitarian crises of the 1990s. Large sections of the international community regarded these interventions as legitimate, despite the lack of prior UN authorization. This is why the gap between the legitimacy and legality of humanitarian interventions appears to widen. The record of interventions suggests that various actors appear gradually more satisfied with replacing the Security Council's endorsement with authorizations coming from regional and sub-regional organizations. As Brian Job duly argued in 2004, "the premise that regional organizations would condition their peace operations upon UN approval did not hold" (236). The ECOWAS intervention in Liberia, which proceeded at Nigeria's initiative, verifies this trend. So does the NATO military intervention in Kosovo, when NATO support was invoked after it became clear that the UN approval would have been impossible to get.

Seeking *ex post facto* authorization from the UN is another notable trend, illustrated once again by NATO's intervention in Kosovo, and by ECOWAS interventions in Sierra Leone and Liberia. Closely related to this is the tendency of the major powers to act unilaterally in anticipation of formal UN authorization. Major players may intervene forcefully to restore peace and respect for human rights when they perceive their national interests at risk, or when the domestic opinion in their countries urges them to react.

The preferences of host governments, on the receiving end of intervention, are also worth considering. Interventions receiving the host state's consent are unambiguous, because the invitation of the host government clearly confers legitimacy to any intervention undertaken without Security Council authorization. Apart from the context of failed states, with no authority in power, there are also cases where the host government is hostile to outside intervention. This can increase the costs of intervention and the risks of harming the very civilians who need to be protected. The most recent example in point is Sudan, where the central government in Khartoum has vehemently refused to allow non-African troops into Darfur, arguing that this would be tantamount to colonialism. Sudan also accepted a regional solution for Darfur, in the form of the AU presence, but has categorically refused any UN input for years. UNAMID, the hybrid mission that took over from AMIS on December 31, 2007, has also been acutely affected by this position. Khartoum's preferences have so far been respected, for fear of greater government reprisals against civilians or other harmful measures, such as denying overflight rights, and facilitating the flow of arms to those resisting the intervening force.

The interventions discussed above suggest a decrease in the number of requests for UN authorization for the use of force. The interventions performed by regional actors seem to support the argument that a legal custom is emerging, according to which interventions proceed without authorization from the Security Council, and subsequent UN approval is sought. Proponents of the subsidiary model between UN and regional actors applaud the noticeable trend of having regional security communities involved in interventions.

Two authoritative alternatives: the UN and regional arrangements

The authorizing agency for humanitarian intervention has varied greatly in the post-Cold War era. Given the Security Council's past unwillingness or inability to authorize interventions to halt humanitarian disasters, there is a clear need of alternative authorization mechanisms in such instances. After the UN image was negatively affected by the 2003 invasion of Iraq, having regional organizations authorize military operations in the territories of their respective member states appeared at times as a more cautious alternative. One key distinction, however, relates to having regional organizations acting within their area of operation or on the border, such as ECOWAS in Liberia and NATO in Kosovo, as opposed to regional agents intervening outside their areas, like the NATO-led International Security Assistance Force (ISAF) in Afghanistan. For impartiality and increased authoritativeness reasons, regional arrangements are preferred to alternatives such as coalitions of the willing. Not only have the latter stronger eroding effects on the source of legitimacy for the international community, but they are also more open to abuse.

Should the UN or regional actors undertake humanitarian intervention? In the mid-1990s, the UN Secretary-General made an appeal to regional actors to play a larger role in peace operations. Invoking the mandate for regional organizations expressed in Chapter VIII of the UN Charter, he pictured a division of labor between regional actors and the UN based on the capability–legitimacy relationship; regional organizations were expected to supply the manpower, while the UN would provide legitimacy by authoritatively approving the use of force. Some, however, argue that the interventions of the 1990s illustrate a significant decrease of the "value" of UN legitimacy in the capability–legitimacy relationship. That occurred once regional organizations became more assertive in authorizing their own interventions without prior UN blessing, partly because of the inadequacies of the UN capabilities to organize and supervise peace missions, as seen in Somalia, Rwanda, and Bosnia. The UN lacked military preparedness for combat roles, faced member states' reluctance to risk the lives of their forces for humanitarian goals, was committed to values of impartiality and non-use of force in cases where these were no longer appropriate, and failed to protect endangered civilians (Roberts 2004: 82). Such UN limitations can only erode the institution's moral authority and legitimacy to react in response to humanitarian emergencies. The expansion of the Security Council's list of activities coupled with the absence of any real UN operational capabilities resulted in the delegation of authority to regional organizations and coalitions of the willing (Weiss 2007: 50).

Relying too heavily on the Security Council for authorization opens up another set of problems, centered on the veto power of the P5. The P5 might choose to use their veto to avoid creating an institutional precedent that could be used against them in the future (Kritsiotis quoted in Voon 2004: 48). Another risk is that governments counting on the support of a P5 state might engage in mass abuses with impunity (Roberts 2004: 85). Even in instances when the Security Council does consider granting authorization, it usually faces the significant problem of a slow decision-making process, which averts intervention from taking place within the right time frame to save lives. Darfur was an example in point in the first couple of years after the eruption of the conflict.

Accordingly, if victims are to rely solely on the UN, they might find themselves in a critical situation, without assistance to halt the human rights violations in due time. As mentioned above, this was the case in Burundi and Sudan, for instance, where the UN had not authorized a peace operation for a long time, despite the obvious need for one.

The UN was severely criticized in relation to the 2003 invasion of Iraq. The fact that the US used force against Iraq without UN authorization was one of the most threatening traumas the institution passed through in decades, and has seriously challenged its image. And yet, it is evident that the damage done to the UN's reputation was smaller than it would have been had it consented to US demands and ratified its war against Iraq (e.g. Price 2004: 267). In the latter case, the UN would have had no credibility at all; no authorization from this institution for using force would have been perceived as necessary, had it been seen as a stamp of approval for the wishes of the major powers. The UN is not to be dismissed so easily, mainly because of the institutional leverage its authorization carries in terms of legitimacy; and especially in the aftermath of the Iraq War states considering intervention look for legitimacy in humanitarian interventions.

Without doubt, the central UN resource in matters of security is its role in conferring legitimacy. Despite the real gap between capacity and legitimacy, the UN remains, in Richard Price's words, "the best arbiter we have of acceptable conduct for the global community" (2004: 264). The UN surveillance over global security is one valuable attribute of this institution, in a context in which the great powers tend to be solely interested in humanitarian emergencies directly related to their areas of interest. The Security Council's authorization of UN forces to avert the serious bloodshed in the DRC, while the rest of the world was focused on the war in Iraq, is a good example in point. Even if more dynamism in addressing humanitarian emergencies would undoubtedly be welcome, multilateral action – or at least UN-authorized unilateral action – is still necessary to ensure a minimal degree of impartiality. Moreover, the presence or absence of Security Council resolutions is for many states the key issue in determining whether or not to take part in an intervention.

Do regional actors do better as agents of intervention? States bordering on a war zone clearly have strong interests in resolving the conflict – in addition to humanitarian concerns – and will thus be more likely to react faster. Furthermore, regional organizations are familiar with the intricacies of local situations and the regional context. The fact that the local actors' territories and economies are visibly touched by the conflict and migration in the area is the most cited advantage of having regional organizations involved in humanitarian crises. Thus, states in the region have a strong incentive to react rather than to remain on the sidelines. Moreover, the shared background and experiences of the neighboring countries facilitate a better understanding of the actors and local cultures involved in the conflict. This can make countries in the region more effective in ending a conflict. Also, regional actors' agendas are not overloaded with the amount of global problems the UN faces, consequently making them a better option to address the crisis at hand promptly. A faster response usually translates into a more effective one, especially if a regional intervention provides the right mixture of knowledge and capability (Welsh 2002: 516).

However, the regional distribution of such characteristics is not uniform. Any quick overview of interventions in the post-Cold War era reveals the significant variations in the organization, conduct and regularity of regional peace efforts. As was the case with the UN, institutional capacity for undertaking humanitarian interventions is central to the discussion of the overall performances of regional actors and their operational choices, but this is discussed at length in the following chapter. For now, only the elements pertaining to the authority question are addressed, particularly in relation to the most committed agents. Some regions of the world, such as northern Asia, do not even have security institutions; others have very weak ones, an example being the Association of South-East Asian Nations (ASEAN); while organizations in other regions are very active, with the African Union and the European Union being the most active in recent years.

Whether regional organizations have at their disposal the legal provisions to undertake humanitarian intervention is also an important question. The European region is the most advanced in this regard: it has NATO, designed to address collective security and defense threats in Europe, and more recently, the European Union (EU), which now also has a common defense policy, is able to authorize and terminate interventions through the European Council, and has carried out successful peace operations. At the opposing end of the continuum are the regional organizations whose legal provisions on collective security are mainly directed toward interstate conflicts and regional aggression acts, rather than at internal conflicts. The OAS is one example, but the Gulf Cooperation Council and the League of Arab States also benefit from legal provisions on collective security which allow them to use force. Other regional and sub-regional organizations enjoy conflict management powers, but mostly for economic-related concerns (Diehl 2008: 72).

The African continent has recently taken big steps to improve its security architecture, which is particularly laudable given that most of the grave humanitarian emergencies are located in Africa.[26] The AU began to codify a norm of humanitarian intervention in 1998, under the "Framework for the Mechanism for Conflict Prevention, Management, Resolution, Peace and Security," which allows for troop deployment in internal conflicts perceived as threats to the region. Through its Peace and Security Council, and with the consent of the AU Assembly, the AU has the authority to undertake interventions and deploy troops. The AU was the first regional organization formally to ratify the normative right to intervene in the internal affairs of member states in instances when the UN is either unwilling or unable to react. Likewise, ECOWAS declared its normative right to intervene in regional conflicts, through the adoption of the ECOWAS Protocol in 1999, which allows it to use force to intervene militarily in a member state when the conflict there becomes a threat to regional security. The Economic Community of Central African States (ECCAS) adopted a similar protocol in 2000.

Such legal provisions in their respective Charters make some regional and sub-regional organizations good candidates for alternative authorizing agents to the UN, at least from the legal point of view. But are regional agents really a panacea? Despite their advantages, they too face dilemmas of legitimacy and capacity. Regional actors can be seriously limited as agents of domestic conflict management. As the operations in Liberia, Sierra Leone, Burundi and Darfur suggested, the AU and ECOWAS depended on significant support and assistance from outside bodies, such as the UN, EU, NATO, and powerful states. ECOWAS was lacking substantial capacity to sustain many of its peace missions and always required outside logistical support. Regional actors sometimes fail to protect civilians effectively in conflict zones because of unclear and disputed lines of accountability and governance. AMIB faced many of the familiar problems the UN faced in the 1990s, including lack of financial resources, proper equipment, and relevant troop experience. As AMIS compellingly illustrates, despite the AU's political will to address the Darfur crisis, its efforts were inadequate for the scale of atrocities occurring in Western Sudan, and for the high numbers of civilians who needed protection.

A common criticism of regional agents of authorization revolves around their inability to take action against the major regional powers, which means that it is highly improbable that interventions will be considered when powerful members are involved in the conflict (e.g. Diehl 2008; Weiss 2007). Consequently, regional agents are regarded as a good choice in response to conflicts between – or within – smaller states, whereas the UN appears to be the agent with the potential to control a regional power. Regional powers are no more altruistic than global powers. Whenever a regional group or a local power chooses to intervene militarily, potential claims of self-interested motives are unavoidable. Several cases in the record of interventions since the 1990s suggest that operations authorized by regional actors are constrained by the interests of the hegemonic member states: NATO became involved in Kosovo once the US chose to react to the conflict in the Balkans; Russia has dominated all the CIS operations; and Nigeria exercised its sphere of influence through ECOWAS actions (Job 2004: 234). Furthermore, struggles can break out between the local hegemon and middle-ranking powers, which may encourage states to side with various rebel groups in retaliation (Olonisakin and Ero 2003: 234). Because of such faults, regionalism could prolong and even intensify domestic conflict, instead of containing or terminating it. This was the case in Burma, for instance, where by strengthening the hand of the government, regional support increased the persecution and insecurity of groups seeking political change. And so, having regional actors intervene militarily is not without risks.

The examination of the advantages and drawbacks of the UN and regional actors as alternatives for authorizing the use of force suggests there is no definite answer to whether one is better than the other. Scholars have argued that the increase in the number of regional peace initiatives is neither good nor bad, and that there seems to be no intrinsic advantage of the UN over regional arrangements in terms of managing conflicts (e.g. Diehl 2008: 83, 134). The examples used so far suggest that the UN and regional actors are capable of both authorizing and undertaking successful interventions, and of failing miserably. The benefits of one authorizing mechanism over the other clearly depend on the specificities of the conflict, the timing of the requests for intervention, the degree of urgency, and the capabilities available at that moment in time, among other variables. Generally, a better division of labor between the "overstretched" UN and regional organizations, or an improved "task sharing" – to use Weiss' (1998) terminology – is the advisable approach in this context.

R2P's answer to the authorization question

The debates on the changing nature of state practice and its impact on codified law represent the core of the dispute over whether intervention can proceed in the absence of prior UN authorization. The overview of post-Cold War era interventions illustrates the need for alternative authorizing loci to the UN Security Council. This becomes particularly apparent in light of the Security Council's past unwillingness or inability to authorize some interventions when needed. Alternative authorizing mechanisms are thus necessary to act as parallel institutional agencies ready to fill the UN gaps, rather than to replace the Security Council. The R2P report correctly identified this requirement, and it is here, I argue, that the major merits of the R2P report's recommendations on authority reside. The ICISS suggests that the Security Council cannot have an absolute monopoly on the authorization of interventions for humanitarian purposes, given previous UN failures to react to humanitarian emergencies in due time and the serious implications of inaction (2001: 53–55). After the overview of the legal and practical arguments, for and against seeing the Security Council as the supreme authorizing body, it becomes evident that the R2P report was correct in suggesting the need for alternative mechanisms to authorize interventions when the Council is deadlocked. This is not tantamount to condemning the UN as unfit to deal with authorization issues. Regional organizations have both failed to take action and succeeded in authorizing interventions when the UN was not able or willing to do so, just as much as the UN's record of interventions includes failures and successes alike.

The Security Council remains the preferred source of authorization for the most legitimate use of force, and the ICISS report certainly emphasizes this. However, the Council is not the singular source of legitimacy, as illustrated by several instances requiring R2P-type action, the most recent high-profile one being Darfur. It is in this context that the R2P report talks about two alternatives to authorize the use of force, namely regional arrangements and the General Assembly's "Uniting for Peace" procedure. Moreover, the record of state practice shows that the international community no longer sees the approval of the Security Council as an absolute must. Interventions since the 1990s also suggest that states seem to respect a "legitimacy ladder" when considering interventions, and climb the necessary stairs accordingly; the Security Council is the most desirable form of authorization, therefore located at the top of the legitimacy hierarchy, followed by regional organizations as the second-best authoritative mechanism.

The R2P report's recommendations confirm the existence of an imaginary legitimacy ladder for interventions when ranking various agents of authorization. The ICISS report refers to the Security Council as "the first port of call on any matter relating to intervention … but not the last one" (2001: 53). Interventions undertaken without Security Council authorization can be legitimized subsequently by acquiring the approval of the Council *ex post facto*, or, in other instances, by the agreement of the host state. As the ICISS report correctly suggests, *ex post facto* authorizations "may offer a way out of the dilemma" if similar cases occur again in the future (2001: 54).

In legal terms, how can the recommendations opening the door to alternative authorizing agents be accommodated within the existing international law?[27] There are grounds for arguing that the limited use of force, solely for the purpose of responding to extreme humanitarian emergencies is not a violation of Article 2(4) of the UN Charter. Accordingly, while humanitarian intervention without Security Council authorization is indeed unlawful, an illegal act can sometimes be morally legitimate, as is the case in domestic law, and so it may be overlooked by the law enforcement authorities or treated leniently (Aust 2005: 232).

The ICISS recommendations on authorization have generated various reactions, ranging from criticism that they add further ambiguity to the application of humanitarian intervention (e.g. Bellamy 2006: 149) to praises for their "imaginative aspects" (e.g. Wheeler, 2005a: 2, 11). According to the first position, R2P increases the ambiguity of the application of intervention "by attempting to legislate for unauthorized intervention in cases where the Security Council is deadlocked [and by] placing great emphasis on the factual elements of each case" (Bellamy 2006: 149). This is accurate as long as one considers solely the aspect of assessing factual evidence for intervention. Indeed, these options are always politically biased, and give the powerful states the opportunity to react in instances where their interests are involved.

Nonetheless, asking what happens when the Security Council cannot agree on collective action is compulsory when discussing the issue of authorization. Thus, such criticisms of the R2P recommendations fail to acknowledge that it was both logically and ethically imperative for the ICISS report to address this question. The two alternative sources identified in the R2P report seem the most legitimate ones after the Security Council, and are in accordance with the legitimacy ladder framed in this analysis. Instead of "ambiguity," the ICISS proposals have the potential to produce results in instances where, otherwise, no action would be taken.

These proposals were too controversial to be retained in any subsequent reference to R2P at the UN. The issue of an alternative authorizing body was left out of the 2004 report of the High-Level Panel, which was the first to embrace R2P after its emergence in the ICISS report, and it was also omitted in the 2005 report of the UN Secretary-General, "In Larger Freedom." As expected, it was not part of the negotiations leading up to the adoption of R2P in the 2005

Summit Outcome Document either. This was a significant retreat from the ICISS report's advantageous proposal. The report of the UN Secretary-General, "Implementing the Responsibility to Protect," emphasizes that measures under Chapter VII must be authorized by the Security Council. It does acknowledge, however, in a paragraph detailing the work of the General Assembly, that this "may exercise a range of related functions under Articles 10 to 14, as well as under the 'Uniting for peace' process" (United Nations 2009a: 9). For obvious reasons, discussions of alternative authorizations were also omitted from the July 2009 General Assembly debate on R2P. As such, all formulations of R2P subsequent to the ICISS report fail to discuss what should happen if the Security Council were unable or unwilling to act.

Even in instances when the Security Council does consider authorizing intervention, it is usually facing a major problem, namely the slowness of its decision-making process and the use of veto by the permanent members (P5) of the Security Council, which averts intervention from taking place within the right time frame to save lives. Apart from being a major obstacle to effective intervention, the P5 use of veto is also of great concern for developing countries, and it fueled recent discussions on Security Council reform. Developing countries argue in favor of Security Council expansion because greater regional representation will give the "weak" more influence in issues related to peace and security, including the use of force.

Security Council reform, though, remains one of the most contentious issues on the broader list of UN reform, and any agreement is unlikely to be reached soon. R2P was linked to the issue during the General Assembly debate on R2P. Before the debate, many supporters feared that states from the Non-Aligned Movement would make acceptance of R2P conditional to Security Council reform. Indeed, during the General Assembly debate, states from the Caribbean Community (CARICOM) argued that action on R2P could only move forward if there was Security Council reform. But the debate concluded with most states acknowledging that the absence of Security Council reform should not be used as an excuse to hinder the implementation of R2P.

Another key recommendation in the R2P report that aims to address this problematic aspect puts the pressure on the P5. The ICISS report urges the P5 to agree to a "code of conduct," and refrain from using their veto when their national interests are not at stake, and especially in cases where there is majority support for authorizing the use of force. In fact, this is hardly ever the case with respect to humanitarian emergencies. The ICISS emphasized that the task is to make the Security Council work better – an idea picked up by the UN Secretary-General in his 2009 report on R2P.

Political controversy prevented the ICISS proposed "code of conduct" from making it into any formal negotiations during the past four UN Summits. The reference to authority for the use of force in paragraph 139 of the final 2005 Outcome Document states, as expected, that collective action is to be taken "through the Security Council." There was no further elaboration, and no reference to the use of veto in the Council. Nonetheless, in his report on R2P, the UN

Secretary-General urged the permanent members of the Security Council "to refrain from employing or threatening to employ the veto in situations of manifest failure to meet obligations relating to the responsibility to protect, as defined in paragraph 139 of the Summit Outcome, and to reach a mutual understanding to that effect" (United Nations 2009a: 27). No "mutual understanding" was reached during the General Assembly debate on R2P at the end of July 2009. However, many states that spoke during the debate criticized past Security Council failures to halt atrocities, and described the Council's inaction as the reason for failures to protect Rwandans, Bosnian Muslims, and Darfuris. Over thirty-five member states expressed frustrations about the conduct of the permanent five members in the Security Council, and called for them to refrain from using the veto in R2P situations. There is, thus, a big gap between the proposed approach to the topic in the ICISS report and the language used after the September 2005 Outcome Document endorsement of R2P at the UN. The lack of any formal agreement on the issue remains deeply problematic.

Since some of the ICISS recommendations were correctly described as equivocal (e.g. Weiss 2007: 108), one might wonder why the report did not use more categorical language on the topic. As the Commission explained, the aim was to produce recommendations embedded in the political realities of the moment, which implied considering what changes were likely to occur in practice. As far as its most radical recommendations go, the ICISS was well aware that "it is unrealistic to imagine any amendment of the UN Charter happening any time soon so far as the veto power and its distribution are concerned" (2001: 51). The R2P report also presented the UN and regional organizations in an accurate light, which was verified by the authorization patterns and legitimacy trends identified earlier. Moreover, it pinpointed some important caveats, mainly related to the negative effects on the UN's future caused by its lack of action. If the Security Council fails to act, individual states will try to do so themselves, either unilaterally or through coalitions of the willing. It then becomes apparent why it is better to have regional alternatives to the UN authorization for interventions, instead of such unilateral and far less legitimate agents.

In practical terms, we are better off perceiving regional organizations as legitimate alternatives to the UN, when the Council is at a deadlock, rather than lamenting that interventions can only take place when the Security Council authorizes them – which is not, at any rate, too constructive. In the legal realm, however, the thorny question of authorization for the use of force remains a contested one. The debate on the legality of an intervention without Security Council authorization and host state consent is as intense as ever. If one considers the authority question from the point of view of those in need of urgent help, then one finds an easy answer to the question of authorization in instances of the gravest humanitarian violations. The lack of reaction in Rwanda is a far more serious threat to international order than action without the Security Council authorization, as was the case in Kosovo: the danger is not too much intervention, potentially under a different authority than the Security Council, but rather too little (Weiss, 2004a: 149; 2005a: 22; 2005b: 236).

The alternative of regional organizations as authorizing agents is also left out of all UN references to R2P, for obvious reasons. Paragraph 139 of the 2005 World Summit Outcome Document suggests that the international community takes collective action, through the Security Council "...on a case-by-case basis and in cooperation with relevant regional organizations as appropriate." References to potential roles played by regional actors are thus discussed in regard to collaborations between the UN and regional organizations to prevent and protect. The Secretary-General's report on R2P also discusses such collaborations, but it does not reference any source of authorization for the use of force apart from the Security Council.

There is some validity to the criticism regarding the potential for abuse emerging from considerations of alternative sources of authorization. However, in instances of egregious human rights violations, of the type covered by R2P, the priority of the analysis should switch from the worries about potential abuses to the realization that convincing agents to react is what matters the most. What was suggestively dubbed "inhumanitarian nonintervention" (Chesterman 2003: 54), namely the lack of political will to act, is the most serious problem to date. As Michael Byers and Simon Chesterman best put it, "states are not champing at the bit to intervene in support of human rights ... prevented only by an intransigent Security Council and the absence of clear criteria to intervene without its authority. The problem ... is the absence of the will to act at all" (2003: 202). Addressing this problem should certainly be a priority in a world devoured by humanitarian emergencies. Its resolve, however, depends on a whole new set of requirements, capability being one of them.

4 Who conducts interventions?

> If an operation is given a mandate to protect civilians, therefore, it also must be given the specific resources needed to carry out that mandate.
>
> (United Nations 2000b: para. 63)

The key question of "who conducts interventions?" is omnipresent in all debates on humanitarian intervention. If there is a responsibility to protect, it is only natural to think that this requires a capacity to protect. While questions of morality were addressed in Chapter 2, and those related to the lawfulness and legitimacy of interventions in Chapter 3, the focus in this chapter is narrowly placed on material capabilities of interveners. No matter how legitimate a case for intervention for humanitarian purposes is, if there is no actor that is both willing and capable of tackling the mission, the victims are left without protection. Even with complete agreement to use force in last resort situations, there may be no capacity to deploy force available to protect in such cases. The lack of operational readiness is one of the main challenges faced when reaction is required in cases of genocide, war crimes, crimes against humanity, and ethnic cleansing.

I examine the question of military capabilities necessary for civilian protection in peace operations from a purely utilitarian perspective. This is rooted in the initial focus of the study on assessing how the R2P framework addresses this contentious issue related to humanitarian intervention. I look at both the actors available and their resources, and at how the ICISS report and subsequent reformulations of R2P have addressed this key question. In line with the responsibility to protect framework, the premise of the chapter is that the use of force under the R2P banner is a measure of last resort. It is evident that the best way to address mass atrocities is to prevent their occurrence in the first place. Indeed, R2P's objective is to decrease the frequency with which the protection of civilians from mass atrocities is dependent on the use of force by outsiders (Bellamy 2009). However, there are instances where the use of force is the only option left to provide protection. As the Secretary-General suggests in his 2009 report on implementing the responsibility to protect, when egregious crimes relating to R2P are committed, "collective military assistance may be the surest way to support the State in meeting its obligations … and, in extreme cases, to restore its effective sovereignty ... the early, targeted and restrained use of international military assets and armed forces may be able to save lives and bring ... stability" (United Nations 2009a: 18, para. 40). In such cases, it is important to have the military capabilities required to act.

The specifics of interventions under the R2P banner

As mentioned in the first chapter of the book, there are important distinctions between peacekeeping missions and operations launched primarily to halt mass atrocities and genocide, considered under the responsibility to protect framework. Peace operations can refer to conflict prevention, peacekeeping, peacemaking, intervention, and peace building, implying various extents of civilian protection considerations. Military operations designed specifically to protect civilians in the four R2P-type scenarios, genocide, ethnic cleansing, mass crimes, and crimes against humanity, are essentially different from peace operations mandated to protect civilians from much lower levels of violence and human rights violations. "The introduction of military intervention by the United Nations as a practical political option" has been described as one of the main contributions of such operations, in terms of solving the predicament between nonintervention principles in internal affairs and the protection of civilians from egregious human rights abuses (Strauss 2009b: 90).

One first important distinction refers to the two types of measures designed to protect civilians: first, there are measures aimed at coercing compliance, which work indirectly, by affecting the benefits and costs of the actors involved; and, second, there are measures aimed at providing direct civilian protection, through military action (Weiss and Hubert 2001). The discussion in this chapter covers the measures aimed at providing direct protection, as pertaining to the focus on the military aspects of the "reaction" component of the responsibility to protect. Very few missions are organized and deployed with a primary objective to prevent or halt mass killings, ethnic cleansing, and genocide, which may be necessary in an R2P-type scenario. Such operations would include situations where there is no viable peace agreement to enforce, where the state authority collapses, where the national authorities have failed to protect the population, where violence becomes extreme and civilians come under direct attack, and the military forces need to stand between warlords and their victims.

The R2P framework can be applied both to situations where there is consent from the host state or the parties involved in the conflict, and when non-consensual use of military force is required. Since the latter is more likely, some elements need elaboration. While acknowledging that the separation line between robust peacekeeping and peace enforcement may be blurry at times, the 2008 UN "Capstone doctrine" clearly explains the main differences between the two. Peace enforcement is the application of a range of coercive measures authorized by the Security Council to restore international peace and security, including the use of military force. This does not require the consent of the parties involved in the conflict, and the Council may utilize regional organizations and agencies for enforcement action under its authority in such cases. Robust peacekeeping, on the other hand, involves the use of force at the tactical level, but with the consent of the host state or of the main parties to the conflict (United Nations 2008: 18–19). Unlike traditional peacekeeping where there is a "peace to keep" and the consent of the parties to the conflict for the deployment of troops is clear, protecting civilians through a military intervention to prevent or halt mass atrocities, consistent with a UN Chapter VII mandate, is likely to take place in non-permissive environments, where military forces address high levels of violence, as was the case in Rwanda in 1994. As such, UN peacekeeping is not an option when non-consensual intervention is needed.

R2P-type interventions are, thus, different from peacekeeping operations and operations at the lower end of the scale of violence. They fall somewhere on a spectrum whose two extremes are traditional peacekeeping and traditional war fighting. At times, they can be referred to as "peacekeeping plus" or "complex peacekeeping," which means that from the beginning of a mission it is expected that problems from spoilers or other causes will emerge during the course of the operation; that military force will be used for civilian protection, under a Chapter VII mandate; and that a rapid "fire brigade" response from a new or extended mission might be needed if mass atrocities occur or are imminent (Evans 2008a: 214). Such missions that deploy in hostile environments and face large-scale violence, with a mandate to use force to protect civilians, have been described as "coercive protection missions" (Challenges Project 2005; Holt and Berkman 2006).

Terminology is important as it triggers different operational requirements. When states commit their troops to military interventions, these troops must also be ready to fight. Depending on the circumstances on the ground, this includes applying deadly force in defensive attempts to protect civilians and the troops' own safety, which in turn requires capable air forces and ground forces, as well as a large logistical infrastructure to support them.[1] Because of imposing specific requirements on the military, such operations pose distinct conceptual, operational and political challenges. The effectiveness of such an operation depends on the structure of the force, the amount of military personnel and equipment available, the speed of the deployment, the doctrine and training coming with the mission's mandate and troops, and the rules of engagement.

But an R2P-type intervention can also resemble a robust peacekeeping operation. In recent years, the civilian-protection element has become embedded in the mandates of UN peace operations. The protection of civilians is standard language in every Security Council resolution that authorizes a peace operation where civilian lives are in danger, and has certainly become "a normative expectation" in today's peace operations (Johnstone and Bah 2007: i). The majority of peacekeeping missions' mandates and rules of engagement have often included language reflecting the R2P concept (Wills 2009: 51). And so, a specific R2P mandate is not required to protect people from mass atrocities (Strauss 2009b: 77). For example, the United Nations Mission in Sierra Leone (UNAMSIL) mandate clearly states its responsibility to protect civilians (Holt *et al.* 2009: 42), while the Security Council deliberations surrounding the adoption of resolution 1706 (2006) authorizing the expansion of the UN Mission in Sudan (UNMIS) into Darfur reflected the international community's sense of R2P (ibid.: 50–51).

The increased need for civilian protection was first addressed in detail in the 1998 "Report of the Secretary-General to the Security Council on the Situation in Africa," which described protection as a "humanitarian imperative" (United Nations 1998). This also marked the beginning of approaching civilian protection as a separate conceptual thematic issue at the UN (Security Council Report 2008: 6). In 1999, Canada put the issue of civilian protection on the Security Council's agenda. This translated into two key Security Council resolutions with implications for future peacekeeping missions, namely, resolution 1265 of September 1999 and resolution 1296 of April 2000. More recently, significant developments came from the General Assembly's recognition, for the first time, that protection of civilians is a challenge for peacekeeping missions and for the UN in general. The 2009 session of the Special Committee on Peacekeeping Operations and its Working Group, whose report referenced civilian protection for the first time (2009b: 24, paras 125–128), is evidence of a much improved environment among member states in respect to such issues. The 2010 session of the Special Committee on Peacekeeping Operations expanded this in its report (A/64/19 2010: 28–30, paras 143–151).

As seen in conflicts like Darfur, the protection of civilians represents the core of recent efforts to operationalize R2P. However, important tensions exist in relation to protection as a military task. For example, military intervention may lead to counterproductive outcomes, even when there is an abundance of political will and resources behind it (Falk 1993: 757). There is a lack of consensus not only about the range of activities regarded as "protection" but also about the "who" and the "how" of protection. A unified interpretation of the concept for protection of civilians in peacekeeping operations is missing (Holt *et al.* 2009: 4). Ultimately, the successful implementation of R2P toward civilian protection is contingent upon several conditions occurring at the same time. These include the existence of one of the four types of mass atrocities triggering R2P, a willingness on the part of contributing states to risk their soldiers' lives to "protect strangers," appropriate training and doctrine to address the specific requirements of non-permissive conflict environments, and sufficient and reliable capabilities to react (Badescu and Bergholm 2009).

The Secretary-General's report on implementing R2P briefly acknowledges such issues, by expressing "appreciation" for member states' efforts to consider the components of capacity for military endeavors to protect civilians, including doctrine, training and command-and-control issues (United Nations 2009a: 27, para. 64). The 2001 ICISS report does not address these aspects in depth. Its supplementary volume discusses current operational challenges resulting from the shift from traditional peacekeeping to coercive protection operations. The ICISS research volume notes that "as obvious as it sounds, well-trained and well-equipped troops are even more necessary for enforcement actions than for traditional peacekeeping" (Weiss and Hubert 2001: 186).

The R2P approach to operational questions of military intervention

The ICISS report focuses on four major categories of principles for military intervention: the just cause threshold, the precautionary principles (right intention, last resort, proportional means, and reasonable prospects), the right authority, and operational principles. The fourth category – directly relevant to the question of capacity – is the focus of the discussion to follow. The final section of the ICISS report – devoted to the "operational dimension" of R2P – addresses this aspect. This part of the report examines the operational principles that would increase the efficiency of humanitarian intervention, and focuses on the importance of clear operational objectives and rules of engagement, a clear and appropriate mandate, a unified military approach, and the availability of adequate resources (2001: 57–67). Effective interventions also require a strong command structure, efficient civil–military interactions, the appropriate use of military power to save as many lives as possible, a willingness to sustain casualties, and an efficient public information campaign (ibid.: 62–64).

The R2P report emphasizes the importance of the protection of civilians after the initial military intervention has established security, by suggesting five "protection tasks" and broad guidelines on the transfer of authority (ibid.: 64–66). Apart from stages relevant to the planning and carrying out of military intervention, the ICISS report also considers operational guidelines for preventive operations and operations following up the initial intervention to establish security. The report concludes its broad discussion of operational principles by suggesting that they deserve increased attention and that a new doctrine be developed by the UN Secretary-General (2001: 66–67). The supplementary volume to the ICISS report addresses this topic in more detail, in the "Conduct and Capacity" chapter (Weiss and Hubert 2001: 177–203).

The literature on peace operations does not specifically address the question of capacity, often assuming the existence of a military capability able to deal with intervention requirements in response to genocide, ethnic cleansing, mass atrocities, and crimes against humanity (e.g. O'Hanlon 2003; Taft and Ladnier 2006). The ICISS research volume rightly highlights this lack of attention to the operational dimensions of military intervention in the analytical literature. As such, it proposes to "identify the operational challenges in applying deadly military force for humanitarian ends" (Weiss and Hubert 2001: 177). The supplementary volume to the ICISS report discusses the need for robust interventions and coercive protection. It expands the brief discussion on "robust capacity" and rules of engagement from the R2P report, and includes an examination of transport capabilities for the troops and equipment (2001: 186–188). Furthermore, it assesses the difficulties faced by the UN in mobilizing troops, caused mainly by the intricacies of getting member states to commit human and financial resources for intervention. It also points to the evident trend that enforcement action has been consistently left to coalitions of willing states (ibid.: 181–182). The need for UN rapid deployment, which remains largely unanswered, is also discussed in this context.

While the ICISS report clearly states its recommendations on the question of authority, it only broadly considers operational issues, without embarking upon answering the specific question of who actually has the capacity to put the "reaction" aspect of R2P that comes closest to humanitarian intervention into practice. Addressing the capacity problem was also one of the most ignored recommendations from the High-Level Panel report, which warned that the protection of civilians in extreme humanitarian emergencies could not improve without increasing capacities (United Nations 2004a). The 2005 Summit Outcome Document does not elaborate on the practical implications of the use of force, other than to reaffirm that missions should have "adequate capacity to counter hostilities and fulfill effectively their mandates" (United Nations 2005a: para. 92).

Both paragraph 139 of the Summit Outcome Document and the Secretary-General's report on implementing R2P talk about the international community's commitment "to assist states in building their protection capacities" (United Nations 2009a: 1). The Secretary-General describes capacity as the most serious of the three main gaps R2P faces before implementation: "Nowhere is the gap more pronounced or more damaging than in the realm of forceful and timely response to the most flagrant crimes and violations ... [h]ere, weaknesses of capacity and the paucity of will ... feed off each other" (United Nations 2009a: 26, para. 60).

The only solutions provided in the 2009 report lack specificity. Cooperation is encouraged, especially in terms of better collaborations between the UN and regional and sub-regional arrangements that need to consider "capacity-sharing and not just capacity-building, as is now the case in mediation support," with the AU–UN ten-year-capacity building program described as particularly crucial in this regard. The Secretary-General urges "redoubling" the UN efforts to ensure that this succeeds and that the African Standby Force reaches its full potential. In his own words, "global-regional collaboration is a key plank of our strategy for operationalizing the responsibility to protect" (United Nations 2009a: 27–28, para. 65). The "Implementing the Responsibility to Protect" report concludes that the UN is still far from developing the kind of rapid-response military capacity clearly needed to handle the fast unfolding atrocity crimes referenced in paragraph 139 of the Summit Outcome. More generally, the UN and its member states remain underprepared to meet their prevention and protection responsibilities (United Nations 2009a: 6).

Such discussions represent only broad assessments of the capacity question, which identify the need for sufficient resources, without expanding on where they are to be found. Despite the discussion of "the operational dimension" of interventions in the R2P report, and the coverage of "conduct and capacity" in its supplementary volume, the framework put forward by the ICISS in 2001 does not consider operational principles in depth. However, instances when the responsibility to protect civilians becomes essential raise questions that go beyond the boundaries set by the ICISS discussions, by demanding who can conduct such missions. The Commission mentions the UN, but does the UN have – or can it quickly assemble – the necessary capabilities required for such missions? If not, what advantages and disadvantages ensue from engaging better equipped actors to conduct military operations to protect civilians from mass atrocities?

The fact that the R2P framework can be tested against the delivery of protection to civilians explains why such questions are important to ask. They go, of course, beyond simply identifying the most militarily powerful actors as agents of intervention, because factors related to legitimacy and doing more good than harm need to be considered as well. At present, the handful of actors that have the capacity to conduct military interventions include the UN, NATO, the European Union (EU), the African Union (AU), the Economic Community of West African States (ECOWAS), and the so-called coalitions of the willing with powerful individual states at the helm, such as the US, UK, and France. I discuss the capacities of these actors, in decreasing order of their respective legitimacy to use force.

Who has the capacity to act?

The United Nations

The UN faces the challenge of preventing or halting mass atrocities more than any other actor. Paragraph 139 of the 2005 Summit Outcome Document strongly emphasizes a collective response to mass atrocities "through the United Nations." International military intervention under Chapter VII of the UN Charter represents the most cost-effective means of preventing a return to war in post-conflict societies (Collier and Hoeffler 2004). Indeed, several studies have shown that UN peacekeeping can play an important role in preventing states from falling back into civil war, and even in preventing mass killings (e.g. Page Fortna 2004; Melander 2009). Hardly enough, however, has been written on the specific requirements of what such operations should do to achieve their goals in terms of prevention and halting mass atrocities.[2] Without doubt, the UN is the most legitimate actor to use force to protect civilians. It is also the first port of call to carry out interventions for humanitarian purposes. The UN peace operations are much cheaper than other forms of international intervention; the approved peacekeeping budget for the July 2009–June 2010 period is close to US$7.9 billion, which represents approximately 0.5 percent of total global military spending.[3] Apart from the United States, the UN has the largest number of military forces deployed in the world. However, the UN has not typically led "peace enforcements" missions, authorized by the Security Council under Chapter VII to use "all necessary means" to protect civilians (Holt and Berkman 2006: 58).

In recent years, UN peacekeepers have been mandated to protect civilians under imminent threat of violence, and almost all missions authorized by the Security Council after 1999 were given Chapter VII "peace enforcement" mandates.[4] The increase in UN peacekeeping activities since 1999, which has further intensified since 2002, is already straining the capacity of the organization. By

2005, the level of UN resources amounted to 110,000 military and civilian police personnel from 115 countries rotated through UN missions in one year. There are currently 125,000 personnel serving on sixteen peace operations led by the UN Department of Peacekeeping Operations (DPKO) on four continents. The number of UN peacekeepers in 2010 suggests a nine-fold increase since 1999. This is also the highest number in the history of the UN to date.[5]

Even if the UN has increased its capacity from 47,883 uniformed personnel in 2001–2002 to 77,002 in September 2006, to 91,382 in January 2009, and 125,400 in May 2010,[6] a significant gap remains between the authorized strength of Security Council-mandated missions and the actual personnel deployed. This is the best illustration of the recurring problem of authorizing missions without being able to generate the required force to put the mandates into practice. This gap also shows that the Security Council may be committed to authorizing a peace operation, while at the same time member states may be unwilling to risk their soldiers' lives in putting the mandate into practice. This is the main danger the UN faces at the moment, one that directly affects implementing R2P in regard to civilian protection. When the head of UN peacekeeping at the time, Jean-Marie Guéhenno, was asked in 2006 whether R2P had any bearing on UN peace missions, he suggested the reference in most resolutions authorizing a peace operation to protect civilians in imminent danger in the areas where they are deployed reflected the emergence of R2P (CFR 2006). And yet, what is required for R2P to be successfully implemented in this context is a strong commitment from member states to back such mandates with the right resources.

However, as Durch *et al.* argued (2003), the UN is only slightly more capable now of mounting peace operations than in 1999. And so, as the High-Level Panel warned, "...the demand for personnel for both full-scale peace-enforcement missions and peacekeeping missions remains higher than the ready supply ... in the absence of a commensurate increase in available personnel, the UN ... risks repeating some of its worst failures of the 1990s" (United Nations 2004a: 68–69, para. 215). Significant risks arise from the increased pace with which new missions are authorized, and there is no better illustration for such challenges and warnings than the three Security Council resolutions passed in August 2006. The trend of the speedy increase in UN peace operations reached its height when, in only twenty days – from 11 to 31 August 2006 – the Security Council adopted three new resolutions: resolution 1701 on Lebanon; resolution 1704 on East Timor; and resolution 1706 on Darfur, which expanded the UN Mission in Sudan (UNMIS) by 17,300 troops and 5,300 civilian police (Security Council Report 2006). The magnitude of such an increase in the demand for troops was unmatched in the history of the UN, and it presented huge challenges for the organization. It is also illustrative of the seriousness of the problem of authorizing peace operations without capacity back-up.

In the case of the AU–UN Hybrid Operation in Darfur (UNAMID), two and a half years after the Security Council resolution authorized 19,315 troops on the ground, only 12,194 were available. Selectivity is built into member states' responses, however. It depends on preferences, as suggested in this instance of the three Security Council resolutions of August 2006, when European countries immediately offered to contribute troops in the case of Lebanon but not for Darfur. Also, UNAMID provides a perfect illustration of another major problem faced in such operations, namely the lack of strategic assets. The international community has not been able to provide the less than thirty military helicopters needed to carry out the UNAMID operations in Darfur, when the global inventory comprises nearly 12,000 (Evans 2008a: 178).

It is evident that the ability of the UN to carry out peace operations depends on the strength of the troops supplied by its member states. But in addition to the regular challenges faced by missions in permissive environments, troop contributors may be further deterred from providing contingents for missions mandated specifically to protect civilians in situations of mass atrocities because of the more dangerous activities involving the use of force in such environments (Holt and Berkman 2006: 64). Moreover, specific national guidelines and conditions under which states are allowed to provide forces can add to the series of difficulties, such as exclusive requirements for UN authorization, and permission to use force only in self-defense.[7]

Apart from circumstances specific to different countries, there are some general trends that make the UN capacity for deployment even more challenging. It is by now a well-known fact that developed countries have reduced their military contributions to UN peace operations in the last ten years. While still important financial contributors, most powerful states, such as the US and the major EU powers, have significantly decreased their troop contributions. For instance, traditional troop-contributing countries such as the Nordic European ones no longer provide thousands of military personnel but only dozens. The supplementary volume to the R2P report rightfully indentified this as a problematic trend at the beginning of the twenty-first century (Weiss and Hubert 2001: 186).

Powerful, developed countries are now more involved elsewhere, in light of the war on terror and their commitments in Afghanistan and Iraq. For several suggestive examples, the US is contributing only eighty military personnel to UN peace operations, Australia fifty-nine, Sweden sixty-two, Canada 142, Germany 287, and the United Kingdom 281;[8] as compared to Pakistan 10,742, Bangladesh 10,212, India 8,771, Nigeria 5,941, and Egypt 5,457.[9] Given that Pakistan, Bangladesh, India, Nigeria and Egypt are, in decreasing order, the first top five contributors, concerns regarding the lack of contributions from developed countries become evident. Although a sensitive topic, it is generally agreed that the effectiveness of troops from developing countries needs to be increased in order to produce successful enforcement operations (Weiss and Hubert 2001: 186). This discussion does not address the issue of doctrine and training in depth; yet, the fact that the bulk of peacekeepers currently comes from the global South weakens UN peace operations because of difficulties in training and equipping personnel to the standard required for the effective protection of civilians. Such problems become more acute in the context of R2P-type situations, which involve an environment where mass atrocities are looming.

The aim of the broad revision of peacekeeping with a special emphasis on civilian protection that currently takes place at the UN is to make the entire organization more field oriented. Discussions on UN reform reignite suggestions related to a UN "standing army" which could be deployed quickly. The idea of having a standing UN peacekeeping force has enjoyed popular support over the years.[10] However, it was never popular within the UN system, for reasons ranging from suspicion among member states about military capabilities controlled by the Security Council, to worries about the potential influence the Secretariat might have on its role, and practical considerations of high expenses related to recruitment, training, and housing troops on a continuing basis. Instead, the UN put in place several standby arrangements to address the capacity problem partially and increase the speed of troop deployments. The now defunct Multinational Standby High Readiness Brigade (SHIRBRIG) was one such initiative.[11] Since SHIRBRIG ceased its operations in June 2009, this might be a good time to redesign a proposal for a standing rapid-reaction force, with a deployment time similar to SHIRBRIG's, under UN command but with volunteer troop contributions from member states.

Even marked by capacity limitations, the UN did intervene in cases where gross violations of human rights were occurring and mandated operations that prioritized civilian protection above all other objectives, as seen in the UN Peacekeeping Mission in the Democratic Republic of the Congo (MONUC) and the UN Mission in the Central African Republic and Chad (MINURCAT). The operation known by its French acronym, MONUC, is one the most illustrative UN operations to date for challenges related to capacity and to employing a wide variety of approaches to the use of force to protect civilians. Deployed in the DRC in 1999 and evolving into a Chapter VII operation with more troops, MONUC epitomizes the challenges for missions that start under-staffed and ill-equipped, address crises during ongoing civil conflicts, cover very wide and unstable regions, and apply force that places the mission between peacekeeping and warfighting.

MONUC demonstrates the challenges of having peacekeepers engaged in coercive protection in "extreme" environments, and of missions with robust postures, like dealing with armed groups that threaten civilians, conducting cordon-and-search operations that then led to reprisals against populations, and pushing militia to disarm or join the Congolese integrated army, which then became a threat to civilians (Holt and Berkman 2006: 157). The capacity limitations of the mission to respond to ongoing mass-scale violence surfaced in the 2003 Ituri crisis, when MONUC was not able to fill the security vacuum left by the rapid withdrawal of the Ugandan army. At the UN's request, the French-led EU Interim Emergency Multinational Force (IEMF), known as Operation Artemis, was deployed to Bunia, the capital of the northeastern region of Ituri in the DRC. After three months of efforts to stabilize the area, it handed back the responsibilities to MONUC.

Similarly, after the UN-authorized European Union military force (EUFOR) completed its mandate to protect civilians and facilitate the delivery of aid in

Chad and the Central African Republic (CAR), the Security Council-authorized deployment of a military component of MINURCAT followed up in March 2009. Both EUFOR and MINURCAT had protection as their primary role, and peacekeepers in Chad were given a strong protection role under the expanded MINURCAT operation. However, three months after the handover, only 47 percent of the MINURCAT capacity was deployed. This was the case even when the transfer of authority from the EU to the UN forces in Chad and CAR saw a number of European contingents "re-hatting" their troops when placing them under UN authority. One inventive initiative in the MINURCAT context could provide good lessons for future operations, namely the UN training of Chadian police forces in eastern Chad to address protection concerns related to the lack of rule of law on the ground. However, UN police faced some serious problems since they were deployed without any logistical support, and even without shelter and supplies at times (Weir 2009: 20). Current efforts at the UN DPKO to establish a standing police capacity with officers forming rapid-response teams are likely to translate into important resources for the UN to address large-scale violence against civilians. This came in response to the Summit Outcome Document endorsing the creation of a standing police capacity to provide start-up capabilities for peacekeeping missions (United Nations 2005a: para. 92), which followed the HLP's recommendation on the issue (United Nations 2004a: para. 223).

Both Operation Artemis and EUFOR in Chad and CAR suggest that regional organizations and member states have acted on behalf of the UN to provide short-term protection of civilians in ongoing crises, when UN capabilities were insufficient for this task. As the UN HLP report (United Nations 2004a) suggests, a strategic partnership between the UN and regional actors is required, through what is called "hybrid missions," namely part UN and part non-UN operations. Experts usually advocate the development of military capabilities at the regional or sub-regional levels to fill the UN military deficit. Paragraph 139 of the 2005 World Summit Outcome Document suggests that collective action is to be taken "in cooperation with relevant regional organizations, as appropriate." As seen in Darfur, the DRC and Kosovo, the UN has collaborated with regional actors in this sense. After the UN, regional and sub-regional actors occupy the next spot in terms of legitimate agents of intervention, ahead of so-called coalitions of the willing and states acting individually to protect civilians.

NATO

NATO is not a regional organization per se, but a collective defense organization, designed to intervene at the direction of its member states, and also having the military capacity to do so.[12] Even if NATO began as a Cold War military alliance whose main purpose was to maintain the security of Western Europe, the last ten years illustrate its transformation into an organization ready to address the wide range of new threats to peace and security, including terrorism, humanitarian emergencies, natural disasters and transnational crimes. In recent years, NATO has started to transform its military, and accepted new members in March 2004 so that it currently numbers twenty-eight states. Taken together, its members' contributions translate into superior warfighting capacity, in terms of personnel, equipment, integrated military command structure, and interoperability.

A notable change in the NATO Strategic Concept occurred in April 1999, with clear implications for its participation in peace operations worldwide: NATO Strategic Concept was approved to have members of the Alliance defend not just themselves, but also peace and security in NATO's region and periphery (Holt 2005: 13). The Strategic Concept provided for NATO to carry out military operations intended to deal with complex emergencies, such as peace enforcement, peacekeeping, conflict prevention and peacemaking. These operations are usually in support of the UN or the Organization for Security and Cooperation in Europe (OSCE). The "Protection of Humanitarian Operations" section of its Strategic Concept discusses the possibility of NATO troops active in genocide situations. Furthermore, NATO doctrine mentions mission tasks that could be applied to civilian protection, such as imposing no-fly zones, establishing safe areas, and creating safe corridors for civilians and aid (Strauss 2009b: 110). After considering the possibility of "non-Article 5 crisis response operations," such as operations under the authority of the Security Council, member states agreed at the 2002 Prague conference to send NATO forces "wherever they are needed," clearly moving beyond the restriction to act in defense of the NATO area (Holt and Berkman 2006: 58).

NATO conducted several peace operations in the post-Cold War period, including the first NATO deployments out of area – Implementation Force (IFOR) and Stabilization Force (SFOR) in Bosnia from 1995 to 2004, the highly controversial Operation Allied Force in Kosovo from March to June 1999, the Kosovo Force (KFOR) in Kosovo from June 1999, and the International Security Assistance Force (ISAF) in Afghanistan since 2001. ISAF marked the first time the Alliance deployed troops outside Europe. However, Afghanistan is not the only example of NATO's involvement outside Europe. The Alliance has been very active in training 1,500 security forces in Iraq and coordinating the delivery of military equipment there, and it also participated in airlifting 5,000 AU troops into Darfur, helping rotate the forces stationed there, and providing training and technical assistance to the AU's mission in Darfur.

The creation of the NATO Response Force (NRF) was a central component of NATO's military transformation toward modernizing the Alliance and its capabilities to address crises rapidly. The NATO Response Force reached initial operational capability in October 2004, with 17,000 troops ready, and its 25,000 rapidly available troops, deployable anywhere in the world within five days, became fully operational in October 2006. NATO doctrine, however, is not clear in regard to the application of force to the protection of civilians under imminent threat, but the NRF emerges as the self-sustaining, highly mobile rapid-reaction force required in such instances. Since it became operational, the NRF has only been used in more traditional operations, such as providing relief after Hurricane Katrina and after the earthquake in Pakistan in 2005.

However, it is the demanding operations like those in Afghanistan that expose the fact that NATO is facing institutional problems, which are not noticeable in smaller and uncontroversial operations like those in the aftermath of natural disasters. As a result of its 20,000-strong mission in Afghanistan, NATO is more recently facing troop-generating challenges. As such, the differences in the willingness of NATO member states to contribute resources and troops to peace operations are similar to the institutional problems the UN faces. NATO's difficulties in raising 2,000 more troops to suppress a resurgent Taliban highlight the fact that many of the world's most capable military forces are presently overstretched.

Given NATO's strong commitment to Afghanistan, it seems unlikely that the Alliance will swiftly answer new calls for humanitarian interventions in places around the world, apart from using the NRF in the initial stages of crises. Another obstacle NATO faces relates to the financial challenges resulting from an increased range of missions undertaken by the Alliance. NATO expects its members to cover the costs of its deployments of troops and equipments abroad, and thus is unable to use the capacities of smaller member states that cannot pay such attendant fees (Taft and Ladnier 2006: 44). Despite such challenges, without doubt, NATO is the organization most capable of rapid response to crises. Recent proposals have also emerged to create a "global partnership" between NATO and non-European states, in order to increase the military capabilities of the Alliance to protect civilians in violent conflict situations. NATO is indeed expanding its relations with countries outside the transatlantic community's borders, such as Australia, Japan and New Zealand (Daalder and Goldgeier 2006).

The European Union

Apart from NATO, the EU is another organization developing its rapid-reaction capability in Europe, which has been the focus of EU peace operations. The most notable exception so far was the 2003 French-led EU Operation Artemis in the DRC. The EU has been described as "still a nascent peacekeeper" (Tardy 2006: 28) compared to NATO, which has fifteen years of experience in peace operations. Nonetheless, the EU presently has the authority to contribute troops to missions covering humanitarian and rescue tasks, and tasks of combat forces in crisis management, including peacekeeping (Holt 2005: 13). It does not, however, have any written military doctrine for troops participating in UN missions. According to Gareth Evans, the EU has the most potential of all regional organizations to put R2P into practice, given its strengths residing in the size of its population, its wealth, its success as a conflict prevention model, and its capacity to use both soft and hard power to influence policy (2008a: 183).

The EU began to deploy troops in 2003 with the preventive Operation Concordia in Macedonia. In 2004, the EU took command of its largest military mission from NATO (SFOR) in Bosnia, namely Operation Althea, which replaced SFOR with the European Union Force (EUFOR). Even though the EU has carried out many other civilian deployments, such as Operation Proxima in Macedonia and the EU Police Mission in Bosnia, they are not relevant to this discussion since they did not involve military requirements in non-permissive environments. Operation Artemis in the DRC is the most impressive EU mission to date, with important implications for the future of this organization in protecting civilians elsewhere.

Operation Artemis – the EU's first military operation outside Europe – intervened in the Ituri region of the DRC in 2003, after MONUC failed to deal with a conflict that erupted in the area when rival militias attacked civilians. After a request from the UN Secretary-General, France volunteered to lead an Interim Emergency Multinational Force (IEMF) to stop the conflict, provided that it would be a Chapter VII mission, with other countries contributing troops, under the EU flag.[13] Operation Artemis deployed 1,400 troops, under a Chapter VII mandate, and it was specifically created as a "temporary" operation, authorized by Security Council resolution 1484 to carry out its mandate between June and September 2003. Operation Artemis provides a good illustration of how operations are conducted amid ongoing attacks against civilians. This deployment was meant to restore security in Ituri, while also buying time for building up the MONUC forces. The mission handed its responsibilities back to MONUC in September 2003.

This French-led EU mission announced the willingness of the EU to contribute troops to stop violence outside Europe. Since Operation Artemis, the EU has established two new missions in the DRC and has also provided training and technical support to the AU mission in Darfur. In October 2007, the UN Security Council authorized the EU mission in Chad (EUFOR) to protect civilians and displaced people from ongoing insecurity in Chad and the CAR, which became operational five months later. Through interventions, interactions with locals, and patrolling, EUFOR established the operational basis that helped the incoming MINURCAT operation, to which it transferred authority in March 2009. These missions had civilian protection as their primary rationale, which makes their lessons relevant to R2P discussions of using force to protect. As such, despite its declared focus on security in Europe, it becomes apparent that the EU has been involved militarily to protect civilians in several key conflicts around the world. Individual EU countries also mounted peace enforcement operations, such as the UK helping UNAMSIL in Sierra Leone in 2000 and France's stabilizing efforts in Côte d'Ivoire in 2002. In spite of its capacity for military interventions, the EU's preference is not for exercising coercive power, but rather for playing a diplomatic role in conflict prevention and resolution and imposing sanctions. The use of military force is the area where it is most difficult to reach internal EU consensus (Evans 2008a: 185–186).

The large-scale initiative of the EU's proposed 60,000 Rapid Reaction Force (RRF) was intended to address the commitment–capacity gap. In 2004, European defense ministers agreed to establish a Rapid Reaction Force of 60,000 troops, to be used for rapid deployment primarily at the UN's request. Initially, this independent defense capacity deployable outside of NATO missions was expected to be in place within three years, but it has been delayed. The EU claims to have around 100,000 troops ready to deploy, but, according to Caroline Earle, only a small percentage of these troops can be committed to EU missions at any time. The reason has to do with the fact that many troops are "triple-hatted" for the EU, UN, and NATO, and therefore counted within the declared capacity of all three organizations despite the obvious unfeasibility of being in more than one place at one time (Earle 2004: 16).

Indeed, operationalizing the RRF proposal appears to have been postponed as European states pursued the multinational battle groups initiative, which was adopted by the EU in 2004 as part of the "Headline Goal 2010." This is a notable example of EU efforts to address crises outside Europe. The battle-group concept involves eleven multinational EU battle groups: EU member states provide for six-month periods, comprising 1,500 self-sufficient and rapidly deployable troops, designed to arrive on the ground outside Europe within ten to fifteen days, and sustainable for thirty days in initial operations, which could be extended to 120 days if appropriately supplied. In essence, the battle-groups proposal emerged out of the model of Operation Artemis in the DRC. These groups were fully operational by January 2007, as two battle groups have been made available on an ongoing basis, to be deployed simultaneously, and then rotated every six months. The first two battle groups comprise troops from Finland, Germany, and the Netherlands, and, respectively, Finland, Sweden, Norway, and Estonia.[14]

Despite the lack of a declared, explicit linkage between the battle-group concept and the EU mandate to protect civilians, such an initiative increases the rapid deployment capacities of the EU. The UN has fully embraced the development of battle groups, describing the initiative as "Bridging Forces," meant to help the DPKO prepare for a new mission or expand an existing one, or as "Over the Horizon Reserve Forces," meant to address emergencies beyond the capacity of the UN itself, but under a UN mandate (Holt and Berkman 2006: 67). However, problems remain, as suggested most eloquently by the lack of EU reaction to the crisis in Darfur. For instance, despite producing seventy official "statements of concern" regarding Darfur by June 2008, the EU has failed to back them up with serious responsive measures (Evans 2008a: 187).

Skepticism thus persists as to how effective such developments of the EU institutional capacity can get for military operations to protect civilians during large-scale ongoing violence, and especially in mass-atrocities cases. The EU was described as still "a relatively small-time military player on the world stage in proportion to its economic might" (Holt and Berkman 2006: 67). Others have suggested that the EU's current capacities make it fit for peace enforcement operations that address short-term crisis and comprise police and rule of law training (Taft and Ladnier 2005). In the near future, it appears highly unlikely that the EU will be capable of carrying out an extensive intervention that could counterpart NATO's capabilities. The EU faces budgetary pressures on the military and an already strained force structure, while ultimately depending on member states to put forward the necessary troops. Even so, the EU remains an important actor when considering mass-atrocities crises.

The African Union

Given the concentration of crises in Africa, and especially in light of the African dictum "African solution to African problems," the AU has a significant role to play in addressing mass atrocities on the continent.[15] The AU's institutionalized exception to non-indifference makes this regional organization all the more critical to protecting civilians from ongoing violence, since its Constitutive Act specifically discusses "the right of the Union to intervene in a Member State [...] in respect of grave circumstances, namely war crimes, genocide and crimes against humanity" (AU 2002: 9, Article 4(h)). The AU was the first regional organization formally to ratify the normative right to intervene in the internal affairs of its member states when such "grave circumstances" occur. An amendment introduced in February 2003 as Article 4(j) of its Constitutive Act added "threats to internal order" to the list of triggers for intervention. Despite a different wording in the AU Constitutive Act from the reference to R2P in the 2005 Summit Outcome Document, the meaning behind Article 4(h) portrays the AU's responsibility to protect civilians from mass atrocities in Africa. Given this foundation, if an effective rapid-reaction force were added to the mix, the AU could become a model for interventions to protect civilians in mass-atrocities cases.

Currently, Africa has the most comprehensive peace and security architecture, in place since 1963 when the former Organization of African Unity (OAU) was founded. The AU has taken unprecedented steps to transform itself into an organization that oversees security in Africa. The AU Peace and Security Council (PSC) has the power to implement the decisions taken in regard to peacemaking, peace-support operations and intervention. The Peace and Security Council incorporates several operational elements, including an African Standby Force (ASF) and a Continental Early Warning System (AU 2002: 5). The ASF represents one of the most significant developments in the African peacekeeping context, with troops and civilian components on call from their own countries, and ready to be deployed in scenarios varying from monitoring ceasefires to military interventions.

The ASF is designed to have five brigades, one from each region of Africa (North, West, Central, East and South), each numbering between 3,000 and 5,000 troops, and coordinated by the PSC. The ASF is expected to be fully operational by 30 June 2010 and ready for deployment either under the authority of a UN Security Council resolution or an AU mandate. Despite the fact that the AU encourages cooperation with the UN, a Security Council authorization is not required for such deployments. In March 2005, the AU proposed a roadmap for the creation of the ASF, which envisions developing the ASF in two phases: in the first phase, until 30 June 2005, the AU was expected to establish a strategic-level management capacity for deploying a political or observer mission within thirty days from an AU mandate resolution; and, in phase two, from 1 July 2005 to 30 June 2010, the AU was expected to have developed the capacity to manage complex peacekeeping operations (AU 2005b).

However, the operationalization of the ASF has been slower than anticipated, and it has focused mainly on the military aspects of peace operations, while the civilian and police dimensions of the ASF framework remain to be developed (e.g. de Coning 2006: 41). At present, most training and development for the ASF is devoted to training infantry battalions. The AU is currently handicapped by inadequate command, control, and support systems, without which the ASF cannot deploy and conduct the complex peace operations required to protect civilians (Marshall 2009: 2–3). Because the AU has yet to complete the formation of the regional brigades, phase one of the ASF roadmap is currently ongoing. And so, it appears that the ASF is not going to become fully operational by the end of June 2010 as initially expected.

Even while developing its security architecture, the AU has been involved in crises on the continent both diplomatically and militarily, as was the case with restoring democracy in Togo and Mauritania, and with more force-focused operations in Darfur, Burundi, Somalia, the DRC, Chad, Comoros and Côte d'Ivoire. Some of these provide relevant lessons for R2P-type interventions, given that the AU deployed troops in cases of imminent or ongoing violence, when the UN was not able to act. In this context, several implications for the future of operations addressing mass atrocities on the continent deserve further consideration. First, while the AU might have the political will to act, it lacks the resources needed to implement robust mandates to protect civilians, as seen with the AU Mission in Sudan (AMIS) and the AU Mission to Somalia (AMISOM). Specifically with respect to using the R2P framework and the AU's willingness to invoke Article 4(h) of its Constitutive Act to intervene, it is interesting to note that the AU chose not to invoke Article (4h) to intervene in Darfur, which was then not an explicit trigger for AMIS (Badescu and Bergholm 2010: 110).

Overall, the effectiveness of the ASF depends on the resources available to finance its mandates, but the serious financial difficulties the AU presently faces might prove problematic when another crisis occurs or is imminent. As with the EU and NATO, capabilities depend on what member states contribute. For instance, the fifteen-member Southern African Development Community (SADC) appears closer to building a robust military capacity, as part of its contribution to the ASF, than the other sub-regional organizations. In terms of effective capacity built up so far, South Africa has made the most rapid progress in meeting the deadline for the first phase of preparations for the ASF. Its comparatively advanced capacities have overall assisted most of the progress of SADC, which has reached 6,000 troops so far. It is generally agreed that no country on the continent, except for South Africa, has the necessary capacities to send in troops, sustain them on the ground, and self-deploy easily on the African continent (Taft and Ladnier 2006: 14; Holt and Berkman 2006: 68).

Previous AU peace operations suggest that even small, unarmed military observer missions have proved too expensive to be financed only from the AU's budget or from the African Peace Fund. This makes external funding crucial.

Being highly dependent on the donor community, however, hardly gives any guarantees that the ASF would work effectively. Relying on external funding to finance the AU peace missions limits the AU's freedom of action in deciding on the strategic and operational aspects of its peace operations. It appears thus that regional solutions might work better where regions are self-sufficient in resources, because if resources are limited and required from outside, they are usually offered with strings attached (e.g. de Coning 2006; Feinstein *et al.* 2006). Another significant shortcoming for the AU is the lack of institutional capacity, especially in terms of human resources available to develop policy and to plan and manage peace operations.

Such operations also depict a pattern of collaborations between the UN and the AU, in terms of sequencing peace operations. This was the case with the African Mission in Burundi (AMIB), which was replaced by the UN's operation in Burundi (ONUB) in 2004, and AMIS, replaced by UNAMID on 1 January 2008. It seems that the AU, or another sub-regional organization, first deploys a stabilization operation, and the UN follows through with a complex peacekeeping operation within ninety to 120 days (Bellamy and Williams 2005; de Coning 2006). One risk with expecting the AU to act first, however, relates to the Security Council's unwillingness to commit to action through the UN, which would not provide the AU with the resources it needs to carry out civilian protection. As such, the organizations might "be played off against each other" (Strauss 2009b: 109).

ECOWAS

ECOWAS' responsibilities with regard to the established mechanism of collective security and peace were delineated in its 1999 "Protocol Relating to the Mechanism for Conflict Prevention, Management, Resolution, Peacekeeping and Security." ECOWAS has the authority to intervene militarily in order to address internal and interstate conflicts, "to alleviate the suffering of the populations and restore life to normalcy in the event of crises, conflict and disaster ... ECOWAS shall develop its own capacity to efficiently undertake humanitarian actions for the purposes of conflict prevention and management" (1999: Article 40). The Protocol suggests that, among other objectives, the mechanism is expected to support the deployment of peace operations.[16]

ECOWAS is a sub-regional organization composed of fifteen member states, which has been involved in peace support operations since 1990, when it established the ECOWAS Monitoring Group (ECOMOG) to intervene in Liberia. ECOWAS has since undertaken peacekeeping operations in Sierra Leone, Guinea-Bissau and Côte d'Ivoire. The Economic Community of West African States (ECOWAS) is another example of an African organization where the sequencing of peace operations can be verified. Since the more recent ECOWAS intervention in Liberia in 2003 showed visible signs of improvement compared to the previous one in 1990–1997 (Taft and Ladnier 2006: 17), some argue that ECOWAS is improving its capacity to deal with crises in West Africa. Indeed,

ECOWAS is developing the ECOWAS Standby Force (ESF), a regionally based 6,500-troop brigade, able to deploy 1,500 troops within thirty days, which are to be followed by the remaining 5,000 within ninety days (Holt and Shanahan 2005: 25).

The ESF will become one of the five regional standby forces conceived under the African peace and security architecture, but the initiative is advancing without training guidance from the AU. Its development, however, remains in the early stages, since ECOWAS is facing serious funding and logistics problems, just as the AU does. Recent field training exercises aimed to evaluate the operational and logistical readiness of the Eastern Battalion of the ECOWAS Stand-by Force spearheaded by Nigeria are encouraging. They took place at the end of April and beginning of May 2010. However, it is still hard to assess whether the ESF will indeed become fully operational to deploy and carry out robust peace operations by December 2010, which coincides with ASF goals for operationalization. ECOWAS suffers from a lack of institutional capacity, the same lack of training and equipment that the AU faces, a lack of clear rules of engagement, and an increased dependency on donor funding, training, and equipment, which all affect its ability to plan and carry out peace operations to protect civilians.

Despite such serious shortcomings, ECOWAS has been described as "the most robust organization in Africa willing to address security issues from a regional stand point … its willingness to use force to stop humanitarian crises has been repeatedly demonstrated" (Taft and Ladnier 2006: 18). This is mainly due to Nigeria's leading role. Nigeria has committed most of the financial, logistical, and human resources required for ECOWAS operations, which shows the importance of having a powerful state involved, and willing to contribute troops and equipment. However, Nigeria also lacks the required logistical capacities for robust interventions, and depends on US and European assistance. ECOWAS still faces significant challenges in mounting the required number of prepared troops for robust interventions, then, just as the AU does. This is yet again another illustration of the gap between having the political will to intervene to stop mass killings – which is quite significant in the case of ECOWAS – and the actual capacity to do so.

The review of regional and sub-regional organizations reflects the unequal distribution of capacities on various continents. Since NATO, the EU, the AU, and ECOWAS have been the only actors capable of taking on human security-related responsibilities, Europe and Africa are the only two regions with the capacity to carry out interventions. The Organization of American States (OAS) is unlikely to consider military intervention, while the Association of Southeast Asian Nations (ASEAN) has only started to debate whether it should play any role in intervening in a member state.

Coalitions of the willing

Coalitions of the willing are defined as groups of states that get together, usually around a pivotal state, in order to carry out a joint mission to address particular crises.[17] None of the various reformulations of the R2P framework between 2001 and 2009 excludes state-based responses to protect civilians in mass atrocities situations. In recent years, multinational forces have carried out the decisions to authorize military force for the purpose of enforcing the peace (United Nations 2004a: 67, para. 210). Ad hoc coalitions of the willing intervening in their region or in former colonies represent a trend of the last fifteen years (e.g. Gray 2005; Bellamy and Williams 2005). Coalitions of the willing may operate with or without proper authorization from the UN Security Council or regional organizations, which affects the legitimacy of the mission significantly. Using ad hoc coalitions of the willing to protect civilians has both key advantages and disadvantages, as seen from the diverse results of several such operations.

On the positive side, a coalition of the willing is, evidently, "willing" to use force to protect civilians and is, thus, seriously committed to contributing troops to a particular mission. Generally, coalitions are led by one powerful country, which accounts for more straightforward command and control arrangements than is the case with multinational organizations. In turn, this also increases the commitment of military and civilian leadership and resources from the lead nation. For instance, if the UN is not able to put R2P into practice by intervening militarily to protect victims from mass killings, Washington can create multilateral coalitions of the willing to intervene to stop the atrocities (Thakur 2006: 63). Coalitions of the willing are generally created in two cases: first, to intervene *after* a UN force has failed to address the conflict effectively because of limited capacity; and second, *in preparation* of a UN operation (e.g. Gray 2005: 215–217). Both instances present obvious advantages resulting from alternative means to provide the necessary military force when the UN or regional organizations are unable to act. Several successful examples can illustrate the advantages of coalitions of the willing carrying out military interventions, especially when given UN authorization.

Although not conducted by a coalition of the willing per se but by an individual state, Operation Palliser is one example of an operation launched in response to a crisis in which the UN lacked the necessary resources to react, but one state had the required capabilities, and was willing to address the conflict. Operation Palliser was launched by the UK in Sierra Leone in 2000, at the request of the UN Secretary-General, as a small and limited operation, directly supporting the ongoing UN Mission in Sierra Leone (UNAMSIL). The rapid deployment of approximately 1,300 troops on 7 May 2000 was initially aimed at evacuating British nationals, but the force also provided short-term training to 14,000 government security forces. The presence of UK troops on the ground and their robust military actions against the Revolutionary United Front (RUF) sent a positive message to civilians that they were going to be protected from the violence unleashed by the rebels.[18] Operational Palliser gave UNAMSIL the necessary time to reorganize and eventually expand its size into a much larger UN peacekeeping force. This is a good example of a short-term military intervention that was capable of protecting civilians.

Coalitions of the willing have also been formed in preparation for a UN operation, such as the French-led multinational force in Liberia in 2003. After the forced departure of President Charles Taylor, the Security Council passed a resolution authorizing member states to form a multinational force to implement the ceasefire in Liberia and prepare for the upcoming UN force comprising 15,000 troops. French troops also took the lead in another operation in Africa in 2003, in Côte d'Ivoire, also authorized by the Security Council. In this case, Operation Licorne was undertaken in collaboration with an ECOWAS force, and operated until the UN was able to deploy its force in the country, under the UN Operation in Côte d'Ivoire (UNOCI). With a Chapter VII mandate, the French and ECOWAS troops were authorized "to take the necessary steps" to reinstall security and protect civilians at risk until the UNOCI force was established in April 2004.[19] Other notable examples of coalitions of the willing acting to protect civilians are the US and French interventions in Haiti, the Italian-led intervention in Albania, the Australian-led intervention in East Timor, and the Australian-led mission in the Solomon Islands, all of which were later followed by either a UN or an EU peacekeeping mission.

The Australian-led intervention in the Solomon Islands in 2003 introduced another trend, namely that of missions undertaken without UN Security Council authorization but with the consent of the host state. This example is also illustrative of the efforts of individual powerful states whose interests are affected by the conflict at stake[20] to build up coalitions of the willing to offer more legitimacy to their missions. In this particular case, Australia called on Fiji, New Zealand, Samoa, Tonga, and Papua New Guinea to form the coalition, and also obtained the written support for this operation from the Pacific Islands Forum (Bellamy and Williams 2005: 169). Even if one country provides the majority of troops and equipment and organizes the mission efficiently, as was the case with Australia, the coalition of the willing format emphasizes the collective dimension of the operation, thus increasing its legitimacy and accountability.

Despite the advantages that such alternatives bring in terms of effective protection of civilians at risk, coalitions of the willing are not without serious problems. They open up the contentious issue of legitimacy, especially if they intervene without UN Security Council authorization, or without authorization from another notable international body, and especially when the invitation of the host country is missing. For obvious reasons, their legitimacy is highly contested. Voluntary coalitions are also likely to face basic challenges in interoperability, resulting from bringing together militaries that do not train collectively prior to deployment. Moreover, a state might pull out of the coalition if faced with a too-dangerous environment on the ground or if the public support at home disappears (Holt and Berkman 2006: 70).

Even so, ad hoc coalitions of the willing can be a useful short-term alternative for dealing with urgent crises. They provide the forces capable of protecting civilians at risk effectively and rapidly, while the world might be waiting for a UN intervention. They usually depend on powerful, militarily capable Western states that look for pragmatic solutions to urgent crises through contributions to hybrid peace operations and interventions taking place outside the UN system. Although such trends are likely to have negative consequences for the UN in the longer term, most of the time such coalitions hand leadership to follow-on UN peacekeeping operations after the emergency crises have been addressed. This diminishes the legitimacy gap, to a certain extent. Since coalitions of the willing can be effective, but also limited in scope, time, and scale, they may contribute to the achievement of the larger UN mandate of civilian protection.

Evidently, the capacity of any coalition of the willing depends on which countries come together to form the multinational force. To reinforce a point made earlier, it is individual states that have the critical responsibility to protect, and ultimately provide the means for any effective use of force. Indeed, there seems to be agreement among scholars that "it is only states [and only a handful] that have the capabilities to fly thousands of troops halfway round the world to prevent or stop genocide or mass murder" (Wheeler 2000: 310; for similar arguments see Thakur 2003; Roberts 2004). This is why coalitions of the willing become a resourceful – though legally questionable – alternative, capable of addressing one of the key concerns when faced with mass killings: how to deploy the required troops to protect civilians rapidly.

Conclusion

The ICISS report advanced the protection of civilians as the primary goal of a military intervention to avert or stop genocide, ethnic cleansing, mass crimes, or crimes against humanity. Such interventions are likely to be located in non-permissive environments, with high levels of violence of the type seen during the 1994 genocide in Rwanda, where coercive protection is needed. Given the specific requirements for civilian protection in non-permissive environments, including coherence, speed, and coordination, such operations are unlikely to be UN led. As seen in the recent record of peace operations, the Security Council has authorized interventions led primarily by multinational forces or regional organizations, and not by the UN itself. This aspect was paramount in formulating this chapter's suggestion that only a few actors can carry out humanitarian interventions. In decreasing order of legitimacy – but not of military capabilities – these are: the UN, several regional organizations, and ad hoc coalitions of the willing. Five organizations are generally capable, to various extents, to carry out such interventions, namely the UN, NATO, the EU, the AU, and ECOWAS.

While we are facing a serious capacity crisis, the demand for peace operations continues to grow, regardless of the fact that it has already exceeded the available supply of qualified personnel. In a vicious circle, this evidently poses additional challenges to an already overstretched pool of capable actors. To make matters worse, although more than 115 countries currently contribute to some extent to UN peace operations, the burden of supplying peacekeepers falls significantly on developing countries. This is problematic for two reasons: first, because developed states who have championed the R2P do not play their part in operationalizing its reaction component; and second, because apart from sheer numbers of troops and force configurations, operational effectiveness to protect civilians also depends on preparation, mandates, and rules of engagement, areas in which developing countries do not have a comparative advantage. Given the growing number of requests for peace operations, it seems likely that the burden will continue to fall on developing countries.

This is further complicated by the fact that the countries with the capabilities to provide well trained and well equipped troops to operationalize the responsibility to protect civilians are reluctant to do so because of commitments elsewhere, such as in Iraq and Afghanistan. The preferences of powerful countries like the US, the UK, and France, who possess sufficient logistics support and planning capacity to avert mass killing in challenging environments, are to act unilaterally or through coalitions of the willing rather than to contribute their national contingencies to UN missions,[21] capturing a major challenge faced by operations designed for R2P-type situations. This impacts on the rapidity and effectiveness of the deployment of forces.[22]

This overview of actors capable to intervene suggests that all face a shortage of trained troops for peace operations. Apart from the reluctance of the West to provide well trained capabilities, the slow progress of various regional capacity-building processes amplifies the current capacity crisis. While regional organizations are expected to intervene to stop mass killings when the UN is inactive, they seem to face the same problems the UN faces, namely financial challenges and difficulties in generating troops from member states. Regional organizations such as the AU, the EU, and NATO operate on a national consensus basis and cannot coerce individual member states to provide forces. They all suffer from similar problems related to command and control issues. Of all of them, NATO remains the most capable organization to intervene for R2P-type operations necessitating civilian protection, as it has both the willingness and the capacity to authorize and manage effective military interventions in non-permissive environments. The willingness to carry out interventions to maintain continental security in Africa, both in the case of the AU and ECOWAS, has been colliding with a chronic lack of resources, equipment, and training, with some critical capacities such as logistical equipment and airlift only being available from nations outside Africa. The significant reliance of the AU and ECOWAS on outside funding and support for their operations exemplifies the shortcomings of having regional organizations in Africa deal with conflicts on the continent.

In successive representations of the responsibility to protect, it is usually assumed that the use-of-force component of the R2P framework is going to be operationalized through the UN. Since it is apparent, however, that the UN does not have the capacity to conduct operations to protect civilians in cases of large-scale violence, and that regional organizations with some capacity also encounter difficulties in generating troops to intervene effectively, strategic partnerships between the UN and regional actors are necessary to address the commitment–capacity gap. After the 2005 World Summit Outcome Document expressed interest in ensuring closer cooperation between regional organizations and the UN, the Special Committee on Peacekeeping Operations concluded in February 2006 that the UN and regional organizations could be vital partners in providing for peace and security. Paragraph 139 in the 2005 World Summit Document discusses the UN's preparedness to take collective action through the Security Council and "in cooperation with relevant regional organizations as appropriate." Acknowledging the importance of having a strategic partnership between the UN and regional actors is one of the merits of post-2005 World Summit references to R2P at the UN. Despite emphasizing early warning when discussing the issue of capabilities, both the report of the UN Secretary-General on R2P and the 2009 General Assembly debate on the topic mentioned the need to strengthen existing capacities and develop new ones at the national, sub-regional, regional, and UN level to be able to respond to mass atrocity situations. Developing the AU Standby capability and the EU rapid deployment capacity are helpful initiatives in this sense.

To sum up the R2P contributions to this debate, we need briefly to return to the 2001 ICISS report. If the report addressed two concerns about humanitarian intervention – on redefining sovereignty and looking at questions of authorization – in enough detail to provide material for assessment, the same cannot be said about the issue of operational capacity. More is covered in the supplementary volume of the ICISS report, but almost no constructive proposals on the topic have emerged since then in relation to the responsibility to protect. The main reason for the silence on this aspect of R2P relates to the conscious effort at the UN to keep the responsibility to protect framework away from considerations of the use of force.

Attempts to appease critical member states (mostly members of the Non-Aligned Movement) who regard R2P as another way of phrasing the old humanitarian intervention enterprise, as well as efforts to advance its acceptance among UN membership, have translated into a move away from direct guidelines pertaining exclusively to the use of force. Security Council resolutions on the topic certainly address the issue of military capabilities for peace operations in greater detail, but never in relation to R2P. It appears that the most extreme manifestation of R2P – the use of force – is not acknowledged as being part of the framework anymore. Most UN documents referencing R2P *and* discussing the issue of capacity in more detail emphasize the need for enhanced early warning.

After the release of the Secretary-General's 2009 report on R2P, the use of force was described as falling under "the third pillar" of the R2P framework. However, the Secretary-General suggests that pillar three is generally understood too narrowly, as meaning solely the use of force. In trying to emphasize the importance of prevention, Ban Ki-moon argues that "if the international community acts early enough, the choice need not be a stark one between doing nothing or using force" (United Nations 2009a: 18). The central message of the Secretary-General's report in relation to the question of capacity is that the world has underinvested in preventive capacities. While this is clearly compelling, the question of reaction in instances where there are no other options left to provide protection but the controversial and contested use of force is critical. Putting together the required number of troops in some last-resort situations remains one of the most challenging tasks in today's increasingly demanding environment to address humanitarian emergencies.

No matter how legitimate a case can be made for military intervention, protection will fail without an actor that is both willing and capable of tackling the mission. Furthermore, operational guidelines need to be provided as well, to make sure effective protection is possible in non-permissive environments most likely to be seen in R2P-type scenarios. Indeed, if the responsibility to protect civilians is to be taken seriously, then, in addition to military capabilities, effective considerations related to training personnel, funding military missions, providing the doctrine, and organizing command and control and rules of engagement are also needed. As Victoria Holt and Tobias Berkman cautiously assess, "until this takes place, the 'responsibility to protect' may remain a mandate that is impossible to execute until the vision aligns with the preparedness of the world's military forces" (2006: 13). It is only reasonable to expect that the responsibility to protect cannot materialize without a capacity to protect.

Part II

R2P's practical dimensions

5 From concept to norm

After establishing R2P's conceptual weight in the previous three chapters, the analysis moves away from theoretical contributions in order to assess the practical dimensions of the responsibility to protect civilians. In this second part of the book, I first follow the normative trajectory of R2P from its emergence in 2001 up to the support it has attracted in principle in the political realm in 2009. This exercise will then allow for a scrutiny of the gaps between R2P's swift evolution on the normative side and the enduring problems on the operational side.

The journey of the responsibility to protect framework for collective action commenced over a decade ago. In this chapter, I look at R2P's normative progress during this period that culminated with two key developments in 2009, namely the UN Secretary-General's report, "Implementing the Responsibility to Protect," and the General Assembly's plenary debate on R2P. I first provide a brief explanation of why norms matter, to introduce the discussion of R2P's norm-building process. This exercise highlights the most important steps along the progressive route that propelled R2P's status from an "idea" in the ICISS report to an emerging norm. I then discuss the stage R2P reached on its normative trajectory, and explain the factors that contributed to this progress. The last section of the chapter explores whether this normative development provides R2P with any legal force, that is, whether it brings R2P closer to a binding norm of international law. In line with this study's focus on the contributions made by the responsibility to protect framework to the debate on humanitarian intervention, I refer in this context to R2P's potential for the collective use of authorized force.

Norms and normative consolidation processes

Norms are defined as shared understandings and values that shape the preferences and identities of state and non-state actors, and legitimize behavior, either explicitly or implicitly (e.g. Kratochwil 1989; Florini 1996). In spite of the many conflicting meanings attributed to the term "norm," when discussing hereafter R2P's status as a nascent norm, I refer to social norms and the existence of generalized standards of conduct that embody collective expectations about proper behavior. When exploring whether R2P is close to becoming a norm of customary international law it is important to understand that legal norms are social norms that have legal implications. They are consequently grounded in shared understandings and are connected to social practice (Brunnée and Toope 2010). Given R2P's declared goal to change the terms of the humanitarian discourse, it is useful to ask how far it has succeeded.

The relevance of international norms is evident in "the war convention" literature, which places normative restraints upon the conduct of war; in "the democratic peace" literature, which emphasizes the normative respect that democracies have toward each other; in "the long peace" literature, which describes unspoken rules emerging out of deterrence situations and evolving into "quasi-law" that coordinates international relations; and in the regime literature, which highlights the role of norms in understanding state behavior. The international theory on "norm debate" is voluminous, with a multitude of models that explain the effects of norms on foreign policy and domestic practices (Cortell and Davis 1996), suggest mechanisms through which norms affect behavior (Onuf 1989), clarify when norms matter, and how they evolve (Florini 1996; Finnemore and Sikkink 1998; Risse 2000). The last category is of utmost interest for this chapter's analysis of R2P's norm consolidation. It is also generally associated with the theory that most supports the argument that norms matter, namely constructivism. Dominant constructivist models describe norm development in the shape of "norm cascades" (Finnemore and Sikkink 1998), "spirals" (Risse *et al.* 1999), "boomerangs" (Keck and Sikkink 1998), or as processes of argumentation, pressure and persuasion, and diffusion (Risse 2000; Checkel 2001).

Summarizing the extensive literature on norms is clearly beyond my scope. I will only refer hereafter to processes of norm emergence and evolution that are relevant to explaining R2P's normative trajectory and its current status in international law, in order to determine its potential to influence decision making and state behavior. I need to introduce one caveat regarding the normative assessment in this chapter: when discussing R2P's normative itinerary, I focus on discourse that helps clarify rather than on compliance as evidence of normative advancement, because of the early stage R2P is at in its "life cycle." The discussion of R2P-type cases in the following chapter will indicate the level of compliance, but the very early stage R2P is at needs to be emphasized to explain the lack of examples of compliant behavior and applications in practice.

Conceptually and policy-wise, the debate over humanitarian intervention has so far taken place on normative grounds (Thakur 2006; Thakur and Weiss 2009). It was precisely its association with humanitarian intervention that made R2P so controversial during the key steps on its normative path, most notorious of which were the negotiations preceding the 2005 UN Summit. Different terminologies are used to describe R2P. For instance, Edward Luck, the UN Special Adviser on issues related to the responsibility to protect still in 2010 refers to R2P as a "concept," mainly for political reasons, whereas the High-Level Panel report called it an "emerging norm" as far back as 2004. However, given its normative content and the three references to it in UN Security Council resolutions, it becomes apparent that R2P has moved beyond the "concept" status. Alex Bellamy (2009), for instance, refers to it as "principle," whereas Gareth Evans (2008a) had previously suggested that R2P was already a "norm."

A systematic assessment of the normative development of R2P is necessary to determine its potential to change state practice and influence civilian protection. It is in this context that R2P can make a positive contribution to the humanitarian intervention debate. Clarifying the status R2P has reached, after passing through the stages of concept, principle, and finally emerging norm, also influences the discourse. Moreover, the importance of this conceptual distinction springs from determining whether R2P alters the meaning of sovereignty or works within the existing parameters of nonintervention norms. To clarify, R2P started as an idea in the ICISS report, and was perceived as a concept in the immediate aftermath of the report's release. Its status quickly became that of a principle close to its adoption in the 2005 World Summit Outcome Document, and R2P became a nascent norm after states accepted its content and pledged to act in accordance with its recommendations. But since some argued that R2P's journey "sounds almost like a fairy tale" (Stahn 2007: 99), a more in-depth examination of the key steps that have marked R2P's normative trajectory so far is certainly needed.

R2P's trajectory: emergence and evolution

A discussion of various steps and inherent reformulations of the R2P framework along its normative trajectory is needed before assessing the stage R2P has currently reached.

Key steps along the norm-building process

As mentioned before, R2P surfaced in an attempt to shed more light onto the contentious humanitarian intervention debate. In 1999, Kofi Annan urged the UN General Assembly to "prevent another Rwanda" and to reach consensus on the issue of humanitarian intervention. In his address to the General Assembly, Kofi Annan requested the international community to "find common ground in upholding the principles of the UN Charter, and acting in defense of our common humanity" (United Nations 1999). In response to his challenge, in 2000 the government of Canada established the ICISS which released its report, "The Responsibility to Protect," the following year. Although the report was completed a few weeks before the September 11 attacks on New York and Washington, its release was delayed until December 2001. The focus of the report was not altered to address the 9/11 attacks, an inspired move in the long run, given that most likely the report's findings would have been less durable had the commissioners been sidetracked by current events (Bellamy 2009: 51).

The ICISS regarded the Brundtland Commission's successful formulation of "sustainable development" as a model of reinventing the terms of a debate. The ICISS report changed the language of "humanitarian intervention" with that of a "responsibility to protect," in order to move away from the impasse reached by the "right to intervene" debate. Additionally, the ICISS removed the adjective from humanitarian intervention to insist that the merits of particular cases be evaluated rather than blindly depicted as "humanitarian" (Badescu and Weiss 2010). The commission was inspired by the revolutionary formulation of "sovereignty as responsibility" initially proposed in relation to the protection of internally displaced populations (see Deng and Zartman 1991; Deng 1993, 1995). The twofold responsibility in this framework – internal and external – draws upon earlier work by Francis Deng and Roberta Cohen on the internal dimension of protection and sovereignty as responsibility (see Cohen 1991; Deng *et al.*, 1996). Despite the fact that the commission never formally acknowledged the origin of this idea, the report reinterpreted sovereignty in terms of responsibility rather than control. As done throughout this study so far, in this chapter, too, the discussion of the critical steps along R2P's normative trajectory focuses on the elements pertaining to humanitarian intervention and the use of force.

The central normative tenet of R2P, as first expressed in the ICISS report, is that state sovereignty entails responsibility and, therefore, each state has a responsibility to protect its citizens from mass killings and other gross violations of their rights. If that state is unable or unwilling to carry out that function, the state abrogates its sovereignty, and the responsibility to protect falls to the international community. In such cases then, collective military action – with the right authorization – could be an option to protect victims within a sovereign state. The two key aspects of the R2P framework – state sovereignty as responsibility and international responsibility in egregious circumstances – will remain a constant throughout R2P's normative evolution, and rightfully so. The 2001 report included three components under the broader "responsibility to protect" umbrella, namely the responsibility to prevent, the responsibility to react and the responsibility to rebuild.[1] In recent representations of R2P, this vision has been altered and refined.

As mentioned earlier, the report proposed five criteria of legitimacy, as a set of benchmarks for reaching consensus in any particular case requiring intervention. Apart from the legitimacy criteria, the sixth condition relates to legality and depicts the right authority for any intervention. The triggers the ICISS identified for action were "large scale loss of life … with genocidal intent or not, which [was] the product either of deliberate state action, or state neglect, or inability to act, or a failed state situation," or "large scale ethnic cleansing" (2001: xii, 32). The ICISS suggests that UN Security Council authorization needs to be sought prior to the use of force. However, the commission also identifies two alternatives for instances when Council's authorization fails in cases "crying out for action," namely the UN General Assembly holding an emergency session under the "Uniting for Peace" procedure, and regional organizations acting under Chapter VIII of the UN Charter. The ICISS report also proposes a valuable "code of conduct" for the permanent members of the Security Council to refrain from using their veto in instances requiring action to stop serious humanitarian crises.

When the discussion started on UN reform, the Secretary-General appointed the High-Level Panel (HLP), which released its report, "A More Secure World: Our Shared Responsibility," in December 2004. The HLP formally put R2P on the agenda for UN reform, and drew at length from the ICISS recommendations on the use of force. It also endorsed R2P as the "emerging norm that there is a collective international responsibility to protect" (United Nations 2004a: para. 203). The HLP also recommended that criteria governing the use of force, closely paralleling those proposed in the ICISS report, be adopted in declaratory resolutions of the UN General Assembly and Security Council (ibid.: paras 206–208). The Russian and Chinese representatives' acceptance of such language, when their governments strongly opposed British attempts in 1999–2000 to reach agreement on such criteria in the Security Council, demonstrates the value of the arguments advanced by key members of the HLP, such as Gareth Evans (e.g. Wheeler, 2005a: 5–6). An innovation in the HLP report was the proposition that the Security Council has the authority, and also the responsibility, to use force preventively to maintain international peace and security.

The High-Level Panel report informed the work of the UN Secretary-General, who was asked to submit to the General Assembly his recommendations for the 2005 UN Summit agenda. Kofi Annan, the UN Secretary-General at the time, endorsed the broad security perspective of the HLP and supported many of its recommendations. After consultations with governments and UN officials and with input from many civil society organizations, the Secretary-General published his report entitled "In Larger Freedom: Towards Development, Security and Human Rights for All," in March 2005. Under the auspices of the General Assembly, governments agreed in April 2005 to negotiate a reform agenda spanning a wide range of proposals intended to provide security for all people. "Security" in this context was broadly defined to include protection from genocide, among other concerns related to poverty, environmental degradation, disease, and freedom from terrorism.

Four elements of this report are significant for the refinement of the R2P framework and its subsequent normative consolidation. The first one relates to a different approach to the possibility for unilateral action in case of Security Council inaction compared to both the ICISS and HLP reports. Whereas these two reports considered the possibility of unilateral action, Annan's report argued that the idea "was not to find alternatives to the Security Council as a source of authority but to make it work better" (Annan 2005a: para. 126). Also, the Secretary-General's report described criteria for intervention as essential for achieving legitimacy and global support for the Council's action (ibid.), just as the ICISS and HLP reports did. In the same subsection on "the use of force," Annan suggested that states should agree whether they "have the right – or perhaps the obligation – to use [force] protectively to rescue the citizens of other States from genocide or comparable crimes" (ibid.: paras 122–123). Introducing the idea that international crimes could activate the use of force – previously portrayed as being triggered by gross human rights violations – was another key element that would matter in subsequent representations of R2P.

Equally important, the Secretary-General's report departed in one significant way from the recommendations of the High-Level Panel, which had an important impact on governments accepting the agenda Annan proposed. The HLP considered R2P a subset of its discussion of "Collective Security and the Use of Force," including the concept under "Using Force: Rules and Guidelines" (United Nations 2004a: paras 183–209). Due to its incorporation in that section, many governments viewed the High-Level Panel's recommendations on R2P as a recharacterization of the humanitarian intervention debate, which increased their fears about unlawful interference in the internal affairs of states. In contrast, the Secretary-General's report separated the normative aspects of the responsibility in paragraph 135 of his report, under the "rule of law" subsection, namely the assertion of R2P as a basis for collective action, from the discussion on the use of force, in paragraphs 122–126. Annan clarified that R2P was not about the use of force, but rather about a normative and moral undertaking requiring a state to protect its own civilians. If a state fails to do so, then the international community must apply a range of peaceful diplomatic and humanitarian measures, with force to be employed only as a last resort. This "decoupling" between the criteria for the use of force and the normative undertaking of R2P might very well have encouraged the endorsement of R2P at the 2005 UN Summit, particularly by those states who were not comfortable with guidelines on the use of force.

The September 2005 endorsement of R2P in the Summit Outcome Document has contributed the heaviest normative weight to R2P's trajectory thus far. This moment marked the first time the concept was endorsed in a universal forum, which was also the largest gathering of heads of state and government to date. R2P's survival until 2005 was "an achievement in itself," and its adoption by a consensus of the General Assembly "momentous" (Bellamy 2009: 67). Very few diplomats, practitioners, and scholars expected R2P to make it into the Summit Outcome Document. During subsequent conversations with Canadian officials, for instance, I learned that the Canadian delegation – no doubt among the most vocal supporters of R2P at the time[2] – seriously doubted that R2P stood any chance of being considered in the negotiation process. While progress had been made on the Outcome Document between March and August 2005, and G77 countries were willing to work toward a compromise on R2P so long as there was movement on development issues they were interested in, R2P's prospects did not look good in the weeks preceding the Summit, and got worse in the last days, amid intense efforts to address the concerns of China, Russia, and the US, and serious last-minute opposition from an influential member of the G77/NAM, namely India.

And yet, R2P survived the very difficult negotiations that preceded the adoption of the 2005 World Summit Outcome Document, especially the intense discussions on R2P taking place until the early hours on the day of the Summit.[3] As a result of the negotiation process, numerous linguistic changes addressing various concerns of member states translated into lengthy sentences with many sub-clauses mirroring successive attempts at compromise. However, agreement on the format to include R2P was finally reached, and so heads of state and government unanimously supported the responsibility to protect in paragraphs 138 and 139 of the World Summit Outcome Document. R2P was included in the section on human rights and the rule of law, and it was given its own subsection title, under the following wording:

> 138. Each individual State has the responsibility to protect its populations from genocide, war crimes, ethnic cleansing and crimes against humanity. This responsibility entails the prevention of such crimes, including their incitement, through appropriate and necessary means. We accept that responsibility and will act in accordance with it. The international community should, as appropriate, encourage and help States to exercise this responsibility and support the United Nations in establishing an early warning capability.
>
> 139. The international community, through the United Nations, also has the responsibility to use appropriate diplomatic, humanitarian and other peaceful means, in accordance with Chapters VI and VIII of the Charter, to help to protect populations from genocide, war crimes, ethnic cleansing and crimes against humanity. In this context, we are prepared to take collective action, in a timely and decisive manner, through the Security Council, in accordance with the Charter, including Chapter VII, on a case-by-case basis and in cooperation with relevant regional organizations as appropriate, should peaceful means be inadequate and national authorities are manifestly failing to protect their populations from genocide, war crimes, ethnic cleansing and crimes against humanity. We stress the need for the General Assembly to continue consideration of the responsibility to protect populations from genocide, war crimes, ethnic cleansing and crimes against humanity and its implications, bearing in mind the principles of the Charter and international law. We also intend to commit ourselves, as necessary and appropriate, to helping States build capacity to protect their populations from genocide, war crimes, ethnic cleansing and crimes against humanity and to assisting those which are under stress before crises and conflicts break out.
>
> (United Nations 2005a)

These two paragraphs explicitly state that there is not only a state responsibility to protect, but also a subsidiary responsibility for the international community "to protect populations from genocide, war crimes, ethnic cleansing and crimes against humanity." This formulation only reinforces the link to international crimes, a step forward from the ICISS report, which suggested that "overwhelming natural or environmental catastrophes, where the state concerned is either unwilling or unable to cope or call for assistance, and significant loss of life is occurring or threatened" could trigger international intervention for humanitarian purposes (2001: paras 4, 33). Despite the fact that the "sovereignty as responsibility" argument could have been more clearly stated, these paragraphs express a willingness to act when agreed thresholds take place. However, the language in the Outcome Document does fall short of what had been requested by the Secretary-General and by the High-Level Panel. For example, it neither affirms that the responsibility to protect is an "emerging norm" of international law nor phrases it as an obligation.

Another element present in previous R2P representations but missing from this formulation is the "continuum" of prevention, reaction, and rebuilding. The reference to the responsibility to prevent is mainly suggested as an appeal (Strauss 2009b: 299). According to paragraph 139, collective action can be taken through the Security Council, on a "case-by-case basis." Clearly, ad hoc arrangements on "a case-by-case basis" are different from the universal prescriptions envisaged in the reports of the ICISS, the HLP, and the UN Secretary-General's "In Larger Freedom." Furthermore, the issue of specific criteria for military intervention was not addressed. And yet, if there was no other way to move the negotiation process forward except by giving up the criteria on the use of force, it is better to have a watered-down version endorsed unanimously than no reference to R2P at all. Although the final text on R2P in the Summit Outcome Document was weaker than R2P's formulation in previous reports due to the numerous compromises and successive linguistic reinterpretations, the language appears sufficiently strong to reveal the endorsement of a new set of principles on national and international responsibility.

In comparison with the terminology used in the ICISS report, the language improved in one way during the bitter negotiations preceding the Outcome Document: while the R2P report argued that action should be taken when countries are "unwilling or unable" to protect their own citizens, the final text in the Outcome Document talks about "manifested failure" to protect, which depicts a more objective standard. Also, even if it does not imply an obligation, the wording in paragraph 139 – "we are prepared to take collective action" – is stronger than what was proposed in the initial draft of the Outcome Document, namely the phrase "we recognize our shared responsibility to take collective action."[4] A reference to acting in "a timely and decisive manner" was also included in paragraph 139, to reinforce the message. While states preserve the primary responsibility for the protection of their citizens, external actors may be mandated to intervene when states fail to act in accordance with their responsibilities. And this "clear acceptance by all UN members that there is a collective responsibility to protect civilian populations … with a commitment to do so through the Security Council wherever local authorities are manifestly failing" was the most "precious" achievement of the 2005 Summit to Kofi Annan (2005b).

After the 2005 World Summit, advocacy efforts focused on persuading the Security Council to reaffirm R2P. Open debates on a draft thematic resolution on the protection of civilians in armed conflict were held in December 2005.[5] After four months of stalemate caused by the Council's difficulties in reaching an agreement on language relating to R2P, in April 2006 the Russian and Chinese reluctance was finally overcome. The result was the Security Council resolution

1674 on the protection of civilians, adopted on 28 April 2006, which "reaffirms the provisions of paragraphs 138 and 139 of the World Summit Outcome Document regarding the responsibility to protect populations from genocide, war crimes, ethnic cleansing and crimes against humanity." This is the first official Security Council reference to the responsibility to protect. The R2P language is further referenced in Security Council resolutions on individual countries. On 31 August 2006, the Council passed resolution 1706, which demanded a rapid deployment of UN peacekeepers in Sudan. The resolution also made explicit reference to R2P, by reaffirming the provisions of resolution 1674 and the provisions of paragraphs 138 and 139 of the 2005 UN World Summit Outcome Document. What makes these references to R2P so important for the principle's normative development is the legal force of Security Council resolutions, unlike all previous incarnations of R2P.

So far then, the 2005 pinnacle and the two 2006 UN Security Council resolutions have been the highlights of R2P's normative trajectory. And yet, during my conversations with advocates, diplomats, and UN practitioners in New York in 2008 it became clear not only that there was no overall agreement over R2P, but rather that R2P was considered "toxic" across the UN. Persistent disagreements among many UN member states on the extent of conditioning sovereignty to civilian protection from R2P crimes, fuelled especially by those Non-Aligned Movement (NAM) states looking to create confusion about what was actually agreed in 2005, constituted the main explanation for this political climate. The fact that some of the major regional powers and key supporters in 2005 switched their positions, such as South Africa, in addition to others' buyer's remorse, did not help either. Some retroactive claims linking R2P to the 2003 invasion of Iraq, and to Burma after the 2008 Cyclone Nargis also increased fears that R2P was solely about military action or regime change. Officials from various offices within the UN Secretariat were not using the R2P terminology for fear of unintended consequences and interpretations.

In 2008, however, the UN Secretary-General, Ban Ki-moon, appointed scholar Edward Luck as his Special Adviser on issues related to R2P, and tasked him with reconceptualizing R2P, developing a strategy of implementation, providing guidelines for UN action in this direction, and building political consensus among member states. Luck started his work with the UN member states and the UN bureaucracy simultaneously, aiming to produce a report for debate in the General Assembly to convince member states to grant the Secretariat resources to carry on the recommendations on R2P from the 2005 Summit Outcome Document. In February 2008, the Global Centre for the Responsibility to Protect was established in New York, as a think tank focused on advocacy, promotion, and research on R2P. In a speech in Berlin in July 2008, the UN Secretary-General, Ban Ki-moon, declared his personal commitment to turning R2P into reality and introduced the "three-pillar approach" to R2P for the first time.

In fall 2008, Gareth Evans' book, *The Responsibility to Protect*, came out. A Task Force on the Prevention of Genocide completed its work, entitled "Preventing Genocide," in December, and provided many recommendations on preventive diplomacy and early warning that could be applied to an R2P toolbox. Plans for a new academic journal dedicated exclusively to the topic also surfaced. The journal, entitled *Global Responsibility to Protect*, published its first issue in January 2009. The number of publications and conferences on R2P in 2008 amounted to "almost a cottage industry." (Steinberg 2009: 433). More importantly, journalists, policy makers, and politicians started to apply the R2P framework to ongoing crises around the world, a point which is explored in more detail in the following chapter. Suffice to say for now that such efforts can be summed under Risse and Sikkink's "adaption" and "arguing" banners in the second and third stages of their spiral model (1999).

If 2008 was marked by the intense efforts of various norm entrepreneurs to put R2P back on the UN agenda, 2009 was even more significant because of two key advances toward translating R2P from rhetoric "to deeds." These were the release of the UN Secretary-General's report, "Implementing the Responsibility to Protect," in January 2009, and the General Assembly's plenary debate on the topic at the end of July 2009. Without doubt, they both propelled R2P further on its normative path.

After the key 2005 momentum in R2P's normative trajectory, the release of the UN Secretary-General's report represents the next significant step adding substance to R2P. In Ban's own words, the report addresses "one of the cardinal challenges of our time … operationalizing the responsibility to protect" (United Nations 2009a: 1). The report outlined the "three-pillar approach" to R2P that Ban first introduced in his 2008 speech in Berlin. The three pillars are: 1) the protection responsibility of the state; 2) the responsibility of the international community to assist states to fulfill their national obligations; and 3) the commitment to "timely and decisive" collective action. In describing the "three-pillar strategy" on R2P, the Secretary-General's report proposes a structure that depends on the equal size, strength and viability of each of its supporting pillars, with no sequence for implementation (ibid.: 2). The proposed view of R2P is "both narrow and deep," meaning that it applies to the four types of crimes, and, respectively, that the spectrum of reactive measures to address these crimes is substantial (ibid.: 8). Luck focused on the prevention and international assistance components of R2P during the consultations leading to the final report, which were obviously more in line with the preferences of the majority of states and, hence, more acceptable. This raised concerns among supporters that the report might move too far from the possibility of coercive use of force in extremis, while attempting to please states that were critical or suspicious of the R2P framework.

Some have argued that the Secretary-General strengthened sovereignty "to avoid the need for military intervention … [thus] distancing R2P from coercive intervention" (e.g. Chandler 2010: 163). That was indeed the intention. The focus in discussions preceding the release of the report and certainly during the subsequent General Assembly debate on the report was placed on pillars one and two. The report does propose to limit the right of sovereign "impunity," and places most emphasis on states' abilities and responsibilities to provide order and stability. However, the Secretary-General briefly contemplates the possibility of collective enforcement measures including coercive military action, authorized by the Security Council under Article 41 and 42, by the General Assembly under the "Uniting for Peace" procedure, or by regional and subregional organizations with prior Security Council authorization (ibid.: 25). It also notes that pillar three is generally understood too narrowly, as focusing mainly on the use of force.

In an attempt to distance itself from the work of the ICISS and appease the NAM countries, the report proposed a different way of thinking about R2P than the one presented in the 2001 R2P report, but the backbone of the framework remained the same. The formulation is also different from the message presented in paragraphs 138 and 139 of the 2005 Summit Outcome Document.[6]

According to Luck, the report provides a first cut at a broad strategy to implement R2P. Given the early stage in R2P's life, it does offer as many questions as answers (Luck 2010: 16). The report is not very specific, for instance, in terms of how the UN is going to mobilize financial, military, and civilian resources when peaceful means of addressing crises fail. Some critics have gone as far as arguing that the current framework of R2P "distances Western powers from responsibility" (e.g. Chandler 2010: 166). However, such a description does not seem accurate because several of the mechanisms proposed in the report focus on the international community's responsibilities to assist, and act when needed.

In relation to the potential use of force, the report certainly downplays it, but picks up an important suggestion from the ICISS report, namely that the permanent five members of the Security Council "reach a mutual understanding" to refrain from using their veto power "in situations of manifest failure to meet obligations relating to the responsibility to protect" (United Nations 2009a: 27). Equally important, the Secretary-General's report also encourages the consideration of the principles, rules, and doctrine guiding the use of coercive force (ibid.: 27). An innovative aspect of the report, which is generally overlooked in discussions on the topic, suggests that at times not governments but armed groups, such as the Revolutionary United Front (RUF) in Sierra Leone and the Lord's Resistance Army (LRA) in Northern Uganda, cause R2P-type extreme violence (ibid.: 19). What matters for the breadth of R2P this study focuses on is the report's acknowledgment in passing that prevention does not always work, and so coercive military action to halt mass atrocities is a possibility in extreme cases (ibid.: 25). This, however, has moved from the headlines in the ICISS report to the position of an afterthought in this one.

The release of the report was expected to be followed by a UN General Assembly debate on the topic. This was postponed for months, until it was finally scheduled for the end of July 2009. The General Assembly's formal plenary debate on R2P was one of the largest debates of the 63rd Session of the General Assembly. It was the first General Assembly debate on R2P, with 108 member states presenting their views. Because of the very high number of speakers signing up to make statements, the deliberations were extended to a third day. In preparation for the debate, the goal of R2P supporters was to deepen and expand the international consensus behind R2P, which actually ended up being the outcome. Civil society emphasized how widely the basic elements of the norm resonated[7] and the need to go beyond verbal commitments toward implementation (Evans 2009).

Initially, many feared the debate would produce a resolution diluting the September 2005 commitment, or translate into normative regress as a result of what the *Economist* described as opponents who "have been busily sharpening their knives" on the eve of the debate (2009). Supporters were worried that such a debate might allow skeptical states to renegotiate paragraphs 138 and 139 and thus detract from finding ways to operationalize R2P. Before the debate, the UN Secretary-General called upon member states to "resist those who try to change the subject or turn our common effort to curb the worst atrocities in human history into a struggle over ideology, geography or economics" (*UN News* 2009).

A troubled start had critics trying to paint R2P in imperialistic colors. This included the "concept note" and opening statement by the Nicaraguan president of the General Assembly, Father Miguel d'Escoto Brockmann, who called R2P "redecorated colonialism" and suggested "a more accurate name for R2P would be the right to intervene" (Brockmann 2009). The President of the General Assembly also organized an informal dialogue before the General Assembly convened its debate and invited four panelists to speak, three of whom were well-known opponents of R2P (Noam Chomsky, Jean Bricmont, and Ngũgĩ wa Thiong'o, with Gareth Evans the only proponent of R2P). Some have described Brockmann's efforts as a "campaign to sabotage R2P" (*Economist* 2009), in light of his efforts to give the debate on R2P a negative spin.

And yet, the remarks by ninety-two countries and two observers who addressed the plenary showed almost unanimous support for R2P. States affirmed that the 2005 World Summit Outcome was not open for renegotiation, and so the debate was mainly positive and forward looking. Almost all states supported R2P's implementation, with only four countries directly questioning the 2005 World Summit agreement – namely Cuba, Nicaragua, Sudan and Venezuela. But even the skeptics were unable to challenge the boundaries of R2P that had been established in September 2005, and some of the states opposing it previously agreed that the 2005 articulation in the Summit Outcome Document represented a "prudent description" of R2P.[8] Remarks from major regional powers that had previously been reticent or even hostile to R2P, such as Brazil, Nigeria, India, South Africa, and Japan, attested to the practicality of much of the three pillars' content, and so appeared especially relevant in this context.

Several key areas of convergence from the plenary debate are important for this discussion. They include agreement on the fact that the responsibility to protect is anchored in existing international law; that mass atrocities within states can constitute threats to international peace and security that could enable the Security Council to take collective action; that R2P applies only to the four crimes identified in the 2005 Summit Outcome; and that it is an ally of sovereignty. No member state could contest the need to address crimes of this magnitude. The role of the Security Council in relation to the use force was among the most debated issues. States expressed frustrations about previous failures of the Security Council to take effective action, and supported the recommendation in the Secretary-General's report for the P5 to refrain from using the veto in situations involving mass atrocity crimes. Some even linked progress on R2P to calls for Security Council reform (GCR2P 2009b: 6–7).

The General Assembly debate over three days in the summer 2009 ended without any resolution and an inaccurate summary from Brockmann, who suggested once again that until the limits are clear, no implementation is possible. However, in spite of disagreement and contestation, the debate showed governmental support for implementing the September 2005 consensus. A resolution was not a necessary outcome of the debate. The hopes of supporters beforehand were to have a constructive dialogue in the General Assembly that would reflect support for the Secretary General's report, for UN efforts to implement R2P, and member states' own commitment to implement R2P. The last never materialized, while no concrete proposals were agreed in regard to the second. The UN Secretary-General concluded his report by suggesting that the General Assembly: 1) welcomes or takes note of his report; 2) defines its "continuing consideration" role mandated in paragraph 139 of the 2005 Outcome Document; 3) addresses the issue of partnerships between states and the international community; 4) considers whether, and, if so, how to conduct a periodic review of member states' progress on implementing R2P; and 5) determine how to oversee the Secretariat's efforts to implement R2P (United Nations 2009a: 30). The General Assembly debate addressed only the first out of these five suggestions of the Secretary-General. This confirmed that R2P is in fact at the beginning of a long, and slow-moving, normative process.

On 14 September 2009, the General Assembly adopted by consensus resolution 63/308 on the responsibility to protect, which is its first resolution on R2P. This short resolution recalls paragraphs 138 and 139 of the Summit Outcome Document, takes note of the Secretary-General's report and the "timely and productive" debate on R2P, and "decides to continue its consideration of the responsibility to protect." It does not mention any concrete plans for the implementation of R2P. Only after the removal of the wording "with appreciation" from the paragraph taking note of the Secretary-General's report was the resolution adopted by consensus (see GCR2P: 2009e). Both the General Assembly debate and resolution adopted in 2009 prove that significant objection to R2P has diminished.

In November 2009, at the eighth open debate on the protection of civilians in armed conflict, the Security Council unanimously adopted resolution 1894, which reaffirms "the relevant provisions of the 2005 World Summit Outcome Document regarding the protection of civilians in armed conflict, including paragraphs 138 and 139 thereof regarding the responsibility to protect populations from genocide, war crimes, ethnic cleansing and crimes against humanity." This marked the third time R2P was referenced in a Security Council resolution. It also confirmed that it is mostly in relation to the protection of civilians that UN member states refer to R2P in public statements before the Security Council.

The stage R2P has reached

The developments since the release of the ICISS report in December 2001 illustrate how R2P has moved from the status of an idea expressed in the international commission's report toward that of a nascent norm, used as a foundation for international public policy. A few weeks after the release of the ICISS report, Kofi Annan, then the UN Secretary-General, praised the report as "the most comprehensive and carefully thought-out response we have seen to date" (2002). After the 2005 endorsement at the UN, R2P was described as a "new declaratory commitment to protect endangered populations" (Wheeler 2005a: 12), a "normative innovation" (Brunnée and Toope 2006: 2), which "became an international doctrine."[9] R2P's rapid evolution is even more surprising given its inherent potential to produce significant change in regard to the use of force, which is one of the most difficult areas of international law. Deciding when states can use force legitimately is also the central normative challenge of world politics (Reus-Smit 2005: 71). The cumulative impact of R2P has been dubbed "the most dramatic normative development of our time" (Thakur and Weiss 2009: 22).

When discussing normative advancement, I focus on discourse that helps clarify rather than on compliance because of the early stage R2P is at in its "life cycle." Even so, Martha Finnemore and Kathryn Sikkink's (1998) "life cycle" model is applicable, as the normative campaign to institutionalize the international responsibility to protect clearly substantiates the major steps in their model's first stage, norm emergence. Tracing the key steps on R2P's trajectory so far also verifies the types of social interactions Thomas Risse and Kathryn Sikkink (1999) identified in their five-phase "spiral model" of norm diffusion as instrumental adaptation and argumentative discourse.

The move from an idea introduced in the ICISS report to a principle whose inclusion in the 2005 Outcome Document was intensely negotiated until the very day of the Summit is illustrative of how shared understandings emerge. They are the result of social learning and interactions, and actors' promotion of particular understandings (Wendt 1999). Shared understandings on R2P were shaped in line with changes in mainstream normative views since the beginning of the 1990s, which have moved toward sovereignty as responsibility and have placed more emphasis on human rights and civilian protection. The most important normative advance of R2P to date – the 2005 endorsement in the Outcome Document – reflects a shared understanding among member states, albeit much debated, of what R2P entails and the four types of crimes it applies to. It is worth testing it against what Finnemore and Sikkink label the "tipping point" in their three-stage life cycle. After their emergence, norms move to a second stage of broad acceptance or "norm cascade,"[10] which is followed by a third stage of internalization. The tipping point between the first two stages is reached when "a critical mass of relevant state actors adopt the norm," namely when at least one-third of the total states in the system adopt it, including most importantly "critical states … without which the achievement of the substantive norm goal is compromised" (Finnemore and Sikkink 1998: 890, 895).

R2P was embraced unanimously at the rhetorical level in September 2005 as evidenced by paragraphs 138, 139 and 140 on the topic in the World Summit Outcome Document. While reaching the threshold rarely happens before one-third of all the states in the system adopt the norm, what also matters is which states adopt it. This is particularly relevant when considering the inequality in terms of normative weight (ibid. 1998: 901). One noteworthy concern in this context relates to the negotiation process resulting in R2P's inclusion in the Outcome Document. Only a small number of powerful countries were actually intensely involved in the negotiation process, which does not necessarily mean that all the 192 UN member states unanimously believed in the accuracy of R2P's principles as reflected in paragraphs 138 and 139. The most powerful ones, though, did. The fact that the General Assembly adoption goes beyond the "critical mass of relevant state actors" suggests that R2P had reached its tipping point, moving into the second stage of Finnemore and Sikkink's model, namely "norm cascade."

Notwithstanding efforts by spoilers, the World Summit Outcome Document's provisions on R2P work to "define the authoritative framework within which Member States, regional arrangements, the UN system and its partners … seek to give doctrinal, policy and institutional life to the responsibility to protect" (United Nations 2009a: 4). An increasing number of states from Latin America, the Caribbean, the Middle East, Eastern and Western Europe, Africa, Asia and the Pacific share the understanding of R2P as outlined in paragraphs 138 and 139 of the Summit Outcome Document (GCR2P 2009e). However, this key push forward for the R2P cart should not be regarded as the pinnacle of the norm consolidation efforts. Instead, it needs to be perceived as the platform for future normative deliberation and interaction (Brunnée and Toope 2010: 204).

While the normative views on how to proceed in the face of mass atrocities have changed, imitation as seen in states' behavior needs to catch up as well. Together with socialization, imitation is one of the characteristic elements in the second phase of a norm's trajectory. Clearly various actors, the UN being the most important of them, are part of the socialization stage R2P has presently reached. Even so, R2P does not yet compare favorably with other humanitarian campaigns a year or two before their consolidation, such as the International Criminal Court, the ban on landmines, and the ban on child soldiers (Badescu and Weiss 2010). Typically the second phase involves the steady accumulation of positive precedents, but R2P is not there yet, as the next chapter will illustrate. The theoretical literature suggests that this stage is reached when supporters convince international and regional institutions to incorporate the nascent norm into their rules or modus operandi. A good example in this sense is the affirmation of the R2P principle in "The Ezulwini Consensus," the AU's common position on UN reform (AU 2005a). Also illustrative is the endorsement of R2P at the African Union (AU) level, although this happened before its inclusion in the Summit Outcome Document.

R2P developments between 2005 and the July 2009 General Assembly debate on the topic reflect how the September 2005 agreement was used as the platform for subsequent negotiations and compromises. Accordingly, the efforts to advance R2P during this period fit the description of the early stages of the "spiral model" of normative progress better, namely denial and tactical concessions (see Finnemore and Sikkink 1998; Risse and Sikkink 1999). Since September 2005, R2P's momentum has stagnated. As part of this stage, characterized by denial, supportive mission representatives and UN officials tasked with working on building consensus about R2P spent more time actually clarifying what R2P entailed and did not entail, as per paragraphs 138 and 139 of the 2005 Outcome Document, than on obtaining diplomatic commitments to implement R2P.

One year before the release of the Secretary- General's 2009 report on R2P, numerous consultations took place between UN Special Adviser on issues related to R2P Ed Luck, member states, NGOs, and various UN departments and agencies to reach consensus on what R2P meant. Such consultations and negotiations on key points related to R2P, and the subsequent drafts of the Secretary-General's report that emerged between the summer of 2008 and the release of the final report in January 2009, showed that consensus could be built around the "three-pillar" strategy. Evidence surfaced that member states claimed that in September 2005 they "killed" the idea of humanitarian intervention in the sense of unilateral and military action.[11] Instead, the agreement reached among member states spoke of a consensus on the "narrowness" of R2P, namely the four types of crimes the principle covered (genocide, war crimes, crimes against humanity, and ethnic cleansing), but with views of "narrowness" as also implying a move away from the idea of intervention.

The July 2009 General Assembly debate on R2P provides additional evidence of R2P going through the early stages of the spiral model. As was also the case before the debates, bargaining among proponents and opponents was prevalent. However, surprises emerged as well, especially in regard to the opponents' reactions. For instance, many of the 118 NAM states broke the tradition by "not explicitly aligning themselves with the NAM statement" (GCR2P 2009b: 4). As expected for this stage, processes of norm-guided identity formation and contestation dominated the debate. Even non-supporters, such as Egypt representing the NAM, remained within the boundaries agreed in September 2005. India, for instance, was another key regional power that changed its position from strong opposition right before the September 2005 Summit to perceiving the representation of R2P in the Secretary-General's report in a favorable light. As Risse and Sikkink argue, "to endorse a norm not only expresses belief, but also creates impetus for behaviour consistent with the belief" (1999: 7).

The focus of the July 2009 debate on R2P in the General Assembly was not on the normative aspects of R2P but on how the Security Council and the UN can act as responsible agents as prescribed in September 2005 (e.g. Serrano 2010: 176). The overall discussions demonstrated member states' desire to move forward. And this reality was further highlighted in mid-September when

General Assembly resolution 63/308 agreed to "continue its consideration." As the UN Secretary-General suggested when welcoming the adoption of this resolution, the statements of support for R2P by member states that had suffered R2P-type traumas are particularly meaningful (United Nations 2009c). By seeking affirmation and reaffirmation through the UN as the organizational platform to propel R2P further on its normative track, its supporters try to create the possibility for R2P to eventually become institutionalized among states, but also within states, which is the final measurement of a "new norm." Given these processes, it appears that R2P's depiction as nascent norm best captures the stage R2P has reached and its current portrayal in the international discourse. It is worth discussing what has accounted for R2P's progress up to this stage.

Factors explaining R2P's normative advancement

Several factors have contributed to the normative advancement of the R2P framework, which include the demand-driven nature of the ICISS report, the concept's emergence in a normative environment marked by greater concern for human rights and humanitarian law, and the efforts of various actors to promote R2P.

The normative fit

The normative evolution of R2P is a perfect illustration of how new norms never enter a normative vacuum, but instead surface in a much contested normative space where they must struggle with other norms and perceptions of interest (Finnemore and Sikkink 1998: 897). Since norms are usually contested, the itinerary of a new idea like R2P depends on its compatibility with the dominant environment. Ideas have to "fit" with the way the world works in order to have any chance of being taken up by important social actors (Raymond 1997; Alderson 2000; Crawford 2002). Normative coherence, then is the first important aspect that deserves attention when assessing the normative development of R2P.

R2P has entered a normative environment where sovereignty and nonintervention norms have been institutionalized. However, the movement toward broader understandings of the term *sovereignty* and greater concern for human rights had already started, which explains the lack of any direct "normative clash" between the R2P framework and the norms of sovereignty and nonintervention. Since the creation of the UN, we have witnessed numerous efforts to shrivel the sovereign domain and to recognize the imperatives of collective action (Brunnée and Toope 2006: 7). The idea of "sovereignty as responsibility" had already surfaced, suggesting that sovereignty entails certain responsibilities for which governments must be held accountable, both to their national constituencies and to the international community (Deng *et al.* 1996: 1).

The derogations from sacrosanct sovereignty made possible the ICISS claim of responsibility to protect as an "emerging guiding principle, grounded in a miscellany of legal foundations ... growing state practice, and the Security Council's own practice" (ICISS 2001: 50). As described in detail in Chapter 2 of this book, state sovereignty has become more contingent on upholding basic human values. That the international community has duties, rather than mere interests in the protection of individuals, has underpinnings in many legal and political undertakings. These include the Universal Declaration of Human Rights, the International Covenant on Civil and Political Rights, the International Covenant on Economic, Social and Cultural Rights, the Convention on the Prevention and Punishment of the Crime of Genocide, the Geneva conventions and additional protocols, and the Rome Statute of the International Criminal Court. Collectively, these international obligations are fostering a "transition from a culture of sovereign impunity to a culture of national and international accountability" (ICISS 2001: 14). R2P emerged amidst growing acceptance that humanitarian objectives advanced in extreme cases of human rights violations were permissible objectives in accordance with international law and could not be held hostage to the norm of state sovereignty, classically understood. The humanitarian intervention theme became intertwined with the broader impact of human rights norms and the concept of human security in the international discourse.

We have been witnessing a "sea change in mainstream normative views since the beginning of the 1990s" in regard to interventions framed and justified along humanitarian terms, which comes in sharp contrast with interventions of the 1970s,[12] for instance (Thakur and Weiss 2009: 40). In regard to the latter, sovereignty was perceived as inviolable and the notion of outside military intervention inside a sovereign state to protect its citizens was far from acceptable. What matters is that normative change is not only rhetorical but also shapes agents' behavior by framing the range of legitimate actions (e.g. Finnemore and Sikkink 1998; Crawford 2002). At the beginning of the twentieth century, the shifts in the security debates from national to human security became a constant when considering the legitimacy of various actions. Human security is now recognized as a key aspect of the international peace and security agenda.[13]

The normative architecture for human rights within which R2P emerged has been characterized by inconsistent respect for the nonintervention principle, and for its corollary, the non-use of force to address humanitarian crises. In the last quarter-century, numerous new challenges have confronted those responding to humanitarian disasters. For example, authorizations for UN military operations went far beyond keeping the peace between opposing parties and monitoring fragile ceasefires; most significantly, many sought to protect and assist civilians caught in the cross-hairs of violence whose basic human rights had been grossly violated (Durch 2006; Howard 2008; Center for International Cooperation 2009). Other initiatives, such as the 1997 Ottawa Treaty banning landmines, have managed to reduce the toll of death and injury from landmines over the last decade (Oxfam International 2008), and the establishment of the International Criminal Court (ICC) and other ad hoc international tribunals have pursued the perpetrators of mass atrocities, including heads of state. The UN Security Council's decision to refer the case of Darfur to the ICC on 31 March 2005, for instance, attests to the recognition of crimes against humanity as global problems.

Another development discussed in Chapter 2 relates to the expansion of the meaning of "threats to international peace and security" under Chapter VII of the UN Charter to include humanitarian concerns, gross violations of human rights, genocide, and other crimes against humanity associated with the most violent forms of conflict. Such expansions lessen the importance of the long-standing assumption enshrined in Article 2(7) of the UN Charter, which denies any right "to intervene in matters which are essentially within the domestic jurisdiction of any state," further challenging the inviolability of state sovereignty. Another illustrative example of changed normative views comes from the increased UN interest in effective mandates to protect civilians in extreme humanitarian emergencies.[14] It has become common practice for UN peace operations after the Brahimi Report to be mandated to protect civilians, which has had a cushioning effect on how states have received the R2P's main recommendations.

When R2P emerged, perceptions on "non-interference" started to change in different regions of the world. In Africa, for instance, the discourse on "African Renaissance" and the increased willingness to engage in issues previously regarded as internal affairs of African member states occurred in parallel with the normative changes described above within the UN. The Constitutive Act of the African Union (2002), which gives expression to the collective security objectives of the organization, established its policy of non-indifference especially through Article 4(h). This permits the Union to intervene in its member states in "grave circumstances, namely war crimes, genocide, and crimes against humanity," through diplomatic and peaceful means, but also allowing the use of force as a last resort. This is a clear result of normative transformations wherein sovereignty becomes conditional on states respecting certain standards of domestic conduct, including respect for basic human rights (Badescu and Bergholm 2010: 110).

This also illustrates that R2P is not a framework invented and associated with the North, which raises North versus South debates, as opponents so often argued about R2P. In fact, as was mentioned in the first part of the book, the AU and ECOWAS embraced the "non-indifference" principle before the September 2005 World Summit, thus giving institutional validity to R2P. To its merit, the 2009 Report of the UN Secretary-General stresses the African roots of R2P in order to explain why the framework should not be viewed and designed as a North–South issue. Furthermore, R2P as expressed in the Summit Outcome Document and the Secretary-General's report is tied to already established international crimes, namely genocide, war crimes, and crimes against humanity, that imply legal requirements for compliance. This ensures R2P's consistency with established norms of international law. Such examples of perceptions framing the normative space in which R2P has emerged make clear that R2P evidences the transformation of the interpretation of sovereignty, but is not itself the reason for this transformation. Also, it is evident that R2P has been shaped by global politics. As such, the nature of the R2P report also deserves consideration when examining the factors that have facilitated R2P's advancement.

The demand-driven nature of the ICISS report[15]

When examining the normative development of R2P, one has to consider the specific nature of the Commission's report. In 2000, the Canadian government appointed the international commission tasked

> to wrestle with the whole range of questions – legal, moral, operational, and political – rolled up in this [humanitarian intervention] debate, to consult with the widest possible range of opinion around the world, and to bring back a report that would help the secretary-general and everyone else find some new common ground.
>
> (ICISS 2001: vii)

The commission demonstrated "remarkable intellectual leadership" (Riddell-Dixon 2005: 1072), evident in the way it reconceptualized the contentious concept of humanitarian intervention. The R2P report shifted the debate from the right of external actors to intervene in the internal affairs of states where gross violations of human rights are taking place to the responsibility of sovereign states to protect their populations in the first place, which proved to be a very clever and efficient formulation.

The role the ICISS played in R2P's normative development is a result of a combination of fine research work and good ideas,[16] on the one hand, and of building political momentum and having the necessary political weight to advance such ideas, on the other hand. If a commission produces work that is only restricted to the former, it risks irrelevance. If, however, it seizes the opportunities to advance its central thesis and receives enough political weight – as R2P did after the release of the ICISS report through the Canadian diplomatic machine – it may become a success, such as the anti-landmine or the ICC campaigns. This is why the ICISS was dubbed "norm broker" (Thakur and Weiss 2009: 35).

The rationale behind the commission's work was to produce a policy-relevant report that would spread the commission's language and circulate the R2P message. What emerged from conversations with Thomas G. Weiss and Don Hubert, the two authors of the supplementary volume to the ICISS report, was the initial goal to produce a report that would avoid the dangers faced by previous reports such as that of the Carnegie Commission on the Prevention of Deadly Conflict or that of the Commission on Global Governance. In such cases, and in spite of very good research and ideas, the major risk is that a commission's report may simply "collect dust" on bookshelves if there is no entrepreneurial force to promote it. With this in mind, the ICISS used the funding available to publicize the "Responsibility to Protect" report, first by shipping 30,000 copies, free, to everybody in the world who expressed an interest in the topic, from foreign governments to UN officials, NGOs and other prominent members of civil society. Also, early efforts included making sure that the R2P concept was part of ministerial speeches, and keeping the issue on the agenda of multilateral and regional fora.

The ICISS was a demand-driven commission, whose rationale for working on the report came from the recognition of failures to protect innocent civilians from the scourge of war or genocide in the 1990s, and the need to find a consensus on the contested concept of humanitarian intervention. The 1994 Rwandan genocide epitomizes such failures and also the need for new policy responses designed specifically to address such crises. The list of egregious crises, however, gets much longer if one considers Cambodia, Liberia, Sierra Leone, Bosnia, Kosovo, and, more recently, Darfur. The need to avoid similar failures of the international community to intervene to prevent or stop atrocities was a pressing question, which increased the demands for an answer when the ICISS was launched.

In his statement to the General Assembly before the July 2009 debate, Luck, the Special Adviser to the Secretary-General on issues related to R2P emphasized that humanitarian intervention was the focus of the General Assembly's debate in 1999 and not in 2009, calling humanitarian intervention a "poor basis for policy and strategy" (Luck 2010: 181). This confirmed the need to invent an effective policy option, and redesign expected reactions to mass atrocity crises. Until its portrayal in the ICISS report, an agreed normative foundation for dealing with mass atrocities was missing.

The need to solve this "problem" certainly helped with R2P's progress on its normative track. Also, the lack of consensus on the issue of humanitarian intervention was the open policy "window of opportunity" that R2P needed in order to come forward. Of course, an open window would never be sufficient to boost R2P further on its normative path; what also mattered was having norm entrepreneurs willing to "couple" the lack of definitive answers on how to deal with mass atrocities with the R2P framework and depict the latter as the envisaged solution to address the original problem. Since advocacy was essential for getting the norm noticed, it is important to discuss in more detail the entrepreneurial roles of various actors, including individuals, states, and civil society, who played a key role in R2P's norm-building process.

The political venue: various actors as norm entrepreneurs

Normative progress is dependent on successful arguments, which are defined as those able to persuade other actors to see a state's actions as legitimate or to adopt a specific course of action (e.g. Crawford 2002). This section looks at key actors involved in promoting R2P, to exemplify either effective individual entrepreneurial leadership, as was the case with Kofi Annan, or norm entrepreneurship, as emanating from countries like Canada. While the lobbying efforts of other actors, such as NGOs, have also been important, civil society did not play the same decisive role in the norm-emergence stage of R2P's trajectory as the first two categories, namely individuals and states acting as norm entrepreneurs.

Individual entrepreneurship

Human agency is critical for the emergence of a new norm. One essential condition for ensuring normative progress is having political entrepreneurs articulate successful arguments, which then enables them to mobilize support for these arguments through good organization. What Henri Dunant did for international humanitarian law and Raphael Lemkin for the fight against genocide best exemplify this condition for norm consolidation. Individual entrepreneurs detect gaps in the existing normative architecture and engage in convincing other actors that the arguments they advance fill these gaps. What it takes for norm advocacy to occur is a would-be entrepreneur who is increasingly dissatisfied with existing standards of international behavior and has strong notions about appropriate standards to replace the existing ones (Thakur 2006: 13). This description accurately applies to the significant role played by Kofi Annan as UN Secretary-General, first through demonstrating leadership in the overall human rights and humanitarian intervention debate, and second in advancing the R2P agenda.

At the 54th session of the UN General Assembly in 1999, Annan, as the UN Secretary-General, challenged member states to prevent "another Rwanda" and to reach consensus on the issue of humanitarian intervention. Annan asked member states to address the dilemmas posed by humanitarian crises where intervention to protect human lives and the sanctity of state sovereignty are in conflict. His by now famous phrase – "If humanitarian intervention is indeed an unacceptable assault on sovereignty, how should we respond to a Rwanda, to a Srebrenica, to gross and systematic violations of human rights?" – triggered the search to produce a new prescriptive framework for the contentious humanitarian intervention debate. This call for action speaks of Annan's ability to sense the potential of intellectual energies outside the UN to solve this problem:

> [In regards to] the intervention issue. I couldn't have done it inside [the UN]. It would have been very divisive … I had to let [member states] digest it but take the study outside and then bring in the results for them to look at it. I find that when you are dealing with issues where the member states are divided and have very strong views, and very strong regional views, if you do the work inside the discussions become so acrimonious that however good a document is, sometimes you have problems … But if you bring it from outside … they accept it.
>
> (Annan cited in Weiss *et al.* 2005: 378)

Furthermore, Annan personally supported ICISS and its findings in the R2P report, which proved essential for keeping the principle on the UN agenda. He did so against the opposition of every one of his senior advisers, who all recommended him to move as far away from this contentious framework as possible.[17] He did not. Annan convened the High-Level Panel on Threats, Challenges and Change (HLP) in September 2003 to indentify challenges to international peace and security and ways in which the UN could be more efficient in addressing these challenges. He invited one of R2P's most active advocates, Gareth Evans, to serve on it. As described earlier, the panel endorsed R2P in their 2004 report and referred to it as "the emerging norm that there is a responsibility to protect."

Annan's decision to convene the HLP was the first factor that significantly changed the normative context of R2P (e.g. Wheeler 2005a: 5).

The Secretary-General's entrepreneurial leadership was further evidenced in his inclusion of R2P on the agenda for renewing the UN. Annan used almost all of the recommendations on R2P from the HLP report in his 2005 report, "In Larger Freedom." He sensed, however, that in order to advance it further he had to distance R2P from humanitarian intervention and the use of force, and so he placed the commitment to R2P in a section on the rule of law, a key distinction from the HLP's discussion of R2P under "the use of force" banner. There is no doubt that the adoption of R2P, first by the HLP, and second in Annan's own report on UN reform, proved critical to placing it on the agenda of the 2005 World Summit (see also Wheeler 2005a; Bellamy 2009).

Annan organized numerous meetings with permanent representatives, where a small mediation team tried to convince delegates of the need to find ways to address previous failures to take action when needed, of the type seen in Rwanda and Srebrenica.[18] Especially during the intensely difficult negotiations that preceded the 2005 Summit, such meetings proved key to keeping R2P on the agenda and eventually getting it into the Summit Outcome Document. The Secretary-General's early support for R2P settled the use of the UN as the ongoing organizational platform for launching R2P further onto its normative track. Given all his efforts to promote and advance R2P, it comes to no surprise that when assessing his legacy as UN Secretary-General, some media suggested that "R2P might be Kofi Annan's most important legacy at the UN" (BBC News 2006).

Apart from Annan, other individuals acted as policy entrepreneurs in the first stages of R2P's normative development, Gareth Evans being one example. Evans has been involved with R2P since its inception, and, without doubt, has been one of R2P's most vocal and active supporters. He served as co-chair of the ICISS, which concocted the term "responsibility to protect," and played a key role in initiating the discussion on R2P and sovereignty as responsibility in this capacity. Evans further promoted R2P when asked to serve on the HLP. He used these opportunities to frame R2P by using language that resonated well with difference constituencies, and with the UN as the organizational platform for promoting R2P.

Evans' efforts to consolidate R2P as a norm and his proximity to the divisive debates on R2P and to the negotiations leading up to the publication of the ICISS report and to R2P's inclusion in the 2005 Outcome Document are explained in detail in his book on R2P (2008a). His statements and speeches, as well as the reports of the International Crisis Group, the NGO of which he was president until very recently, are perfect illustrations of his efforts to advance the nascent norm. Furthermore, Evans played a critical role in the informal interactive dialogue that the President of the General Assembly organized immediately before the July 2009 General Assembly debate on the topic to clarify member states' comprehension of what R2P entailed. Out of the four invited panelists, Evans was the sole proponent of R2P and, thus, the only one left to defend its merits.

Since taking office, the current UN Secretary-General, Ban Ki-moon, also played an important role in keeping R2P on the UN agenda, by picking up from where Annan's entrepreneurial leadership efforts left R2P within UN circles. In the year-long campaign searching for Annan's replacement, Ban was the only candidate who talked about the responsibility to protect. Once he became UN Secretary-General, Ban showed his commitment to continuing the promotion of his predecessor's legacy (Thakur 2009). Ban tried to consolidate R2P within the bureaucracy by presenting it as one of his key concerns, and referring to R2P's implementation as one of his priorities as Secretary-General (UN News 2008a). To help with such efforts, he also appointed two new positions related to translating R2P into practice. In May 2007 he announced the appointment of Francis Deng as the Special Adviser for the Prevention of Genocide to replace Juan Mendez,[19] and upgraded his position to Under-Secretary-General (USG; and in February 2008 he appointed Ed Luck as his Special Adviser with a focus on the responsibility to protect, at the level of Assistant Secretary-General. He later declared his intention to propose a joint office which would incorporate the mandates of both Deng and Luck, but this has not yet been finalized.

At the time, these appointments created debates among member states. The General-Assembly's Fifth Committee negotiations on these appointments concluded with a compromise agreement to upgrade Deng's position to USG but to omit the expansion of his mandate to include "prevention of mass atrocities" as Ban had suggested in addition to "prevention of genocide." Debates on Ed Luck's appointment were much more intense, but in the end he became a Special Adviser. Because of strong opposition to the inclusion of any R2P terminology in his title, agreement for the appointment was solely on "Special Adviser," with no reference to R2P. The UN Secretary-General was later criticized for dropping "R2P" from Ed Luck's title to appease member states critical of R2P. However, Ban remained focused on implementing R2P and was very supportive of Luck's efforts to bring consensus on the topic among various UN constituencies. Drawing on Luck's efforts and reflections, Ban released his report, entitled "Implementing the Responsibility to Protect," on 12 January 2009.

Less than a year passed between Luck's February 2008 appointment as Special Adviser for matters related to R2P and the release of the Secretary-General's report on R2P in January 2009. The UN Secretary-General tasked Luck with reconceptualizing R2P, designing the strategies and instruments to operationalize it, and building political consensus on R2P among member states. Luck was appointed as a special adviser without a specific job description in his title, and with no staff or salary – being paid a symbolic 1 USD per year – and did not work from inside the UN, but from the International Peace Institute. His work on two sides simultaneously, namely with the UN bureaucracy and with member states to complete these three tasks, places him on the individual entrepreneurship list for key efforts to advance R2P since early 2008.

On the UN front, Luck has focused on addressing the deep divisions within the Secretariat about R2P, perceived by many parts of the UN system as a threat by competing for funds and political attention, and because of its controversial and polarizing nature. For a few months in spring 2008 he worked closely with the UN contact group established to develop a conceptual framework that the key policy-planning officials (who were part of the group but coming from various UN agencies and departments) would agree to. This process also involved consultations with heads of different UN agencies and departments. The agreed conceptual framework was expressed in a short paper laying out R2P's legal status, its relationship to different parts of the organizations, and its "narrow" scope. The conclusion of the concept paper proved timely as it allowed the UN Secretary-General to introduce this agreed framework on R2P in his Berlin speech, in line with the initial goal to have him do so before the NAM meeting in Teheran at the end of July 2008. This was important in order to counteract the expected goal of NAM states to discuss sliding backwards on the 2005 agreement at their meeting.

Luck designed the powerful metaphor of the "three-pillar approach" to R2P right before the Berlin speech, and has used it ever since to frame conversations and negotiations with member states on R2P. This certainly fits the theoretical depiction of the classic norm entrepreneurs' advocacy efforts. Since August 2008, Luck single-handedly revised and rewrote numerous drafts of "Implementing the Responsibility to Protect" before the final report of the Secretary-General was released in January 2009.[20] In the meantime, the Special Adviser also met regularly with UN member states, trying to build up consensus behind R2P, promote it, and explain its key components. The main challenge he faced was to package R2P as including the use of force only as a last resort, which was the only way to win the support of NAM states before the expected General Assembly debate.[21]

In his efforts to build consensus on the various dimensions of R2P, Luck lobbied permanent representatives in New York to embrace R2P by focusing on what was guaranteed to sell with member states, namely the first two pillars, and avoided referencing proposals for action that could have been perceived as threats by both the NAM and developed countries. While it is understandable that the focus on pillar one and two, and specifically on prevention – the least controversial of all R2P dimensions – might have been the only way to build consensus and move R2P forward, the final framework as represented in the Secretary-General's report does downplay the importance of pillar three and the use of force when everything else fails. As such, it comes as no surprise that the report was criticized for diluting what had been described as the central feature of R2P, namely its "reaction" component (e.g. Thakur 2009). Luck's role in the future is likely to remain important for the advancement of R2P, as he needs to continue to explain R2P-related processes to member states while also developing the toolbox for their implementation.

States as norm entrepreneurs

"Persuasion by norm entrepreneurs," the key mechanism in the first stage of a norm's "life cycle" (Finnemore and Sikkink 1998: 895), is reflected in the efforts

Canada made to advance R2P up to the September 2005 highlight on the nascent norm's trajectory. The Canadian government was correctly dubbed "R2P's state champion" (Thakur and Weiss 2009: 34), for being the main advocate of R2P in the first four year since the release of the ICISS report.

Canada's role as norm entrepreneur began with its decision to answer Annan's call to member states in fall 1999 to find a compromise on humanitarian intervention, by establishing the ICISS in September 2000. This decision is a perfect example of entrepreneurial leadership (Riddell-Dixon 2005: 1074). By assuming leadership in building up a new norm, Canada expected to shape the outcome. In sponsoring the ICISS, and later on in promoting R2P, Canada has built on its ongoing commitment to multilateralism, human security, and especially on its focus, in recent years, on promoting civilian protection. In 1999 and 2000, during its non-permanent Security Council membership, Canada lobbied for the adoption of two UN resolutions on civilian protection – Security Council resolutions 1265 and 1296 – that marked the Council's first-time recognition of the need to protect civilians in general, and not just humanitarian workers. Canada was thus already influential in introducing concerns about the safety of civilian populations, human rights law, and international humanitarian law into discussions at the UN.

Canada started its advocacy campaign for R2P as soon as the ICISS report was released in December 2001, by promoting it both at home and abroad, among UN officials, other states, and the NGO community. The Canadian government invested significant resources of time, money, and reputation in the R2P campaign. An office inside the Global Issues Bureau within the Department of Foreign Affairs and International Trade Canada (DFAIT) was specifically mandated to promote the R2P framework, to advocate the adoption of the recommendations in the ICISS report, and to build a constituency of support among "like-minded" friends. Numerous conferences and events were organized at home and abroad in an attempt to promote the concept, educate Canadian officials and members of civil society on the ICISS report, and persuade other states to adopt R2P in various resolutions and declarations. In line with its reputation as active promoter, many Canadian embassies abroad conducted briefings on R2P. Apart from raising the issue of R2P bilaterally, Canada also raised it in multilateral forums, such as *La Francophonie*. Canadian officials used powerful rhetoric to make sure the R2P language was included in declarations, official documents and political statements, and placed on the agendas of various conferences and workshops on security.[22] By calling attention to R2P and to recommendations from the ICISS report in its own statements, Canada helped "build" the language of R2P.

Attracting civil society to promote R2P was part of the Canadian government's strategy. From 2001 to 2005, Canada funded civil society roundtable discussions all over the world using money from a 10 million-dollar human security program fund that DFAIT had directed toward policy development on various human security issues, including R2P. DFAIT sponsored several NGOs to seek feedback on the potential role of civil society in promoting R2P, such as the

World Federalist Movement–Institute for Global Policy (WFM–IGP), the primary organizer of NGO support for R2P, and a Canadian NGO, Project Ploughshares, whose work included developing a series of consultations in Africa on R2P.[23]

Through persuasion, Canadian initiatives were directed toward convincing a critical mass of actors to embrace R2P. These efforts culminated with Canadian officials' work behind the scenes for months in preparation for the 2005 World Summit to ensure that R2P would be included into the Outcome Document. During the protracted negotiations of the last days before the beginning of the Summit, Canadian Ambassador to the UN Allan Rock implicated influential third parties and asked Canadian Prime Minister Paul Martin to discuss personally the issue of R2P with the strongest critics. In the final forty-eight hours before reaching an agreement in the negotiations, Martin made personal phone calls to five heads of the most strongly opposing governments in the General Assembly, including Pakistan. As a result of this last-minute personal diplomacy by Paul Martin, in at least three of the five cases the permanent representatives in New York indicated the following day that they were under instructions from their capitals to change their position on R2P.[24]

Canadian efforts were particularly noteworthy at the time since Canada did not have many state allies in promoting R2P. However, since the Conservative government of Stephen Harper took power in 2006, support for R2P has disappeared.[25] The Nordic countries, especially Sweden and Norway, as well as the UK, and several other members of the European Union countries were norm supporters that Canada regarded as allies in the first stage of R2P's life cycle. While the UK, for instance, was a supportive advocate of R2P and played a leading role in the negotiations preceding the 2005 World Summit, its image was tainted after Tony Blair's speech linked R2P to the war on terror (*Guardian* 2004).

Another important factor that influenced the outcome of the 2005 World Summit was the support for R2P from a few key African countries, such as South Africa, Rwanda, and Tanzania. Rwanda and South Africa in particular took a firm stand in the General Assembly and argued that R2P was not a Western, interventionist concept, but one that referred to protection in general and was thus essential for dealing with such problems in Africa. Such declarations from South Africa and Rwanda made it really difficult for opponents from the NAM to portray R2P as an interventionist concept. The persistent advocacy of sub-Saharan African countries, led primarily by South Africa, and the embracement of limited-sovereignty principles by key Latin American countries played an important role in the inclusion of R2P into the 2005 Outcome Document.

Later on in the R2P campaign, namely in preparation for the 2009 General Assembly debates on the topic, the efforts to promote R2P included coalition building among supportive states. The forty or so state members of the "Group of Friends" of R2P in New York, co-chaired by Rwanda and, until very recently, Canada, is an example in point. Apart from the UN, NGOs are also used as organizational platforms for norm entrepreneurs, especially since their efforts may, at times, be more focused on promoting specific norms than those of international organizations.

The role of civil society in promoting R2P

NGOs have participated in advancing the R2P framework. The role of civil society, however, has not been as decisive as the previous two categories of actors in the early years of R2P's "life cycle," although their efforts have intensified in the recent years of the campaign. In the years preceding the 2005 World Summit, the primary organizer of NGO support was the World Federalist Movement–Institute for Global Policy (WFM–IGP). WFM–IGP coordinated the NGOs working on R2P, both in New York and internationally, convened roundtables with humanitarian organizations, such as CARE International, Oxfam International, and World Vision; with human rights organizations, such as Amnesty International and Human Rights Watch; and with faith-based organizations, such as the Quakers, Mennonites, and Unitarians; and engaged in consultations about the ICISS report to determine whether its principles could be useful to civil society and how they could be included in advocacy campaigns.

The "Responsibility to Protect – Engaging Civil Society" (R2P–CS) project, led by WFM–IGP and Oxfam, soon emerged. R2P–CS played an important role in building awareness about R2P, lobbying permanent representatives in New York, and continuing the global consultations series. The consultations showed widespread support among NGOs for the expansion of the notion of sovereignty to include protection and for the international community to commit to a continuum of protective measures that emphasize prevention and treat force as a last resort. The roundtables indentified a "three-track" approach to potential civil society engagement in advancing the R2P agenda, focused on persuading decision makers of the moral imperative to react to R2P-type crises; gathering information about crises and creating political will for action within governments; and advocating for the strengthened capacity of international institutions to act (Bellamy 2009: 72). However, most NGOs consulted showed little interest in advocating a doctrine aimed at justifying military interventions (Pace and Deller 2005: 21–22). The few exceptions are the International Crisis Group (ICG), Human Rights Watch (HRW), Amnesty International (AI), and Oxfam, which have constantly invoked the language of R2P in their reports, and advocated the use of force in instances like Darfur.[26] After the September 2005 Summit, though, more of the leading human rights NGOs started to pressure the Security Council to act based on the R2P commitment.[27]

New civil society groups focusing on R2P advocacy and research emerged around the world, and worked on generating ideas about ways in which NGOs and governments could implement R2P. Since the R2P report found an immediate constituency in Africa among international commentators, lawyers and NGOs, and particularly in sub-Saharan Africa, Project Ploughshares, a Canadian NGO, worked in collaboration with another NGO in Kenya, on a three-year project and developed a series of consultations in East, West and Southern Africa on R2P. Similarly, WFM–IGP worked with NGOs in Mali and Nigeria, to explore what R2P meant for different layers of power and authority in Africa, and to propose establishing a regional network of NGOs to coordinate R2P advocacy in Africa. A comparable initiative took place in the Southeast Asia.

At this stage in the norm-building process, NGOs' efforts to promote R2P varied significantly, depending on the "type of responsibility" they were comfortable advocating. Most of them accepted the first key aspect of the R2P report, namely state sovereignty as responsibility, but disagreed on the format of the international responsibility in cases of egregious circumstances. The R2P Coalition, launched in September 2006 in Chicago, was one notable civil society initiative that signaled a potential change in this sense. Its mission was to convince the American public and leaders to adopt R2P as a domestic and foreign policy priority. Its effective advocacy campaign persuaded the Illinois State Assembly to adopt a resolution affirming R2P and suggesting that the US government implement it.

There is no doubt that the longer-term implementation of the R2P report requires the cultivation of support from civil society. On this side, a coalition of global NGOs including ICG, Oxfam International and HRW, with the support of several governments and foundations, launched the Global Centre for the Responsibility to Protect (GCR2P) in February 2008 in New York. The GCR2P is a think tank conducting research and advocacy to promote a better understanding of R2P, build support for it, inform advocacy on specific country situations, provide assistance to key R2P supporters ranging from NGOs, governments, and international institutions, and design research on implementation concerns to support efforts to build up the capacity to operationalize R2P. The GCR2P has four regional associates: the Asia-Pacific Centre for the Responsibility to Protect (R2P Asia-Pacific) with offices in Australia and Indonesia; The Kofi Annan International Peacekeeping Training Centre (KAIPTC) in Ghana; Fundación para las Relaciones Internacionales y el Diálogo Exterior (FRIDE) in Spain; and the Norwegian Institute for International Affairs (NUPI) in Norway.

The launch of the International Coalition for the Responsibility to Protect (ICRtoP) in January 2009 marked another major step in coordinating the civil society advocacy efforts. The WFM–IGP serves as the secretariat for the Coalition, which integrated the R2P–ECS, together with its useful website resource and network of collaborations, to raise awareness of the need for operationalizing R2P. The composition of its Steering Committee, including Asian, African, Latin American, and international NGOs, speaks for the coalition's diversity. Its goals are to strenghten normative consensus on R2P, push for international and state actors to develop capacities to address R2P-type crises, and mobilize NGOs to press governments for action in country-specific cases. Given the similarities with GCR2P's goals, more collaboration between the two would be beneficial in the future.

They both worked separately in the first half of the 2009, after the release of the Secretary-General's report on R2P, to mobilize their respective advocacy networks before the General Assembly debate on the topic in late July 2009. Their efforts at this stage qualify as important contributions toward normative progress. In preparation of the debate, they picked up the mantle from previous norm entrepreneurs and mobilized around the "three-pillar approach" in the Secretary-General's report. Their collective efforts resulted in mobilizing constituencies in advance of the July debate by organizing various press conferences to explain what R2P entails and by meeting with state officials to encourage their support for the norm.[28] The ICRtoP focused particularly on building support in the global south, with three press conferences organized in March and April 2009 in Mali, Ghana, and Tanzania.[29] One of the key challenges for civil society to get organized beforehand was the lack of any confirmed date for the debate, which kept being pushed back until the very month of July when it eventually took place. The date of the debate, finally scheduled to start on 23 July 2009, was only confirmed on 9 July 2009. This was but one small problem among more significant challenges to build consensus that civil society faced before the debate.

After discussing the factors that have contributed to R2P's emergence and progress, it is appropriate to look at how close this normative progress has brought R2P to a new international customary law norm.

Does R2P have legal force?

The key idea behind R2P is that egregious human rights abuses are no longer a matter of sovereign concern, but belong to the international domain. The framework is controversial not only because it touches upon very sensitive issues like sovereignty, nonintervention, and using force, but also because of its possible impact on the rules governing use of force. R2P is important because of its potential to reform foundational elements of the international legal order (Slaughter 2005: 619). At this point in R2P's life cycle it is too early to assess whether it will live up to this potential, but it seems appropriate, in light of this chapter's focus, to assess R2P's legal characteristics.

To begin with, it is difficult to identify *erga omnes* and *jus cogens* norms with certainty. While there is agreement on the existence of norms from which no derogation is permissible, namely peremptory, or *jus cogens*, norms, there is no agreed representation of all the norms included in this category. Equally important for this discussion is the category of *erga omnes* norms. They overlap with *jus cogens*, but they are concerned not with states' obligations, but with the legal interest of states in compliance. There is agreement, however, that the prohibition of genocide,[30] rules governing basic human rights, and the right to self-determination have *erga omnes* effect. Similarly difficult is identifying state practice that relies on the peremptory character of legal norms (Brunnée 2007: 37–38, 40). And yet, state practice along with *opinio juris* shape customary international law. Custom, international treaties, and general principles of law are the sources of international law, according to Article 38 of the Statute of the International Court of Justice (ICJ).

The General Assembly adopted the 2005 Summit Outcome Document referencing R2P by resolution, which represents a non-binding recommendation for member states. Even as a non-binding text, a General Assembly resolution includes normative declarations that could contribute toward the development of international treaties, by framing principles for future agreements. States may place normative agreements in non-binding or political instruments such as declarations or resolutions in order to use political pressure to induce dissident states into conforming behavior (Shelton 2006: 319). Compliance with non-binding norms may sometimes lead to the creation of customary international law. The UN Convention on the Law of the Sea, which initially started as a US declaration in 1945, is an example of soft law becoming absorbed into international law. Because other countries started to apply the same doctrine of extending sovereign control to cover all natural resources of their continental shelf, this declaration became law within ten years.[31]

A quick look at R2P as articulated in paragraphs 138 and 139 of the 2005 Summit Outcome Document suggests that the framework's possible legal content derives from references to existing legal obligations. Under customary and treaty-based international law, states are obliged to prevent and punish genocide, crimes against humanity, and war crimes. Ethnic cleansing, while not specifically defined as a crime in international law, can fit within the framework of one of the other three clearly defined crimes. The ICISS report first noted how R2P is grounded in a miscellany of legal foundations (2001: 50). The fact that paragraphs 138 and 139 tied R2P to a set of established international crimes reflect the norm's consistency with existing norms of international law. In fact, the 2009 report "Implementing the Responsibility to Protect" clearly explains how the provisions that underpin R2P are "firmly embedded in pre-existing treaty based and customary international law" (United Nations 2009: 5, para. 3; 12, para. 8).

R2P's trajectory is part of the broader normative evolution toward reshaping sovereignty and collective concerns. R2P proposes obligations owed to both persons and states, something that has the potential to produce a "tectonic shift in the definition of sovereignty" (Slaughter 2005: 627). If applied properly, R2P implies that a state is obliged to protect its own people, and is also accountable to other states if it fails to do so. Furthermore, and most importantly, other states have the responsibility to assist the state concerned to address the violations, and also to intervene. Unlike the ICISS approach, which suggested that instances involving "large scale loss of life, actual or apprehended [or] large scale ethnic cleansing, actual or apprehended" are triggering events for intervention, the Outcome Document limits action to "international crimes." It also requires the actual commission of the crime, not the threat. By focusing on the narrow category of international crimes encompassing the four types of crime, and thus narrowing R2P's domain to violations of *jus cogens* that refer to firmly entrenched norms, the drafters of the Summit Outcome Document have actually strengthened R2P, making it harder for states to escape their responsibilities (Brunnée 2007: 51).

Drawing extensively on the ICISS recommendations, the HLP suggested in their report that guidelines on the use of force could "maximize the possibility of achieving Security Council consensus" and "minimize the possibility of individual Member States bypassing the Security Council" (United Nations: 2004a: para. 206). Many, however, perceive the codification of a legitimate humanitarian exception to the ban on the use of force as dangerous, for prompting states to use humanitarian justifications for military acts that were in fact designed to fit their narrow national interests (e.g. Chesterman 2003: 27). Even proponents of R2P strongly disagree over the merits of incorporating criteria of legitimacy within the R2P framework.[32]

Nonetheless, agreement on the principles on the use of force would establish a straightforward benchmark against which to verify the accuracy of states' humanitarian claims. The predicament, rather, is that no agreement on a workable set of codified criteria for intervention is in sight, which leaves the parameters for recourse to force open to political determination. This is certainly problematic when considering the legal force of R2P. Guidelines, as proposed by the ICISS or HLP, would clearly increase the legality of the R2P norm by replacing the "case-by-case" decision-making process proposed in the Outcome Document. Gareth Evans described the failure to adopt criteria for the use of force as "the only disappointing omission from the Outcome Document" (2008a: 48), but this issue proved too contentious when the Outcome Document was drafted. Even if the Outcome Document does not elaborate on criteria for the use of force, there seems to be agreement that the principles of proportionality, right intention, just cause, right authority, last resort, and reasonable chances of success usually guide deliberations on the use of force. Legal scholars have argued that, among these, necessity and proportionality are actually well-established components of the regime governing states' legitimate use of force under the UN Charter (e.g. Gardam 2004).

The preparedness "to take collective action" expressed in paragraph 139 of the Summit Outcome Document resonates well with the concept of state responsibility, which is articulated in the International Law Commission (ILC)'s Draft Articles on Responsibility of States (United Nations 2001). The Draft Articles on State Responsibility argue that when a state breaches a peremptory norm of international law, other states are obliged to cooperate to stop the breach through lawful means. Failures to implement the obligations expressed in international legal norms trigger legal sanctions. None of the versions of R2P expressed, in turn, in the ICISS and HLP reports, the Summit Outcome Document, and more importantly, in the 2009 report of the UN Secretary-General discusses the fundamental question of what should happen if the international community, through the Security Council, fails to exercise its responsibility to protect. Since the wording in paragraphs 138 and 139 is not specific enough to hold states accountable for their inaction, and non-compliance of a political body (Security Council) cannot be challenged, the "manifest failure" condition might provide an alternative way of assessing collective action options.

The Security Council is the legal authority for the use of force, as suggested in the various representations of R2P, ranging from the ICISS and HLP reports to the 2005 Summit Outcome Document and the Secretary-General's 2009 report. However, the Outcome Document, the point of reference for a legal assessment of R2P, does not imply an obligation to act. Most problematic is the cautious phrasing of paragraph 139 – "we are prepared to take collective action ... on a case-by-case basis" – which illustrates members' unwillingness to agree on the Council's firm duty to act. This critical aspect certainly weakens the legality of the responsibility to protect framework, raising questions about the use of force element of R2P in particular. That is because it leaves room for political assessments and interpretations of what the condition of national authorities "manifestly failing to protect" implies and announces a potentially inconsistent application of R2P by the Security Council. What makes this even more problematic is the fact that the Security Council is increasingly seen as less legitimate by developing countries. Without doubt, efforts to promote a collective legal responsibility to protect by improving the Council's decision-making process will be negatively affected not only by NAM, but also by the permanent members of the Council who envisage their space for political assessments shrinking (Brunnée and Toope 2010: 212).

In addressing this point, it is important to emphasize that R2P introduces the idea that states have not only legal obligations, but legal responsibilities as well. This was described as the "greatest innovation" of R2P (Brunnée 2007: 50). But since the responsibility to protect against genocide, war crimes, crimes against humanity, and ethnic cleansing is rooted in existing law, its violation should trigger responses similar to cases of *jus cogens* violations, in light of the established obligations that the state involved in perpetrating the crimes stops and the other states cooperate to end the violations. According to the law of state responsibility, states have a legal obligation to act; that is, not to stand by when genocide, war crimes, crimes against humanity, and ethnic cleansing occur. In other words, R2P "makes explicit what international law, arguably, already requires" (ibid.: 50).

The responsibility to protect is limited to "genocide, war crimes, ethnic cleansing, and crimes against humanity." As such, the 2005 Outcome Document linked R2P to international crimes but also to norms that, arguably, have *jus cogens* status and *erga omnes* effect. The law of state responsibility establishes consequences for breaches of *erga omnes* and *jus cogens* norms, so R2P could be strengthened by the fact that it refers to general precepts of international law (Brunnée 2007: 49). On the other hand, by building upon established norms with consequences for non-compliance, if R2P mobilizes action and actors pursue it to induce compliance, they also act toward consolidating the already established norms. As such, R2P offers an opportunity to improve the implementation of existing legal obligations to protect populations from genocide, war crimes, crimes against humanity, and ethnic cleansing. Normative progress, then, becomes mutually reinforcing.[33]

Conclusion

In spite of the general endorsement of R2P in 2005, claims that its status amounts to an international norm have been met with resistance (e.g. Stahn 2007; Strauss 2009a). R2P represents a new way of thinking about mass atrocities, which proposes obligations owed to both persons and states, and is indicative of evolving international customary law. As soft law, R2P currently marks a stage in the formulation of custom or treaty.[34] The R2P framework, in its various expressions that culminated with the Secretary-General's "three-pillar approach," is silent on the question of how to deal with violations of the responsibility to protect. The uncertainty surrounding the consequences of non-compliance sheds doubt on the idea that R2P is an emerging hard norm of international law (Stahn 2007). R2P has not yet been included into a binding normative instrument, and its endorsement at the UN provides the foundation for taking action when political will exists.

R2P's rapid normative evolution is indeed surprising given that the framework touches upon very sensitive issues like sovereignty, nonintervention, and the use of force. As the previous section clarified, the responsibility to protect has not yet achieved the status of a legally binding norm and no new collective legal obligation has been created. However, in light of its established normative foothold, the question of whether R2P should be adopted in a binding manner misses the point. R2P has already created a platform that clearly details how what used to be a state's internal business is now of international concern, and could become, in extremis, appropriate terrain for the Security Council, thus shifting classical interpretations of the UN Charter on the issue. It is expected that the policy agenda proposed in the Secretary-General's report for implementation will inform the work of the UN, shape states' decision-making processes, and influence behavior in response to civilian protection.

If normative status is of concern, supporters might push for a UN Declaration on the Responsibility to Protect in the near future, similar to the Declaration on Principles of International Law Concerning Friendly Relations and Cooperation among States, the resolution adopted by the General Assembly in October 1970.[35] Building precedents is a necessary element before one can talk about R2P as an established norm. A new body of cases – hopefully positive ones, where the Security Council responds effectively, but at least a few negative examples as well – are likely to occur in the near future before an opportune moment for another norm-building step will emerge at the UN. The necessary practice is missing, but R2P is still at a very early stage on its normative path. If state practice builds on a continuum of actions to prevent and stop mass atrocities, and *opinio juris* is created over time, R2P could eventually emerge as a norm of international customary law. At this point, however, having a binding endorsement of R2P does not appear to be critical. After all, the prohibition on torture or the prevention of genocide has already attained *jus cogens* status, and yet they are not respected universally. So the legal stamp does not necessarily make a difference in practice.

Rather than thinking about R2P as a legal tool, the framework should be used as a political tool. This could shape the much-needed agenda to set off political options for actors like the UN to protect victims of grave violations of human rights. As argued in regard to the mutually reinforcing normative process between R2P and the established norms of international law it is tied to, implementing R2P could strengthen existing legal obligations. What is clear is that the only way to push the responsibility to protect further on its normative path is by applying the framework to new R2P-type situations. Agreement on principles or legal considerations does not count for the civilians on the ground who need protection; only implementation makes a difference. It is the "narrow and deep" framework of R2P adopted in September 2005 that animates the discussion of the main challenges to implementing R2P addressed in the following chapter.

6 From normative development to implementation

The rhetoric of international institutions, states, civil society and advocacy groups invoking – rightfully or not – R2P in conflicts in Darfur, in the eastern region of the Democratic Republic of the Congo (DRC), in post-election Kenya, in the aftermath of Cyclone Nargis in Burma, and more recently in Sri Lanka and Guinea suggests that R2P language is gaining increased recognition. However, reactions to such invocations also show that R2P continues to activate the same contentiousness regarding the use of force for humanitarian purposes as that triggered by the debates on humanitarian intervention. So far, responses to conscience-shocking situations have depended on political conditions and interests at stake in the conflicts in question, as well as on the willingness and capabilities of various actors – whether international or regional organizations or individual states – to react. The broader question of whether R2P can overcome such ad hoc and reactive ways of offering civilian protection in extreme humanitarian emergencies merits further consideration. There is still no universal acceptance of the responsibility to protect, and no coherent vision for its implementation, but the fact that R2P continues to be debated among proponents and opponents should be a reason for celebration for its supporters.

While R2P has gained terrain in principle, the key questions relate to its implementation.

The pace of R2P's normative progress, as described in the previous chapter, has been impressive, but the practice has yet to catch up with it. This chapter begins with a brief overview of several cases where R2P has been considered: the conflict in Darfur; post-electoral violence in Kenya; after the humanitarian disaster of Cyclone Nargis in Myanmar; the conflict between Russia and Georgia over South Ossetia; and the political and economic implosion in Zimbabwe. A look at these crises illustrates the particular mechanisms included in the R2P toolbox. It also provides the background for discussing the main challenges R2P faces, comprised in the second section of the chapter, and the lessons for implementation, in the third section. The Secretary-General has identified three major gaps, namely "in capacity, imagination, and will" (United Nations 2009: 26, para. 60), and commentators generally concur on the existence of three key challenges: conceptual, institutional, and political (e.g. Evans 2008a; Applegarth and Block 2009). I add two more challenges to the last three, so that my list also comprises operational challenges, and a very significant gap between expectations and capacity. The last section of the chapter considers ways to close these five gaps and, accordingly, to put procedural flesh on the normative skeleton described in the previous chapter.

Cases where R2P has been considered

There is no point in discussing the responsibility to protect framework in relation to mass atrocities such as Srebrenica or Rwanda that occurred before R2P surfaced in 2001, but previous such failures illustrate the effects of the incapacity to protect civilians, and so, the need for new rules. R2P has been considered in relation to several cases, and a brief review of these cases reveals key challenges and lessons for the operationalization of R2P. Misapplications and abuses of the R2P terminology are important too, for the different kind of message they carry in regards to challenges, so they are discussed as well.

The 2003 invasion of Iraq

Although not a humanitarian intervention per se, the 2003 invasion of Iraq affected the overall perception of R2P significantly. As one of the most persistent misunderstandings about what R2P stands for, the use of force in Iraq has worked toward undermining global support for the responsibility to protect. The United States and the United Kingdom justified the war in Iraq *ex post facto* as a "humanitarian" undertaking. Finding no evidence of weapons of mass destruction (WMDs) or links to Al-Qaeda, their rationale switched to humanitarianism and overthrowing a brutal regime, with Tony Blair in particular invoking "the responsibility to protect" Iraqi populations from Saddam Hussein's tyranny.[1] Some questioned whether the responsibility to protect was itself a casualty of the Iraq War (Feinstein *et al.* 2006), with others arguing that Iraq "almost choked at birth" the emerging R2P norm (Evans 2004).

The US and UK's humanitarian justifications reinforced the suspicions of skeptical developing countries that such a principle could be used by strong against weaker states (Chandler 2002; Ayoob 2004). Meanwhile, proponents warned that using Iraq as an example of humanitarian intervention risked draining the legitimacy of such enterprises (Thakur 2006: 262). In 2003, the human rights violations in Iraq did not cross the threshold into mass atrocities that required the invocation of responsibility to protect.[2] Had it existed at the time, R2P could certainly have been invoked in the late 1980s for crimes committed against the Kurds, or in the early 1990s against the Marsh Shi'ites. However, the fact that the key condition – the gravity of the threat at the time of the invasion – was missing enabled commentators to indicate the misrepresentation as soon as the principle was invoked (e.g. Roth 2004). Since Iraq 2003, supporters of the responsibility to protect have constantly had to face the Iraqi situation when promoting R2P, which means that they have devoted significant energy and time explaining the difference between the invasion of Iraq and the R2P framework and application, instead of focusing on specific strategies and policies for implementation.

The Darfur crisis

The crisis in Darfur, a region roughly the size of France in western Sudan, resembles a textbook illustration of a government that is "unable or unwilling" to live up to its responsibility to protect its citizens, and also of an international community "unwilling or unable" to take on the default responsibility envisaged by the R2P framework. Although the conflict in the area has been long-standing, the current crisis in Darfur started in February 2003, when two rebel groups, the Sudan Liberation Movement/Army (SLM/A) and the Justice and Equality Movement (JEM), attacked Sudanese government posts in response to decades of political and economic marginalization and neglect. In retaliation, the Arab-dominated government in Khartoum armed and supplied the Janjaweed militia to attack Darfur's ethnic groups.

The UN referred to Darfur at the end of 2003 as one of the world's worst humanitarian crises. By the spring of 2004, mass atrocities and crimes against humanity were widely known to be occurring in Darfur, and the number of "war-affected" (the UN's term for those killed, raped, displaced, malnourished, etc.) civilians stood at one million. By June 2005, the number had reached 2.9 million (Prunier 2007: 148–152). In seven years, an estimated 200,000 to 400,000 civilians died, either from violence, war-related famine or disease (Wills 2009: 61). Darfur provided an evident test case for R2P – that is, a "first test case" (Mepham and Ramsbotham 2006: 2) since the endorsement of R2P at the 2005 World Summit.

Before showing its support for an AU-led peace operation for Darfur, the UN Secretariat regarded the possibility of a multilateral military intervention in Darfur as unfeasible (Badescu and Bergholm 2009: 295). The government in Khartoum rejected any UN presence in Darfur. In July 2004 the AU deployed sixty observers and 300 troops to Darfur as the African Union Mission in Sudan (AMIS), and in August 2004 it started the Abuja negotiations for inter-Sudanese peace talks. In March 2005, the UN Security Council referred Darfur to the International Criminal Court (ICC) and established the UN Mission in Sudan (UNMIS), which was tasked with reinforcing AMIS and implementing the Comprehensive Peace Agreement (CPA) intended to end the conflict in southern Sudan.

"Three years too late" (Mepham 2006), the Security Council passed resolution 1706 of 31 August 2006, assigning a 20,000-strong UN peacekeeping force to replace the AU mission. On 31 July 2007, Security Council resolution 1769 established the African Union/UN Hybrid operation in Darfur (UNAMID). UNAMID officially took over from AMIS in December 2007. In July 2008, the Security Council extended UNAMID's mandate for another year, followed by another extension on 6 August 2009 for one more year, until 31 July 2010. According to the latest data available from the UN Department of Peacekeeping

Operations (DKPO), from the authorized strength of 19,555 military personnel and 6,432 police, as of February 2010, 16,852 troops and 4,675 police officers are on the ground. This represents roughly 86 percent of the authorized troops and 73 percent in terms of police on the ground in the almost three years since UNAMID was established. UNAMID's composition still respects the concerns expressed by the Sudanese government in the sense of maintaining a predominantly African character. UNAMID continues to face shortfalls in critical transport and aviation assets, and it seems unable to react rapidly to atrocities.

Several peace talks took place in Doha, the first in February 2009, when the Khartoum government signed an initial peace agreement with JEM. After the Doha peace process stalled, two other attempts in the beginning of 2010 looked promising, but not for long: in February 2010, the Sudanese government and the JEM signed a pact aimed at ending hostilities, and in March 2010 a new coalition of eleven rebel groups, called the Liberation and Justice Movement (LJM), signed a framework agreement that included a three-month ceasefire. One rebel group, the Sudan Liberation Movement (SLM), however, was not part of the Doha peace talks, and later the JEM suspended its participation in the peace process after accusing Khartoum of breaching the cessation of hostilities agreement.

UNAMID's tasks have recently become more challenging because of the increase of violence in Darfur surrounding the April 2010 elections. It is hard to see how R2P can be implemented at the hands of UNAMID without overriding sovereignty, because of the strong anti-UNAMID government attitude. The ICC involvement in the crisis has not been without problems either. In response to the ICC issuing an arrest warrant for President al-Bashir in March 2009 on charges of war crimes and crimes against humanity, al-Bashir expelled thirteen foreign and three domestic NGOs assisting the people of Darfur. But as commentators rightfully pointed out, it is hard to argue that people cannot be saved in conflict situations for fear that their governments would interrupt the access of humanitarian aid to camps that are already the targets of attacks (Strauss 2009b: 116).

The calls for protection in Darfur were framed within the language of the responsibility to protect, and rightfully so. R2P helped to mobilize international attention on the conflict in Darfur, as well as to achieve recognition of its severity. However, it failed to activate sufficient political will for states to agree on an explicit and convincing response in line with the R2P framework for action. The best illustration in this sense is the fact that the Security Council conditioned the deployment of a Chapter VII operation on the approval of the Sudanese government. The Council member states were divided over the actions within the UN's mandate, even after the International Commission of Inquiry on Darfur established in February 2005 that war crimes and crimes against humanity occurred in Darfur on a wide scale.

Had the responsibility to protect framework been applied, a more systematic action plan would have been in place by now, to include several policy options, and clear documentation to establish the "manifest failure" of the government of

Sudan to protect civilians in Darfur, and consequences for the crimes committed. The most visible parts of the response, AMIS and UNAMID, represented symbolic measures that, to some degree, allowed world leaders to claim that they were acting in response to Darfur. It is apparent that Darfur's population has been let down by the civilian protection offered by AMIS and, so far, by UNAMID. The response to Darfur made the debates on R2P flourish. While some have argued that R2P is failing as a framework (de Waal 2007), others argued against proclaiming the overall failure of R2P as an emerging norm based on one case, no matter how pivotal that case might be (Badescu and Bergholm 2009).

Post-election violence in Kenya

Following the disputed December 2007 presidential elections in Kenya,[3] the country's several dozen ethnic groups took to the streets, and the subsequent demonstrations and escalating violence that resulted in 1,300 deaths and 600,000 displaced civilians threatened to slide toward carnage and ethnic cleansing. Collective efforts in early 2008 brought this to a halt, and showed the beneficial effects of rapid and consolidated international action.

The largest ethnic groups in Kenya are the Kikuyu, representing 22 percent of the population; the Luo, with 13 percent of the population; and the Kalenjin, with 12 percent. In the 2007 elections, Raila Odinga, the leader of the Orange Democratic Movement (ODM), challenged the incumbent president, Mwai Kibaki, a Kikuyu, and his Party of National Unity (PNU). While Odinga appeared to be leading in the number of votes, Kenya's electoral commission announced Kibaki as winner. Violence erupted immediately after the release of the flawed election results and, in response, the Kikuyu-dominant army and police used excessive force.

Desmond Tutu and Francis Deng, the UN Special Adviser on the Prevention of Genocide were the first to make references to R2P in relation to the 2007 post-election violence in Kenya (UN News 2008c). The UN Secretary-General reminded the Kenyans of their legal and moral responsibility to protect the lives of their citizens, regardless of ethnic, racial, or religious origin, and to prevent future violence, but did not repeat this reference to R2P in his subsequent statements (Strauss 2009b: 118). Early January 2007, the Chairman of the AU and President of Ghana, John Kufuor, asked former UN Secretary-General Kofi Annan to mediate as the leader of a small panel which also included former Tanzanian president Benjamin Mkapa and the former first lady of Mozambique, Graça Machel. After initially rejecting mediation by either the UN or the AU, Kibaki and the PNU ultimately accepted the mediation team, which arrived in Kenya on 22 January 2008. As a result of "the 41-day mediation marathon," a political power-sharing proposal for Kenya's first coalition government saw the creation of the post of prime minister with some executive authority for Odinga (Weiss 2010: 23). He was sworn in on 17 April 2008. The arrangement brokered by Annan was essential in bringing the parties to the table and stabilizing Kenya after the flawed elections. The R2P reaction prevented civil war but did not address instability in the longer term. Indeed, post-mediation progress has been slow and insufficient, and early in 2010 the power sharing came close to collapse.

The R2P was used implicitly rather than explicitly, so the best way to describe its input is "as background music that contributed a sense of urgency, motivating Africans, the US, and the EU to enter the fray with seriousness and due speed" (Weiss 2010: 24). Scholars and commentators have argued ever since that Kenya illustrates the successful application of the R2P prevention logic, calling it a "model of diplomatic action under the responsibility to protect principles adopted by the UN" (Human Rights Watch 2008: 67).

After Cyclone Nargis, Myanmar[4]

On 3 and 4 May 2008, Cyclone Nargis submerged Myanmar's Irrawaddy Delta, producing the worst natural disaster in the country's recorded history. According to various estimates, the crisis affected between 1.5 and three million people, with death toll numbers ranging between 100,000 and 200,000 (Hoagland 2008; Beyrer and Genser 2008; *International Herald Tribune* 2008a; *New York Times* 2008a). Despite the scale of the disaster, Burmese authorities at first refused to allow access to international aid workers, insisting on control over all aid operations. Ten days after the cyclone, less than a quarter of the requisite aid was entering the country, and that was being distributed ineffectively (Asia-Pacific Centre for the Responsibility to Protect 2008: 2).

The response of the Burmese generals presented humanitarians with an acute quandary, namely how to assist civilians when a government refuses its consent. On 7 May 2008, frustrated by the position of the authorities in Burma, the French foreign minister, Bernard Kouchner – who had been at the forefront of debates on humanitarian action since he founded Médecins Sans Frontières (MSF) in the late 1960s – invoked R2P as a basis for a Security Council resolution allowing the delivery of emergency aid without the government's consent. Kouchner indicated that based on Council's authorization, the French, US and British navy presence on standby could get involved (*International Herald Tribune* 2008b).

Kouchner's oratory and desire to raise the profile of the Myanmar crisis fit perfectly with his long-standing tactic of seeking publicity for causes to which he is personally committed.[5] But Kouchner's proposition found no support at the UN. The responsibility to protect also was largely absent in the mainstream media, even in France. After an initial op-ed (Nougayrède *et al.* 2008: 4), commentary was less about Kouchner's argument and more about the lack of support internationally, even from President Nicolas Sarkozy.

Some thought that Kouchner's proposed course of action would be counterproductive, making aid more problematic and mediation by the Association of Southeast Asian Nations (ASEAN) more difficult. Under-Secretary-General for Humanitarian Affairs, John Holmes, pointed to the impracticality of the proposal, and argued that air drops or other military activities would not be beneficial with insufficient people on the ground (*New York Times* 2008b). Holmes also described Kouchner's call for R2P as "unnecessarily confrontational" (BBC News 2008a). The Special Adviser on issues related to R2P, Edward Luck, argued early on that "linking 'the responsibility to protect' to the situation in Burma is a misapplication of the doctrine" (BBC News 2008b). Most supporters of R2P opposed Kouchner's proposal, mainly because it would complicate ongoing humanitarian relief efforts and "not help the R2P case" (e.g. Thakur 2008a).

Conversely, others have argued that Burma could have been an R2P case (e.g. Cohen 2009) because the natural disaster did turn into a human-made disaster. A few media commentators argued that Kouchner was right to call on the Security Council to act under the R2P banner, and suggest that states respect their commitments (e.g. Daalder and Stares 2008). Missing from media accounts, however, was a clear view about the most appropriate way to forcibly deliver aid. A military invasion was out of the question, but some suggested that the US and France – the two states with ships waiting in the nearby waters, loaded with food, water, medicine and heavy-lift helicopters – should airdrop aid to victims (*New York Times* 2008a). And yet, R2P requires "reasonable chances of success," which in this case were doubtful as food, sanitation, and medical supplies would have remained on pallets without boots on the ground, local transport to reach remote settlements, and trained personnel.

The refusal of the generals to allow external relief after the cyclone would not, in itself, trigger the application of R2P. However, if such actions had led to massive deaths and displacement, then the responsibility to protect framework would have been relevant. The advocates of R2P had to consider carefully the details of this crisis, especially as the original ICISS report included under threshold criteria "overwhelming natural or environmental catastrophes, where the state concerned is either unwilling or unable to cope, or call for assistance" (ICISS 2001: 33). Unlike the 2001 ICISS report, however, only genocide, war crimes, crimes against humanity, and ethnic cleansing act as triggers, as stated in the 2005 World Summit decision. In this case and despite the gravity of the crisis, the indicator of doing more good than harm led to the conclusion that Myanmar was not an R2P situation.

Russia–Georgia's conflict over South Ossetia

After being invoked in relation to post-Cyclone Nargis Myanmar, R2P returned to the spotlight in August 2008 for the five-day war between Russia and Georgia over South Ossetia. With only 3 percent of the total Georgian population, South Ossetia had seceded in 1992 and had been functionally separate since. Georgia tried to retake the breakaway region by force several times after the unilateral declaration of independence. The Organization for Security and Cooperation in Europe (OSCE) monitored unstable areas and facilitated economic rehabilitation projects, while Russian troops acted as peacekeepers to monitor the 1992 ceasefire. This arrangement maintained a tenuous peace, but it also served to exacerbate the conflict in so far as Russian peacekeepers backed the South Ossetian claim for independence, and Moscow facilitated immigration by people of Russian heritage. Despite Georgia's protests, most South Ossetians now have Russian passports; and Moscow accelerated their issue in the months preceding the military confrontation (BBC News 2009). The agenda, clearly, was to encourage the people of independent South Ossetia to vote in favor of fusing with the Russian republic of North Ossetia.

On 7 August 2008, Georgia began its offensive to regain control over the breakaway province, arguing that it was acting against violent secessionists and Russian aggression. Georgia's claims that Russian forces were the first to enter South Ossetia were false. One day after the Georgian artillery fire and air strikes against the capital of South Ossetia, Tskhinvali, Russia responded by sending large numbers of troops into South Ossetia, launching bombing raids and quickly outflanking Georgian military forces and expelling them from the enclave. Nearly 100,000 people were driven from their homes, with Russia citing 1,600 South Ossetian civilian casualties; a number disputed by Georgia, which claimed that some 200 were killed and hundreds wounded (Antidze 2008). An independent commission appointed by the EU to investigate the war found that 850 people were killed, and 35,000 of the 100,000 who fled their homes remained displaced more than one year after the war (Independent International Fact-Finding Mission on the Conflict in Georgia 2009).

Both President Dmitry Medvedev and Prime Minister Vladimir Putin argued that Russia had the legal right to move into South Ossetia to prevent the genocide of South Ossetian separatists and to defend Russian citizens and its own peacekeepers. Medvedev's and Putin's genocide argument found echoes from its ambassadors to the UN and to NATO (Deleroz 2008; Reuters 2008). The foreign minister, Sergei Lavrov was the first to justify Russia's use of force as an R2P exercise in an interview with the BBC News on 9 August, when he argued that "the laws of the Russian Federation make it absolutely unavoidable to us to exercise the responsibility to protect" (BBC News 2008c).

Western states regarded Moscow's characterization as false, and condemned it because of the apparent irrelevance of R2P to Russian military actions. Not only was the genocide claim empty, but the Russian intervention was also disproportionate; it violated R2P criteria for an appropriate scope and intensity of response as well as international humanitarian law. Moreover, the main justification for intervening in South Ossetia – protecting Russian citizens – was a classic case of self-defense under the UN Charter, Article 51. The fact that Russian troops had moved deep inside Georgia made it even harder for Moscow to justify its claim that troops and tanks reflected a genuine humanitarian impulse, especially because the military exercise was reported to be popular among 80 percent of Russians. Moscow used R2P internationally to legitimize its intervention, but public enthusiasm less reflected humanitarian rhetoric than a forceful stance against Georgian President Mikheil Saakashvili.

Further evidence of Russia's false humanitarian claims emerged from a similar incursion in Abkhazia. Moscow argued that sending additional ground troops into another breakaway region was preventive and reassured the local population that the scenario in South Ossetia would not be repeated (Kendall 2008). Within days, Russian troops had expelled Georgian forces and controlled both South Ossetia and Abkhazia. On 26 August 2008, Russia officially recognized both provinces as independent sovereign states and implemented a ceasefire brokered by the French president, Nicolas Sarkozy.[6] Besides Russia, to date only Nicaragua has recognized South Ossetia.

The release of the report by the Independent International Fact-Finding Mission on the Conflict in Georgia, established to investigate the 2008 war between Russia and Georgia,[7] sparked nothing but debates on the causes of the war. On the one hand, the report concluded that Georgia caused the five-day war and that its attack on the South Ossetian capital was not justified under international law. On the other hand, Russia was also responsible for the war in that the Georgian attack followed months of Russian provocation; and Russia escalated the conflict through the massive deployment of troops and pushing far into Georgia, also in violation of international law. The report also suggested that Russia's initial military actions in defense of its personnel in South Ossetia were justified, but that its subsequent actions were not (Independent International Fact-Finding Mission on the Conflict in Georgia 2009).

The growing crisis in Zimbabwe

Zimbabwe is a country bordering collapse, but not because of war or natural disaster; rather, the deliberate acts of its leaders have driven it to this state. Zimbabwe's descent into a generalized political, humanitarian, and economic crisis accelerated rapidly toward the end of 2008. As a result, many commentators have rushed to call for international action under the responsibility to protect banner, including prominent African figures like the prime minister of Kenya, Raila Odinga, and Nobel Laureate Archbishop Desmond Tutu (Steinberg 2009: 439).

Irresponsible sovereignty and violence in Zimbabwe have been sustained by a small elite since Robert Mugabe came to power in 1980, with the Zimbabwe African National Union – Patriotic Front (ZANU–PF) using violence and intimidation to govern. The political speech of the ZANU–PF leaders has been dominated by hate and supremacist discourse (Slim 2010: 158). In 2000, Mugabe began a fast-track land reform and resettlement program to redistribute white-owned farms. This, together with Operation Murambatsvina in May and June 2005, the "slum clearance" program, left hundreds of thousands of farm workers displaced, and destroyed the houses of 700,000 people who were then forcefully displaced. Around one million people are internally displaced and 3.4 million have fled abroad (IMF 2005). Ineffective diplomacy and sanctions best describe the international efforts to address the crisis in Zimbabwe to date.

The hardships caused by political violence, forced displacement, and food shortages intensified after the disputed March 2008 presidential and parliamentary elections. Thabo Mbeki, then president of South Africa, brokered a power-sharing deal that saw Mugabe's opponent, Morgan Tsvangirai, eventually become prime minister in February 2009, while Mugabe remained president. Once tensions increased significantly and the government rejected any advice or pressures from the outside, the deteriorating situation started generating intense debates on whether mass atrocities were taking place. They had previously occurred in Matabeleland in the 1980s. The lack of serious pressure and action from international and regional actors, however, was more troubling because Mugabe knew he was safe from sanctions such as expulsion from African bodies like the AU and the Southern African Development Community (SADC). Also, he knew that a potential Security Council referral to the ICC or the Council's consideration of Zimbabwe as a threat to international peace and security were unlikely.

After careful consideration, proponents of R2P such as Thomas Weiss question: "If not the crisis in Zimbabwe, then what would qualify as an R2P self-induced atrocity?" (2010: 27). While some have argued that the seriousness of the crisis, due to cholera, displacement, starvation, and the health system's collapse, could translate into crimes against humanity, others claimed that mass atrocities were already taking place, because of the level of violence Mugabe's regime used against supporters of the opposition (Steinberg 2009: 440). Determining whether the thresholds triggering R2P have been reached in Zimbabwe remains the first essential question in the process. If the gravity of the situation does not amount to such crimes, then there are other measures available to address crises, without having to invoke the R2P language.

The gaps between the normative and the operational dimensions of R2P

The six situations described above are those most cited for the application of R2P by media commentators, diplomats, policy makers, and scholars. Each of the cases considered here illustrates important challenges that need to be addressed if R2P is to be implemented effectively. In line with the focus of this study on humanitarian intervention-related elements, the discussion covers those challenges related to mobilizing support for the "reaction" component of R2P. They are discussed along five categories of gaps between the normative and the operational dimensions of R2P: conceptual, political, institutional, operational, and the significant divide between expectations and capacity. However, these categories are linked to each other: for example, increasing conceptual clarity has a direct impact on mobilizing political will; in turn, political will shapes the institutional capability to offer protection, while influencing operational preparedness as well. And so, there are, inevitably, overlapping elements among these five categories of gaps. For instance, determining the kinds of situations R2P applies to is a key conceptual challenge, which might require an "R2P watch list," discussed, in turn, in relation to diminishing the expectations–capacity gap. Similarly, considerations related to capabilities are included in the discussion of institutional and operational challenges, but such elements also affect significantly the divide between expectations and commitment.

The conceptual challenge

Almost five years after the adoption of the World Summit Outcome Document, and one year after the release of the UN Secretary-General's report on *Implementing the Responsibility to Protect* and the General Assembly debate on the topic, plenty of confusion still remains about the scope and limits of R2P. As the case studies illustrate, there is still no international consensus, not even among supporters of R2P, on how to operationalize it. The retrospective application of R2P to the 2003 invasion of Iraq confirmed skeptics' fears that humanitarian action language would be used to justify unilateral use of force directed at regime change. After the July 2009 debates in the General Assembly, however, it appears that R2P is currently undergoing reinterpretation. The conceptual gap is critical for the implementation of R2P, and so it also represents one of the biggest deterrents to further normative consolidation.

The different terminologies, used even by supporters when referring to R2P, add to the confusion: while politicians and civil society representatives describe it as a norm (e.g. Evans 2008a; International Coalition for the Responsibility to Protect (ICRtoP), other NGOs and scholars call it a principle (e.g. Bellamy 2009; Steinberg 2009), and some UN officials continue to refer to it as a concept, for political reasons (e.g. Luck 2010). As suggested by cases like the war over South Ossetia, language is important precisely because it can be abused to fit the interests and actions of a powerful intervener. Language is also important for the message it carries when studies seeking to "operationalize the responsibility to protect principles" describe their efforts as directed towards "mobilizing the will to intervene" (Montreal Institute for Genocide and Human Rights Studies 2009).

One key area where uncertainty persists is that of the exact meaning of R2P. And yet, paragraphs 138 and 139 of the Summit Outcome Document clearly define the scope of R2P as a framework aimed at preventing and halting four of the most serious crimes, namely genocide, war crimes, ethnic cleansing, and crimes against humanity. They are all defined under international law, so, theoretically, there should not be any misunderstanding as to which crimes R2P seeks to address.

However, as seen in the response to the crisis in post-Cyclone Nargis Burma, most commentators correctly pointed out that R2P was designed in relation to mass atrocities, and not to natural disasters. The UN Secretary-General and his Special Adviser on issues related to R2P have emphasized this aspect when speaking out against prescribing an R2P-type scenario for Burma. At the same time, others have argued that even if it started as a natural disaster, Burma turned into a human-made disaster, with the crimes committed potentially amounting to crimes against humanity (Cohen 2009: 255). Roberta Cohen pointed to another implication of such an interpretation: invoking R2P could actually translate into forcing the Security Council to consider steps to animate political and humanitarian action (2009: 255). This argument links conceptual interpretations to questions of agency. Moreover, another unclear aspect, as seen in the Darfur and Myanmar cases, relates to the relationship between R2P, humanitarian access, and humanitarian principles, and especially to explaining how R2P affects the latter.

Equally unclear is the "toolbox" of instruments implied by the R2P framework. The UN Secretary-General suggests that R2P's "response ought to be deep" (United Nations 2009a: 8, para. 10), with "deep" referring to the instruments available under the three-pillar approach. Among these, confusion still surrounds the instruments assigned to the "reaction" component of R2P. Suggesting that R2P is tantamount to humanitarian intervention continues to be one of the biggest misunderstandings about R2P, fed especially by opponents who try to discredit it as a framework for action. As made clear in the previous chapters, "reaction" under the R2P toolbox does not necessarily imply military action, but can also involve less coercive measures, such as political, diplomatic, legal pressure, economic sanctions, or referral to the ICC. Kenya is certainly a good example in point. Invoking R2P in post-Cyclone Nargis Myanmar, on the other hand, did raise questions about the level of interventionism R2P implies. Without a doubt, in cases where crises break out and prevention fails, coercive military action might be the only option to stop mass atrocities. The R2P framework would clearly not be complete without this last-resort option, but the mechanisms included under the use of force dimension of R2P need to be clearly explained; if the options available in the toolbox and their content are unclear, states might not want to be part of other efforts either, such as early-warning or capacity-building endeavors.

It is no secret that R2P's status as an emerging norm makes it easy to diffuse, but also more prone to abuse, even if proponents argue that it is more difficult to manipulate than the humanitarian intervention concept. The examples of the invasion of Iraq and the Russia–Georgia war over South Ossetia are illustrative in this sense. However, if consensus is reached on what R2P entails and when it is to be applied then the framework's longer-term progress is guaranteed.

The political will challenge

The lack of political will is the most commonly heard explanation for inaction in the face of mass atrocities, and one that directly affects the remaining three challenges. The disconnect between multilateral norms and loud rhetoric and the disturbing realities of ignored conflicts and conscious-shocking violence on the ground is usually blamed on political unwillingness to act. As the ICISS report eloquently suggests, "unless the political will can be mustered to act when action is called for, the debate about intervention for human protection purposes will largely be academic" (2001: 70). So mobilization, rather than lamentation, is what matters most (Evans 2008a: 224), which explains why it is critical to find ways to create and sustain the political will for implementing R2P over time.

Of all the case studies considered in this chapter, Darfur best illustrates the most problematic elements associated with the challenge of generating the necessary political will to act. Seen through the lens of the international response to Darfur from 2003 onwards, one first observation is that the UN Security Council was not willing to consider intervention in Darfur without the consent of the government in Khartoum. Powerful states have tried to lobby Sudan to consent to UN troops; however, for political reasons, Khartoum has not been seriously threatened by potential consequences should it fail to comply with the UN's demands. For instance, the US' interests in Sudan revolve around oil and intelligence exchange, which meant that Washington preferred to keep the government of Sudan on side in the "war on terror" and to avoid fueling anti-Western terrorist activities. These priorities trumped concerns over the gross human rights violations in Darfur. Furthermore, Russia and China wanted to protect their lucrative oil interests and arms trade with Sudan, and so threats of more widespread sanctions by the Security Council were likely to be vetoed by China or Russia (Williams and Bellamy 2005: 36–40). The reality is that implementing the last-resort element of R2P, the use of force, depends on the political will of UN member states, especially the permanent five with veto powers in the Security Council.

Another challenge Darfur illustrates so plainly is the lack of consistent political will from powerful states, especially from those that have declared their support for R2P in principle, to commit military forces in ways that would challenge the traditional meaning of sovereignty. The reality is that no state is interested in adopting an aggressive approach to protecting civilians, so nonconsensual interventions are going to be very rare in the future. What is going to be much more common is coerced intervention, as seen in East Timor in 1999, where consent for the Australian-led intervention emerged only after huge pressures were imposed on the Indonesian government. Reluctance to challenge the sovereignty of the government of Sudan characterized not just the UN, but all actors involved in supporting, first, AMIS and, later on, UNAMID. The AU, for instance, would never have considered deploying AMIS without consent from Khartoum, and all its subsequent actions in Darfur were taken with the government's consent.

The protection of civilians amidst armed conflict is a political endeavor. Having specific political interests to intervene in a particular context does not always have negative connotations. Past experiences have shown that actors reacting to crises requiring the use of force are in fact more likely to succeed in saving lives when they do have some political incentives, in addition to humanitarian ones (e.g. Seybolt 2007). Finding ways to highlight this challenge is particularly relevant for the focus of this study on the "reaction" component of R2P.

The institutional challenge

The case studies briefly examined at the beginning of this chapter point to serious institutional deficiencies in implementing R2P, at the level of the UN, through regional organizations, and in terms of existing domestic government resources for the states concerned. The problem is the lack of institutional structures available to facilitate R2P-oriented policy making. The 2009 report of the

UN Secretary-General, "Implementing the Responsibility to Protect," recognizes the UN's institutional deficiencies, but leaves it to the General Assembly to discuss R2P further. It does not provide suggestions on reforms to address this challenge.

The domestic government structures in Sudan, Kenya, Myanmar, Georgia, and Zimbabwe were certainly not equipped to support decision making on R2P in line with the first pillar of the framework, namely the state's own responsibility to protect. The idea to have states design their own implementation plans is infinitely more challenging for countries that do not respect the fundamental human rights of their citizens. Societies most likely to commit the four types of crimes covered by R2P are the least amenable to the institutionalization of R2P measures. Consequently, as seen in some of the case studies above, when states are not capable to address or halt mass atrocities, the expectation is that regional or international actors will step in to do so.

In Kenya, for instance, a mediation panel acted to stop the post-election violence, with UN and AU assistance. Kenya's neighbors were critical in pushing for a political settlement. The AU worked fast to identify three well-respected African mediators to negotiate the way out of the violent crisis. The UN Secretariat supported Annan's mediation efforts, but going through the UN would have delayed the process much longer. This crisis showed that what was missing on the part of the UN was an integrated approach among the Secretariat, the Security Council, and the agencies involved in the crisis to assess the crimes committed in Kenya and their consequences. For instance, the report of the Special Adviser on the Prevention of Genocide was not shared extensively within the UN, which meant that no common assessment took place. Furthermore, the UN was not prepared for emergencies, and did not consider a continuum of actions in case the government in Kenya failed to meet its responsibility to protect (Strauss 2009b: 120).

Another institutional challenge relates to establishing effective collaborations among regional and international actors. As seen with AMIS in Darfur, the UN chose to support an AU-led peace operation for Darfur, while knowingly placing the main burden of response upon Africa, which remains unable to provide the necessary troops and funds for a large-scale civilian-protection operation. Post-Cyclone Nargis Myanmar, on the other hand, helps to clarify useful patterns of collaboration and a division of labor among actors. One proposition was that the "bad cop" Kouchner made it possible for the "good cop" diplomats and humanitarians to be more effective than they would have been otherwise (Thakur and Weiss 2009). The Association of Southeast Asian Nations (ASEAN) persuaded the government to allow access for relief and rescue teams. ASEAN led the Tripartite Core Group – a collaborative effort between the UN, ASEAN, and Myanmar – that worked to facilitate post-Cyclone Nargis cooperation between Myanmar and other actors. While in this case a regional body placed pressure on Burma to accept outside assistance, crises like Zimbabwe illustrate the lack of any regional initiative or support to address the grave ongoing problems in the country. It is therefore important to design policy-making processes and structures that avoid the problem of institutional overlap, but also make sure there is action when needed.

One challenge when focusing on UN decision-making procedures relates to consistency. The crisis in Darfur is a good example in this context as well. The UN is not consistent with the consequences it designs when parties fail to comply with its recommendations or resolutions. Darfur is a cautionary tale in terms of the improvement that is possible after robust diplomatic efforts, as seen in 2004 with Security Council resolutions 1564 and 1574. These resolutions first let the government of Sudan itself try to provide protection, while allowing human rights monitors into the country, and also providing good access for aid agencies. However, since early 2006 the diplomatic effort has failed to remain consistent, especially as a result of the lack of any common position among the five permanent members of the Security Council, which only sent mixed signals to the parties in the conflict.

The Security Council decision-making process represents another key challenge. Darfur also shows how, despite General Assembly and Security Council resolutions on the protection of civilians referencing R2P, the Security Council has yet to consider how these resolutions play out in response to specific crises. Many voices from the global South argue in this context that as long as the Security Council remains outdated and represents the world order of 1945, it cannot be trusted to act as the sole body that authorizes or fails to authorize the use of force. The Council's reform is a huge issue with African, Asian and Latin American countries, but its resolution is likely to take a very long time. Addressing the challenges related to developing effective institutional capacities is a prerequisite for mobilizing resources to answer the operational challenges to implement R2P.

Operational challenges

All the gaps identified in this section are linked to each other. Apart from the lack of sufficient institutional structures in place, operational challenges are also explained by failures of political will to translate capabilities into resources and training to fulfill R2P mandates. The various operational challenges considered here inevitably require the continuation of political will through the decision-making, resource deployment and action phases. A critical challenge results from the fact that the principles proposed in R2P debates and concepts of civilian protection generated in the humanitarian and human rights community are often not well translated into practical policies and directives for military and policing elements of peace-support operations. Despite the consensus reached in September 2005 regarding the international community's responsibility to protect civilians, at a practical level little agreement exists on what constitutes effective protection by third-party military forces. It is still not clear when the use of force in pursuit of civilian protection is justified, what degree of force should be applied, and when responsibilities for protection should be transferred to local authorities. Even where consensus is reached, inconsistencies still remain with respect to national forces' approaches under UN or regional command (Wheeler and Harmer 2006). Without policy and doctrinal guidance on how to conduct R2P-type interventions, troops on the ground today risk facing the same dilemmas their predecessors encountered in Rwanda and Bosnia.

Of all the conflict situations explored in the first section of the chapter, Darfur best captures the major operational challenges to the implementation of the use of force component of R2P. These challenges range from limited military capacity and equipment, and insufficient training to protect civilians under imminent threat, to lack of military doctrine and vague mandates and rules of engagement. Although peacekeepers have not explicitly been deployed to Darfur to implement R2P, their mandate provisions to protect civilians came in response to the ongoing debates about the need for commitment to the responsibility to protect. Both AMIS and UNAMID have operated with far fewer resources and troops than would have been reasonable to expect in this context. The response of the international community to the conflict indicated how AMIS provided a convenient excuse for Western powers to avoid direct involvement in Darfur (Cohen and O'Neill 2006: 52). For example, donors did not follow through on the recommendation in the March 2005 assessment to provide AMIS with attack helicopters (United Nations 2005c). The mobility of AMIS was highly dependent on the vehicles, civilian helicopters and fixed-wing aircrafts provided by donors. The lack of attack helicopters in the subsectors of Darfur was a substantial obstacle to protecting civilians.[8]

In contrast to AMIS, UNAMID's primary mission objective is civilian protection. However, there was no strategy in place to prepare the UNAMID leadership or its troops for this task in any comprehensive way. As Alex de Waal (2007: 1047–1049) argues, the planning for UNAMID rested on flawed assumptions, and also lacked a strategic goal. For example, the AU–UN joint assessment missions did not carry out a comprehensive field assessment of all armed parties, nor did they build the necessary confidence between these parties. According to UNAMID's force commander at the time, Martin Luther Agwai, even if the mission were at full deployment, the peacekeepers would not stand between rival armies and militias engaged in full-scale combat (cited in Adada 2008). This is reflective of the UN Secretariat's unease with UNAMID's position: the peacekeepers have no peace to keep, and the UN's role is not to wage war (Badescu and Bergholm 2009: 301). This also speaks volumes about the general tensions inherent in current operations mandated to protect civilians.

The peacekeepers in Darfur were ill prepared and insufficiently supported for the task of protection, while the political process was not afforded enough time or resources. Both AMIS and UNAMID were deployed to Darfur with vague mandates, especially in regard to civilian protection, in an attempt to mask the disagreements among UN member states on the issue. Neither the AU nor the UN managed to change significantly the criminal behavior of the government of Sudan against civilians in Darfur; indeed, they were only present in the area because they had respected Khartoum's requirements. Both organizations have lacked the political authority to set the terms for their operations or to enforce their freedom of movement. Except in several instances of courageous initiatives, the two missions had limited civilian protection success. Also, troop-contributing countries had differing understandings of what peacekeepers were permitted to do militarily.

Such challenges specific to providing protection to civilians in Darfur point to broader operational gaps that need to be addressed if future operations under the R2P banner are to succeed. The policy gap with respect to what protection in non-permissive environments entails is one such challenge. Although the Security Council has used the language "to protect civilians under imminent threat of physical violence" consistently since the 1999 operation in Sierra Leone, and made it standard language for peace operations afterwards, the UN failed to examine how mission leaders and peacekeepers had addressed this aspect of the mission. A consistent understanding of what the Security Council means by protection mandates has yet to surface (Holt *et al.* 2009: 213–215).

In his report on implementing R2P, the Secretary-General suggests that states "may want to consider the principles, rules and doctrine that should guide the application of coercive force in extreme situations" (United Nations 2009a: 27, para. 62). A critical implementation concern relates to whether troop contributors have the doctrine[9] necessary to respond to mass atrocities situations, where civilian protection is the immediate goal of the mission. Although some British, NATO, AU and UN doctrines mention the protection of civilians, no specific guidance is provided on *how* to protect civilians. And so, the ad hoc approaches to civilian protection have resulted in operations without the preparation and assets necessary to address protection crises (Giffen 2010: 7). Apart from doctrine, political strategies and rules of engagement are also needed to guide decisions at the tactical level in terms of when troops should act, how to determine the risks and consequences of using force, and whether this might contribute to an escalation of violence against civilians. The rules of engagement, in particular, influence the assumptions about what a mission allows in terms of using force to protect civilians and what peacekeepers are expected to do.

Another key operational challenge relates to having well-trained personnel for missions whose central task is to protect civilians, given that the environment and the required decision-making processes are different from traditional combat or more traditional peacekeeping scenarios. Some have argued that even in the absence of explicit doctrine, a well-trained military would still be capable of reacting effectively, if the mission and what is expected to be accomplished on the ground is stated clearly (Holt and Berkman 2006: 132).

The shortage of capacity rapidly available to address R2P-type scenarios is clearly one of the most critical operational challenges. Apart from basic capabilities related to equipment and civilian, police and military personnel, capacity concerns also cover mobility and training for troops on the ground, and strategic reserves. One notable aspect of operations with specific requirements to protect civilians, versus more traditional peacekeeping operations in permissive environments, is that such requirements add a potential deterrent for troop contributors.

Mandates to protect civilians frequently require the use of force and engagement in dangerous activities. As discussed in Chapter 4, the organizations most likely to deploy troops with a mandate to protect civilians are either not able to lead military interventions because of the lack of political will to operationalize designed military campaigns, the case in point being the UN, or are not yet ready to manage complex peace operations, as seen in the discussion on the AU and ECOWAS. Military analysts agree that NATO troops, especially from the wealthiest developed nations, are the most combat ready and best equipped. However, their numbers are too small to meet today's rapidly increasing needs to protect civilians from large-scale violence. Various commentators have estimated that only 10 to 15 percent of the nominal troop strengths of European ground forces are operational, and after taking troop rotation into account, 5 percent becomes the more realistic number (e.g. Durch cited in Ward 2006).

None of the cases explored at the beginning of this chapter, when R2P was correctly invoked, provides suggestions for any particular methodology to be applied during crises. In terms of operational challenges, it seems that despite all the money states spend on their militaries, "the international society is still not prepared to conduct effective responses to mass killing that prioritize the needs of the victims" (Williams 2006: 181). The operational challenges are serious, and it takes determination and commitment, mainly on the part of supporters of R2P, to address them.

The gap between expectations and capacity

The divide between expectations and capacity is arguably the most serious challenge R2P faces before implementation. This is not a separate gap per se, but a combination of the previous four challenges, resulting from a mixture of conceptual confusion, political indifference, and a lack of institutional and operational structures and capabilities to make R2P a reality. In light of the capacity limitations discussed in relation to the key institutional and operational gaps, it seems critical to manage the public expectations about what the R2P framework can accomplish. That is because we have been witnessing unrealistic expectations about the use of R2P and about what it can achieve.

The main implementation gap in such cases results from a perception problem: missions to protect civilians obviously create expectations on the part of civilians that they will be effectively protected. To pick the example of Darfur, the expectations were set too high in regard to what the AMIS and UNAMID operations could have actually achieved in active conflicts such as the one in Darfur, especially in light of their vague mandates and the shortage of proper resources and troops on the ground. And yet, the civilian protection components of UNAMID's and MONUC's mandates, together with the presence of uniformed personnel on the ground, sent a signal to populations and human rights activists that there was commitment to protect civilians from ongoing violence.

However, there are various interpretations of what protection entails, as discussed earlier. There is a full spectrum of protection tasks, ranging from guarding and escorting to stabilizing entire areas of operations. Even if 20,000 troops are deployed to the DRC with a mandate to protect civilians in a territory that is larger than Western Europe, their ability actually to provide protection on a day-by-day basis is stretched. In turn, this creates very serious expectation and public perception problems. Another perception predicament results from the largely unguided interaction between the military and humanitarian actors on the ground. Both sets of actors deliver "protection" but are far from reaching a joint understanding of what protection actually means or what it requires. This becomes particularly problematic since the humanitarian and human rights communities[10] have developed various guidelines for their protection work, which are not aligned with those of the military actors.[11]

As discussed with respect to operational challenges, the responsibility to protect terminology itself causes interpretation problems, in terms of how the mandate to protect and the rules of engagement are understood and interpreted by force commanders and troops on the ground. Furthermore, once commentators begin to use the R2P language more often in relation to conflicts erupting in places like Sri Lanka, Guinea and the Gaza Strip, expectations that R2P will be applied to such cases rise as well. The challenge in this context is to make sure the cases discussed in the media indeed qualify as R2P-type scenarios.

The way forward: diminishing the gaps

As the case studies showed, and the discussion of challenges confirmed, there is a significant gap between the rapid evolution of R2P on the normative side and the enduring problems on the operational side. What structures, strategies and policies are needed so that we will not face the "mind the gap" catchphrase in regard to R2P anymore? This section looks at what supporters could do to ensure R2P is implemented properly and also to bring those ambivalent or opposed to R2P on board.

Closing the conceptual gap

There are many ways in which supporters of R2P could increase its conceptual clarity, at four levels: within the UN, in regional organizations, in national governments, and through an effective advocacy network involving transnational civil society exchanges of information. One potential approach relates to encouraging public debates on whether R2P should be applied to certain cases. The lack of consensus on R2P's application to crises such as Zimbabwe in late 2008, and more recently, Sri Lanka in the first half of 2009 and the September 2009 massacre in Guinea, could prove beneficial by translating into debates which, in turn, increase clarification. Agreement is more likely to be reached after debating and verifying whether application would be within the parameters prescribed by the R2P principles.

Publicizing examples of successful R2P enterprises is another way to build more knowledge about R2P and the costs associated with its implementation.

Identifying concrete examples where the international community has been engaged in effective support labeled as an R2P-type exercise can also clarify what options are included in the R2P toolbox. The early 2008 successful mediation effort in Kenya is one such example.

Drawing attention to misrepresentations of R2P such as those seen in Myanmar, South Ossetia, and Iraq helps to reduce the conceptual gap in two essential ways, by suggesting first that R2P should not be seen narrowly, and second, that R2P should not be viewed as the protection of everyone from everything (Badescu and Weiss 2010). Visible contestation by diverse actors is also important not only as public diplomacy but also as a means to influence domestic and international opinion. For instance, Moscow's weak attempt in August 2008 to justify its military actions in South Ossetia as in line with R2P failed to convince international audiences. Russian claims were recognized as false not only because of transparent self-interest but also because of the unseemly rapid resort to military force without even a semblance of diplomacy.

Clarifying that R2P is not only about the use of military force and is not a synonym for humanitarian intervention was especially relevant after the rhetoric of the US and UK morphed into a "humanitarian" justification for the war in Iraq when WMDs and links to Al-Qaeda proved non-existent. The South Ossetian case was also helpful in that humanitarian concerns were so transparently absent. The responsibility to protect is above all about taking timely preventive action, about identifying situations that are capable of deteriorating into mass atrocities and bringing to bear diplomatic, legal, economic, and military pressure. We require reaction long before the only option remaining is the US Army's 82nd Airborne Division; equally important are additional commitments after deploying outside military forces.

Publicizing misapplications also shows why widening the focus of R2P has the potential to dilute its utility. The hostile reactions against Kouchner's claim that the Burmese junta's actions after Cyclone Nargis should trigger an R2P-type response demonstrated why the R2P framework cannot be applied too widely. Supporters of R2P need to emphasize the importance of not broadening its application beyond the mass-atrocity threshold. It is evident that civilians need to be protected in crises resulting from economic loss, assaults on human dignity, or significant human rights violations, but the causes and manifestations of such crises have to be carefully considered, to verify the relevance of the R2P framework. While ethically it may also be tempting to say that we have a responsibility to protect people from HIV/AIDS, for instance, if R2P covers everything, it means nothing. The 2003 Iraq war, too, made the responsibility to protect more fraught and, temporarily, more toxic, but it eventually helped to reinforce the boundaries of the framework (Badescu and Weiss 2010). It also clarified why human rights violations – if they fall short of mass atrocity crimes – do not justify an R2P-type reaction. Equally important, Iraq shed light on the confusion between the emerging norm and the doctrines of pre-emptive use of force (Nardin 2005).[12]

A necessary condition to increase conceptual clarity relates to R2P supporters reaching agreement among each other on the scope of R2P and on how to implement it. Disagreement among high-profile proponents, public figures, diplomats, or scholars, while constructive at first, ends up blurring the perception of what R2P actually entails. One example relates to the need for guidelines on the use of force, which some advocates see as necessary (e.g. Evans 2008a), while others do not (e.g. Bellamy 2009). So long as fragmentation persists among proponents of R2P, their message is weakened and it becomes even more difficult to convince skeptics and critics of what R2P means in practice. Pro-R2P states then need to coordinate better, in order to have a coherent strategy on R2P progress in the short term and in longer-term efforts towards implementation. Their communications within international and regional venues as well as during interactions with civil society should be consistent and provide clarity on R2P thresholds, applications to country situations, and the toolbox available.

The Group of Friends of R2P at the UN – now co-chaired by Rwanda and Netherlands, with the latter replacing Canada in March 2010 – has played an important role in this regard. But the lack of coordination among supporters suggests that they could certainly be more effective in providing shared conceptual clarity, generating proposals for R2P implementation, and encouraging dialogue on R2P among UN missions and their respective capitals on the previous two issues. It is evident that R2P can be effectively implemented only if UN missions coordinate with their capitals on strategies and proposals for action, because it is ultimately individual governments that need to understand clearly what R2P entails and how to exercise it. Regular meetings of the Group of Friends are important in this sense, because they help to generate productive discussions yielding proposals for action and to create a consistent message among R2P supporters. Not holding regular meetings carries a double risk: first, losing critical momentum towards engaging in coordination when important developments on R2P occur;[13] and second, missing the opportunity to discuss potential scenarios as new R2P situations arise. A similar role is necessary for civil society coordination.

Emphasizing the need for greater Southern state engagement is closely related to such activities, and strategically essential for reaching agreement across the North–South divide on what R2P entails. One of the most persistent misunderstandings about R2P, which is constantly highlighted by NAM states, is that the responsibility to protect is another tool of Northern propaganda and imperialism. The fact that most of the discourse on R2P has been initiated in the North feeds such perspectives. Closing the conceptual gap is possible only if it is jointly addressed by the North and the developing world.

Civil society attempts to attract outspoken R2P supporters in Africa and Latin America in preparation for the General Assembly debate in July 2009 showed a good start in this direction, but a louder voice from the global South needs to be heard in order to remove completely imperialism-related criticism. A good example of efforts to link R2P to Southern voices – African in this case – comes from the supporters' push for another General Assembly meeting to discuss R2P in July 2010, when the presidency of the Assembly is held by the Libyan diplomat Ali Abdussalam Treki. The next president of the General Assembly, Joseph

Deiss of Switzerland, would certainly be very proactive on R2P in line with his country's support for it so far. Waiting, however, one more year to have another General Assembly session on R2P hosted by a president of the Assembly from Switzerland could translate into yet another association with an initiative from the North. This also relates to political will considerations, which belong to the next category of challenges R2P faces before effective implementation.

Mobilizing political will

Having a shared understanding of what R2P entails, synonymous to reaching normative consensus about its meaning, increases the chances of generating the necessary political will when a potential R2P crisis arises. Mobilizing political will, however, is so challenging precisely because it requires long-term resource commitments and not too obvious, or substantial, political returns.

One way to address this challenge is to involve states that support R2P in domestic and international public diplomacy campaigns publicizing the need for and benefits of the framework. This can be done within the UN, and in settings outside the UN, through regional organizations, other multilateral forums, civil society networks, and through dialogue among states. Finding the places in the world where R2P "resonates" best can increase the chances of effectively placing R2P on official agendas. A good example in this sense is the African regional context. Integrating R2P into regular meetings and collective programs of regional bodies such as the African Union can boost political support for R2P.

Within the UN, addressing this challenge necessitates convincing member states to redefine their interests in collective action in the long term. The lack of reaction in response to mass atrocities is likely to weaken the UN's global authority and encourage states' unilateral action bypassing the Security Council decision-making process. It is along these lines and also based on emphasizing basic values that UN officials, and especially the Secretary-General, could provide reasons that are convincing enough for member states to act. Effective leadership from someone in the system is always required to raise the profile of a potential R2P-type situation, ensure continuous attention to the case, and rally support for addressing it. The UN Secretary-General can play an important role in this sense, especially in light of his powers to bring matters to the attention of the Security Council.

Outside the UN venue, supporters should create a capital-to-capital partnership in support of R2P that would coordinate planning and encourage intergovernmental cooperation. An example of such an international partnership that was formed in 2005 and worked successfully in terms of providing effective planning, cooperation, and strategy could be used as model, namely the International Partnership on Avian and Pandemic Influenza (Applegarth and Block 2009: 49). Also important is to have countries that have acted as norm entrepreneurs adopt R2P domestically.

Continued promotion of R2P is key to generating political will. Equally important are supporters' efforts to fund civil society organizations to advance

R2P. Some of the initial supporters have vanished, but new ones have emerged. For instance Canada, which played a critical role as norm entrepreneur until the September 2005 endorsement of R2P at the UN, stopped investing in the promotion of R2P once the Conservative government of Stephen Harper came to power in 2006. Sadly, in this case, the R2P campaign suffered because of its close association with the previous government of Paul Martin, who strongly supported the responsibility to protect, and so Harper's absolute dismissal of R2P was rooted in the desire to distance the current government from the foreign policy advanced by its Liberal predecessors. New supporters, nonetheless, have emerged, such as Croatia, Uruguay, Mexico, and Japan. When faced with a potential R2P-type scenario, supporters also need to call on the Security Council to pick up its responsibility to protect.

Taking such a difficult political action as committing significant resources to something that might not have relevance at first to one state's national interest requires intensive and excellent lobbying techniques. Since powerful states' support is so important for providing various resources needed to implement R2P, it is of the essence to convince them that R2P does not threaten their interests. Supporters should actually try to mobilize political will by explaining how mass atrocities abroad can also pose a direct threat to a state's national interest. A helpful example in this case is the report of the Genocide Prevention Task Force, co-chaired by Madeleine Albright and William Cohen, which concluded that preventing genocide was central to the interests of the US, and also an "achievable goal" (2008). The success of the enterprise began to take shape when the Obama administration created the position of "director for war crimes atrocities and civilian protection" within the National Security Council to address the recommendations of the Task Force in relation to mass atrocities. Apart from the traditional security and economic dimensions of one state's interest, there is another path to the mobilization of political will that might work better, judging by the very slow, but obvious, recent changes in today's interdependent world: a state's interest in being perceived as a good international citizen.

Appeals to this aspect during diplomatic negotiations, international campaigns or transnational communications could also emphasize the political implications – in the absence of the legal ones – of inaction in R2P-type situations, such as stigma and shaming. State leaders, however, are usually risk-adverse. The Clinton administration's inaction in Rwanda is one example: it followed events in Somalia, where the administration was strongly criticized after the much-publicized incident of eighteen US rangers killed in Mogadishu. And yet, studies have shown that domestic public opinion is well ahead of decision makers both in the North and the South in terms of showing willingness to take action in the face of mass atrocities (Evans 2008a: 232). The Chicago Council on Global Affairs and the Program on International Policy Attitudes – World Public Opinion conducted a survey in 2007 in collaboration with polling organizations around the world, interviewing people from both developing and developed countries that included roughly 56 percent of the world population.

The survey showed very strong support for the idea that the Security Council has a responsibility to intervene militarily to protect people from gross human rights abuses.[14]

The role of civil society in mobilizing political will is significant, perhaps more so in regard to this particular challenge than the other four gaps discussed in this chapter. Bottom-up civil society action together with media coverage can mobilize national and international public opinion. Civil society networks have direct links to national governments, which makes them able to pressure the latter to act. Their statements are not limited by political considerations as is the case with pro-R2P states' campaigns to mobilize political will among others. NGOs can then direct their discourse at key national policy makers in their respective countries, or work collectively with the Group of Friends of R2P, as international coalitions of NGOs like GCR2P and ICRtoP in New York are doing. Most importantly, through their transnational networks, they can coordinate their agendas to consolidate calls for action. Civil society efforts are particularly important in addressing this challenge because of the options they have at their disposal for mobilization: apart from public events used as educational tools and platforms to foster action, they are called to do confidential briefings to provide strategic advice and can also do advocacy behind the scenes. The Arria Formula briefings, for instance, allow NGOs on the ground to report directly to the UN Security Council in respect to situations of potential concern.

In turn, increased political commitment is more likely to provide international and regional actors with the necessary resources for implementation, which has the potential to translate into an improved protection agenda.

Addressing the institutional gap

There are two ways to diminish the institutional gap that hinders the effective implementation of R2P: the first one implies reforming the existing structures within institutions at the national, regional, and international level – some of which might be already engaged in R2P-type activities, but without applying the responsibility to protect framework; and the second one relates to creating new structures that would facilitate the R2P decision-making process.

Changes at the domestic level unmistakably determine institutional and operational readiness, and best reflect political willingness in the long run. Progress towards implementation is directly related to R2P becoming embedded in the national culture, stances, and government structures of most states, but certainly of those pro-R2P to begin with. At the domestic level, R2P should be included into existing programs, policies, and foreign policy strategies. R2P terminology needs to infiltrate foreign policy briefings, national strategy documents, and also be referenced by public officials. One example of such an inclusion into national documents comes from France's reference to R2P in its June 2008 White Paper on Defense and National Security, which details its military strategy for the next fifteen to twenty years. Similarly, the US referenced R2P in its 2010 National Security Strategy.[15]

Ideally, various offices and programs within domestic government structures would collaborate under a common responsibility to protect agenda. Since R2P needs a "home" within existing structures, one office – and government officials, respectively – could be designated explicitly to integrate R2P across the government, and bring together various stakeholders needed for successful implementation. Once this takes place in several states, an international network of high-level officials emerges, which would generate a constituency interested in implementing R2P when new crises arise (Applegarth and Block 2009: 44–45).

New structures may also be created to assist with the R2P decision-making process. A standing interagency mechanism producing standardized assessments of emerging crises to verify whether they fall under the R2P framework is an ideal option in this context because it would be directly linked to key decision makers and thus allow for swift action when crises emerge. The example of a position recently established in the US administration, within the National Security Council, speaks of such a structure. On 13 April 2010, David Pressman was appointed the first-ever director for war crimes atrocities and civilian protection, which is a National Security Council position created by the US president, Barack Obama. This came in response to the recommendation on establishing standing interagency mechanisms for mass atrocities prevention, included in the report of the Genocide Prevention Task Force (2008), co-chaired by Madeleine Albright and William Cohen. Equally important, this development has occurred in the same year that the US referenced R2P in the 2010 National Security Strategy. Pressman will be coordinating and supporting the US government's efforts to respond to mass atrocities around the world, with Darfur, Burma, and Zimbabwe, among others, already on his agenda. His mission is to create a structure within the US national government to fight mass atrocities, working alongside the Departments of State, Treasury, Justice, and the intelligence community.

Similarly, regional actors can also integrate R2P into their programs and policies, and reference the R2P language and analysis into documents on security strategy. Instructive lessons for other regional organizations come from the European Union (EU)'s efforts to mainstream R2P within its various institutions, and also from the foundation R2P already has within the AU. A progressive example of including R2P into regional organizations' documents can be found in the EU's Report on the Implementation of the European Security Strategy, "Providing Security in a Changing World," released in December 2008. But even when the R2P rationale is not directly publicized, regional actors can take action against misbehaving member states, as was the case with the AU's refusal in 2007 to give its revolving chairmanship to the Sudanese president Omar al-Bashir because of the crisis in Darfur.

When discussing institutional developments to implement R2P, the UN is an obvious focal point, especially in respect to potential requirements to reform some of its fundamental components, such as Security Council membership, and the use of the veto by the five permanent members of the Council,[16] but also in terms of creating an administrative structure to allocate resources required for R2P implementation. To begin with, the key principles of the responsibility to protect framework should be circulated among UN agencies and departments whose work relates to mass atrocities. Recent improvements within existing UN structures create the space for such developments. One example is the creation of the Mediation Support Unit within the Department of Political Affairs, after the need for strengthened capacity in this area was expressed at the 2005 World Summit. Similarly, operationalization of R2P could be explored in the context of the structures developed within the departments of Peacekeeping Operations and of Field Support. Proposals for an interagency and interdepartmental committee to meet regularly, discuss specific conflict situations, develop joint country strategies, and offer general recommendations on issues related to R2P have been considered. Through a system-wide approach, the Executive Committee on Peace and Security, the Integrated Task Force, and the Policy Committee should be able to provide the necessary know-how and resources to respond to emerging crises (Strauss 2009b: 124–125). In his 2009 report on R2P, The Secretary-General proposed modifications to the UN's early warning capabilities, and mentioned more specific proposals were to come.

The Policy Committee of the Secretary-General considered the responsibility to protect at its meeting at the end of March 2010, and agreed, among other items on the R2P agenda, to mainstream R2P within the agencies sitting in the Policy Committee, and to move ahead with the proposal for a Joint Office working on genocide prevention and the responsibility to protect. Proposals for establishing the Joint Office as a special political mission would see the office of Francis Deng, the Special Adviser to the Secretary-General on the Prevention of Genocide, work together with Edward Luck, the Special Adviser on issues related to R2P, but it is unlikely that the title of the office will be changed soon.[17] This initiative, which has been discussed informally for a while but hampered by resource allocations and funding considerations, is significant for the office's potential to serve as a coordinating hub for all R2P-related activities, and facilitate making R2P a component of standard operating procedures across UN departments and agencies.

Another area of concern, specifically in regard to authorizing the use of force, is the Security Council decision-making process and the use of veto by its five permanent members (P5). One of the most problematic examples in this sense comes from the lengthy Security Council debates over the deployment of peacekeepers in Darfur, and the Council's insistence on securing the consent of the government in Khartoum for the UNAMID deployment. This seemed tantamount to negating the commitment to R2P, given the involvement of the Sudanese government in the very crimes that the Council was seeking to stop. Increased willingness to respond fast by considering country situations at the first signs of mass atrocities is needed on the part of the Council. This requires a shift from previous instances of not accepting situations such as Uganda, Somalia, and Zimbabwe onto the Council's agenda. The implications of paragraph 139 of the Summit Outcome Document are clear when mentioning the Council's sought-after readiness to accept a situation on its agenda if that would provide protection for populations from the four types of crimes.

The Secretary-General also plays an important role in alerting the Security Council on conflict situations in need of immediate attention. He can collaborate with his Special Adviser on the Prevention of Genocide, the High Commissioner for Human Rights, the Under-Secretaries-General for Political Affairs and Peacekeeping, and the Emergency Relief Coordinator on information pertaining to such cases. The 2009 report "Implementing the Responsibility to Protect" actually emphasizes the Secretary-General's "obligation to tell the Security Council ... what it needs to know, not what it wants to hear ... [as] the spokesperson for the vulnerable and the threatened" (26, para. 61). Furthermore, a critical requirement relates to the P5 voluntarily refraining from using their veto in cases involving ongoing or imminent mass atrocities. In his report on R2P implementation, the Secretary-General also urges the P5 to refrain from employing or threatening to employ the veto in situations of manifest failure to meet obligations relating to R2P, and also to reach a mutual understanding on this (United Nations 2009a: 26–27, para. 61). The P5 should also agree to respond fast and without threats of a veto when a resolution identifying an R2P-type crisis is passed by two-thirds of the General Assembly.

Out of the P5, France and the UK are likely to agree to a veto refrain, which they have not used in a long time. The US has begun to be more engaged, as seen with the National Security Council position to deal with war crimes atrocities and civilian protection, and Russia and China need to be convinced by either stigma or peer pressure. Russia's opposition to any references to R2P stemmed from its belief that this was synonymous to civilian protection, but once the distinction between the two was made clear it finally agreed to the R2P reference in the Security Council resolution 1894 of November 2009 on the protection of civilians in armed conflict.[18] China's contribution to UN peacekeeping efforts around the world – which it sees as a visible and effective way to meet its obligations to the UN – is significant (ICG 2009: 11–13). Lobbying efforts in regard to the non-use of veto could be built along the lines of China's motivations for this contribution, which rest on national interests that include, among others, image building and multilateralism. It is clear that many reforms are needed, but getting closer to an efficient institutionalization of R2P would in turn facilitate the mobilization of resources, policies, and actions necessary to implement R2P.

Diminishing the operational gap

Operationalizing the use of force is directly dependent on the existence of political will and the institutional structures discussed above. They make possible the policies and actions necessary to implement the tactical civilian protection dimension of the R2P framework. Since the UN faces the challenge of preventing or halting mass atrocities more than any other institution, it needs to lead the efforts to close, first, the policy gap. The Department of Peacekeeping Operations (DPKO) should develop a concept of civilian protection to support the planning and preparedness for future peacekeeping missions. This should be centered on the goal of the mission to prevent or halt systematic and widespread physical harm against civilians, and discuss the use of the military, police, and other mission resources either for the day-to-day strategies of ongoing operations or for planning to address potential crises threatening civilians' lives (Holt *et al.* 2009: 216).

Doctrine for the use of military force to respond to threats to civilians is an important aspect to consider in this context, mainly because a better understanding of what is involved in using force helps to clarify political debates and reach greater consensus on acting swiftly when needed. Recent developments are somewhat encouraging. The peace support operations doctrines of NATO and the UK, which address widespread human rights abuses and ethnic cleansing, and the AU doctrine which also refers to genocide, are illustrative of how military doctrine has begun to address the importance of protecting civilians from violence. The US doctrine for stability operations and counterinsurgency also emphasizes the importance of providing security for the civilian population. The 2008 UN Peacekeeping Operations Principles and Guidelines, known as the Capstone Doctrine, refers to civilian protection as a key task for most multidimensional peace operations, and also as a justification for the use of force beyond self-defense.

While these documents acknowledge the importance of protecting civilians, they fail to provide detailed guidelines on how to actually do protection, leaving it up to those designing and implementing such missions to develop the operational plans required to provide protection (Giffen 2010: 12). Accordingly, the UN and regional organizations' efforts to develop doctrine on the protection of civilians must specify how the military components of multidimensional operations are to be applied effectively to protect civilians, how protection should be prioritized in relation to other potential objectives of the mission, and how to manage the consequences and risks associated with either action or inaction when protecting civilians (Giffen 2010: 13).

An excellent example of an initiative to incorporate preparedness into military doctrine is found in the Mass Atrocity Response Operations (MARO) Project (2010), which provides military planners with guidelines on the main operating tasks, and on developing and planning missions in response to mass atrocities. Determining the intervening force's measure of responsibility for civilians, both in terms of tasks and duration, is one very important preparation requirement for an R2P-type mission. Clear guidance is needed on whether the intervening force is expected to provide emergency assistance to stop the killing, and thus deal only with the symptoms of ongoing violence, or whether it should act beyond the cessation of mass atrocity and help with the provision of services and restoration of governance, equivalent to addressing the causes and potential effects of ongoing violence. Choosing between the two approaches clearly influences the amount of political will required to intervene in the first place, the type of preparation and training the intervening force needs, and the planning of international divisions of labor between robust military forces and potential agents taking on the initial mission (MARO 2010: 36–37).

Addressing the capacity gap should be another focal point for the efforts to operationalize R2P. Capacity building for R2P obviously covers the full range of mass atrocity prevention and response, including the development of early warning systems, preventive diplomacy capacities, and military capabilities. Given my focus on the use of military force, only the last element will be considered here. As discussed in Chapter 4, there are no easy solutions to solving the capacity crisis caused by the ever growing demand for civilian protection operations, the slowness of regional capacity building, and the reluctance of Western states and major R2P supporters to supply well-trained troops. The capabilities likely to be provided for operations to address mass atrocities will certainly be unable to match the US 82nd Airborne Division deployment time, namely three days anywhere in the world. However, the EU's 1,500-strong battle groups deployable to crises outside Europe within fifteen days from the decision to intervene, and the NATO's response force, which can number up to 25,000 troops and start to deploy after five days' notice, represent potential options in this context. In the meantime, outside partners need to intensify their efforts to help the AU build its standby force (ASF), and provide it with lift and logistics support when the AU tackles crises on the continent. If states pledge to contribute troops to address mass atrocity situations around the world, as was the case with the US calling for an increase in the number of troops available worldwide for "conflict intervention,"[19] they should follow through with their commitment. This is particularly important for developed countries, in terms of providing more troops and advanced support, such as heavy transport and medical units.

Commentators seem to agree that better collaborations between the UN and regional and sub-regional organizations represents the best option available at the moment to increase capacity to act with regard to R2P-type scenarios. The predisposition of each of these actors to relinquish responsibility on the basis that the others would act, as seen repeatedly in past failures to protect, should be replaced by a commitment to work together more effectively to provide troops and equipment. One proposal to address the shortage of uniformed personnel is to revive the notion of "white helmets," the retired military personnel with protection capacity. With sufficient training, "white helmets" might become an option for civilian protection operations. According to Thomas Weiss, "if occupying forces or outside militaries do not provide … protection … then 'civilian' personnel with military expertise must" (2003: 3). Beyond the basic capabilities related to military troops and equipment, improved capacity for rapid and efficient action would also require intelligence assets and better technological capacities able to intercept and jam cell phone communications and satellite transmissions.

Even if the required military personnel is made available, contributing countries should also ensure that the troops they provide are sufficiently trained to perform in the challenging environment of large-scale atrocities. At the national level, training centers should include the responsibility to protect in their training modules, as they now cover issues such as sexual exploitation (Strauss 2009b: 134). A standardized training program should be developed for troop contributors in order to overcome the discrepancies in capacity between contingents from different countries and ensure that troops share a similar understanding of their role in a mission to protect civilians (Weir 2009: 9). Furthermore, states should ensure that the troops deployed are able to function at the pace described in the mission's operational requirements. At the UN, the DPKO Integrated Training Service should draft pre-deployment training elements to brief troop contributors on missions mandated to protect civilians. The DPKO Training Service should also check the modules used in major training centers on rules of engagement for the use of force to protect civilians and the implementation of Security Council mandates (Holt *et al.* 2009: 219–220).

Also, more efforts at the national levels are needed in order to enhance the overall operational standards of peace operations mandated to protect civilians. The initiatives of the US, the UK and France in this sense should be replicated by other countries with advanced militaries. In 2004, the US established the Global Peace Operations Initiative whose goal is to train 75,000 peacekeepers, mainly from Africa, over fifteen years. Troops from a dozen African countries have been trained under this program to date, including approximately 14,000 troops deployed to Darfur. The Africa Contingency Operations Training Assistance is another program through which the US contributes to international training. Through such programs, millions of dollars are spent each year on developing military peacekeeping capabilities in potential troop-contributing countries around the world (Feinstein 2007: 35; Weir 2009: 9). Similarly, the UK is involved in training 17,000 African troops as peacekeepers. Since 1997, France has also been involved in training and developing the military capacity of the ASF, under the Reinforcement of African Peacekeeping Capacities program. All these are options available to address the challenges related to doctrine, operational policies, training, and capacity that need to be overcome to operationalize R2P.

Closing the expectations–capacity gap

After considering the most important challenges R2P faces before implementation, closing the expectations–capacity gap should take priority over the other four in the long-term strategic thinking on R2P. Only by doing so would the most accurate vision for its implementation be reached. Despite the complexity of the challenge, the solution is extremely straightforward, namely decreasing the inflated expectations about what R2P can achieve at the same time as increasing the level of commitment and capacities available to make R2P work. Decreasing expectations and increasing capacity would also narrow the gap between rhetoric and action. Since I have already addressed the latter element of this rapport, namely how to increase capacities with respect to the institutional and operational challenges covered earlier, I am going to focus on "expectations" hereafter. There are several ways to minimize the unrealistic expectations the public, media, diplomats, and policy makers have at times about R2P.

The responsibility to protect is a commitment states have made to protect their own populations from genocide, war crimes, crimes against humanity, and ethnic cleansing, to assist other states to fulfill their responsibilities, and, when appropriate, to support collective action through the UN Security Council. And so, the R2P framework addresses four specific types of crimes, while covering a continuum of measures ranging from prevention to reaction and rebuilding. Because of its breadth, R2P might be perceived as too ambitious. At times, supporters' messages about what R2P is able to achieve certainly are, as seen, for example, in Gareth Evans' subtitle to his book on R2P, "ending mass atrocity crimes once and for all" (2008a). The R2P framework is not going to be able to achieve this goal, no matter how morally satisfactory it sounds. Such arguments, then, risk to be stamped as wishful thinking, just as the post-Holocaust "never again" dictum proved to be.

R2P's boundaries need to be ingrained into public discourse so that both supporters and opponents agree to one vision of what R2P stands for. As Alex Bellamy argues, it is important to recognize the distinction between what the responsibility to protect is and what its supporters would like it to be (2009: 196). R2P is not necessarily about the use of force, and there is no better example to prove this than the successful application of the preventive dimension of R2P in post-election Kenya in early 2008. But when the debates switch to the "use of force" component of the R2P framework, it is paramount always to emphasize that this was meant as an exceptional response to the four exceptional circumstances. If understood as such, by both academics and politicians, the calls to apply it to conflicts covering a wide spectrum of human right violations would subside. A clear set of guidelines providing a template for a "watch list" of potential R2P-type situations is needed to avoid invoking R2P simply as a technical exercise. This should contain the expectations to apply the framework to crises that are not of "R2P concern" because the thresholds for invoking R2P were not reached, as we have seen with previous calls in the media. Established standards are also helpful in this sense because governments know what is expected of them in terms of protecting their own populations, and how their performances are going to be measured against such standards.

It is important, too, to set modest expectations in terms of what R2P can achieve. As Darfur best illustrates, the "success" or "failure" of R2P on the operational side should be examined within reasonable expectations of success, and especially after giving careful consideration to circumstances on the ground. It is always important to define the scope of what is possible to achieve in particular situations where R2P is contemplated. The previous discussion of the operational challenges R2P faces at the moment explains why this is the case. Supporters still struggle to assess the impact of the responsibility to protect on ongoing large-scale conflicts. The affirmation of R2P at the UN, for instance, does not seem to have made a meaningful difference yet to the displaced and threatened civilians in Darfur. It did, however, have an impact on the work of the DPKO, according to the former head of UN peacekeeping, Under Secretary-General Jean-Marie Guéhenno. When asked if R2P had any bearing on the DPKO work, Guéhenno suggested that "in most resolutions authorizing a peace operation there will be a sentence to the effect that our forces will protect the civilians in imminent danger in the areas where they are deployed, which reflects the emergence of the [R2P] norm" (Guéhenno cited in CFR 2006).

Another way to minimize the inflated expectations about the responsibility to protect relates to emphasizing that R2P is just one tool among others available to address conflict situations. Very few exceptional cases of the Rwanda type are likely to emerge in the future. These aside, other responses are available in the international toolbox to address various types of conflicts or serious human rights violations around the world. International investigation and prosecution is one such tool. In Sri Lanka, for instance,[20] where some spoke in favor of applying R2P in early 2009, calls for investigation of the conduct of hostilities and the role of the military and political leadership on both sides of the conflict have recently been made, with the International Criminal Court (ICC) appearing as the best option here. However, Sri Lanka is not a member state of the ICC and the UN Security Council is unlikely to refer the crimes in Sri Lanka to the ICC in the short term. As such, a UN-mandated international inquiry was proposed, together with calls for countries having jurisdiction over the alleged crimes to pursue investigations (ICG 2010).

Ultimately, closing the expectations–capacity gap would translate into getting R2P right in practice. But this exercise first requires that R2P be right conceptually, an aspect discussed in relation to the first challenge introduced in this chapter. Decisions on how to protect civilians involve not only operational considerations, but also normative choices. In turn, acting on such decisions to protect shapes the normative climate in which actors would confront future choices to implement R2P. Indeed, the normative and operational potential of R2P is significant. However, the discussion of the gaps between the normative and operational sides of the responsibility to protect confirms that R2P is still a nascent norm, which states need to internalize in order to speed up the very slow progress on implementation to date. This also shows why expectations need to be downsized accordingly. Given that actors still debate the practical mechanisms through which to implement it, R2P remains at the very inception of its long normative path. Because of R2P, however, it is now normal to expect that state sovereignty is no longer a shield behind which states can hide to commit mass atrocities. While this is a big realization in itself, further refinement of its implications and commitment by states are required for R2P to become an organizing code of conduct for the international community.

7 Conclusion

Supporters of the responsibility to protect have gone to great lengths to distance it from the concept of humanitarian intervention, arguing that instead of being centered on the use of force, R2P covers a wide spectrum of measures ranging from prevention to post-conflict rebuilding. While this is an accurate depiction of R2P's breadth, this book has focused on the responsibility to protect in relation to the use of force. The central rationale was to look at why R2P emerged in the first place. The responsibility to protect represents the culmination of the quest to solve the humanitarian intervention puzzle. In spite of extensive deliberations since the early 1990s, no consensus has been reached on the principles governing humanitarian intervention. The issue had proven conceptually unhelpful and politically unfeasible, hence the need for a novel approach to move beyond the impasse it created. In the words of the Commission that produced the R2P report, "external military intervention … has been controversial both when it has happened – as in Somalia, Bosnia and Herzegovina and Kosovo – and when it has failed to happen, as in Rwanda" (ICISS 2001: vii). As the UN Secretary-General later argued in his report on R2P, "humanitarian intervention posed a false choice between two extremes: either standing by in the face of mounting civilian deaths or deploying coercive military force to protect." Ban described both as "unpalatable alternatives" (United Nations 2009a: 6, para.7).

This book has looked at the search to develop a more acceptable account of the principles and mechanisms associated with the use of force, and so has focused on the contributions made by R2P to the debate on intervention. Another starting point for the book was the assumption that the humanitarian intervention approach was not able to address the protection gap in today's world. The responsibility to protect emerged because of the necessity to fill this obvious normative gap regarding ways to address the needs of the victims in mass atrocity situations. This shows why R2P is not just a theoretical issue, but one "of deadly urgency" (Annan 2005a: 25). Its relevance is explained by the fact that it proposes a more viable way of engaging with protection issues than the humanitarian intervention framework.

In almost a decade, the responsibility to protect has gone through successive reformulations. It evolved from an "idea" proposed in the 2001 ICISS report to a nascent norm embraced unanimously by world leaders in September 2005, which was then redesigned into the "three pillar approach" in the UN Secretary-General's 2009 report, and was later discussed in the first General Assembly debate on R2P in July 2009. Despite several important variations during these transformative years, the backbone of the framework remained the same: state sovereignty entails responsibility, which means that each state has a responsibility to protect its citizens from mass killings and other gross violations of their rights. If that state is unable or unwilling to carry out that function, the state abrogates its sovereignty, and the responsibility to protect falls to the international community. Thus, two aspects of the R2P framework have remained unaltered throughout R2P's various reformulations: state sovereignty as responsibility, and international responsibility in egregious circumstances. R2P's conceptual novelty came from the way in which ICISS posed the underlying question of the report to the countries opposing the basic tenets of intervention: If humanitarian intervention was not an acceptable answer, then what would such countries envision if the international community was faced with "another Rwanda"? The September 2005 World Summit moment revealed that the responsibility to protect formulation, as opposed to the humanitarian intervention one, worked, since member states were able to agree on the former but never on the latter.

However, R2P as envisaged in paragraphs 138 and 139 of the 2005 World Summit Outcome Document is different from the original ICISS representation of R2P. Out of political necessity, the 2005 formulation of R2P left out several important ICISS propositions, such as the inclusion of criteria for the use of force, the refrain of the P5 from using their veto in Security Council deliberations, the possibility of military action without Council authorization, and the continuum of measures under the ICISS R2P umbrella that included prevention, reaction, and post-conflict rebuilding. No wonder commentators dubbed the World Summit representation "R2P lite" (Weiss 2007: 117). And yet, the R2P language was sufficiently strong to be regarded as an endorsement of a new set of principles on national and international responsibility. The adoption of R2P in 2005 represented a significant ideological and normative shift affecting the way in which states' responsibilities, as set forth in the UN Charter, are implemented. Paragraph 139 turned the use of the Security Council's pre-existing authority to resort to collective military action into a political responsibility when faced with mass atrocities. Also, the unanimous agreement at the World Summit clearly circumscribed the limits to the UN Charter's prohibition on outside interference in the domestic jurisdiction of member states. Given the history of the debates on humanitarian intervention, R2P's inclusion in the Summit's Outcome Document is significant. Indeed, this marked R2P's most important normative advance to date, and it is this representation of R2P that I have used as reference point for the implementation-related discussions throughout the book. The 2009 report of the UN Secretary-General, "Implementing the Responsibility to Protect," details the representation of R2P along three pillars: the protection responsibilities of the state; the responsibility of the international community to assist states in fulfilling their national obligations; and the commitment to timely and decisive collective action consistent with the UN Charter. One significant change in the discourse on R2P with respect to the use of force is noticeable here: for political considerations, the Secretary-General's report downplayed intervention; and so, R2P moved from central stage in the ICISS report to an afterthought in this report.

Almost five years after the adoption of the World Summit Outcome Document, and one year after the release of the UN Secretary-General's report on implementing the responsibility to protect and the General Assembly debate on the topic, plenty of confusion still remains about the scope and limits of R2P. As the case studies from Chapter 6 illustrate, there is still no international consensus, not even among supporters of R2P, on how to implement the responsibility to protect. While the responsibility to protect framework remains contested at present, the most significant concerns relate to the use-of-force element of the third pillar of R2P. Some states are still worried that great powers might abuse R2P and the Security Council will apply it selectively. Apart from being its most contested dimension, the use of force also faces the biggest challenges before implementation as compared to the other tools comprised under pillars one and two. And yet, it is inevitable that the use of force will remain a key element of the international conversation on the responsibility to protect not only because of such lingering concerns but also because R2P emerged after all as a response to the humanitarian intervention debate, because it will be used as a diplomatic tool in extreme situations, and because it carries great potential to protect civilians. To get a complete overview of the contributions made by the responsibility to protect to the debate on intervention, I have focused on two main areas of analysis in the book, both centered accordingly on the use-of-force aspect of R2P. First, I have discussed how the responsibility to protect framework addresses the most contentious themes on intervention, and, second, I have explored how it might operate in practice.

Theoretical contributions

The first part of the book provided the theoretical foundations of the responsibility to protect, while clarifying the differences between R2P and humanitarian intervention. Three of the most contentious questions that reoccur in all debates on humanitarian intervention were discussed: How can the alleged conflict between the norms of sovereignty and nonintervention and the norms demanding respect for human rights be reconciled so that humanitarian intervention becomes permissible? What is the right authorization for humanitarian intervention? Who has the military capacity required to translate an authorized intervention into practice?

Out of the three key issues of sovereignty, authority and capacity, the biggest conceptual breakthrough proposed by the R2P framework came from "sovereignty as responsibility." Although this revolutionary formulation was not an ICISS invention but one that originated in the 1990s work on the protection of internally displaced populations, it was R2P that placed it under neon lights. As a result, there is now universal agreement that state sovereignty is no longer a shield behind which states can hide to commit mass atrocities. From all R2P representations, the 2001 report framework provides the most comprehensive discussion of sovereignty and nonintervention in relation to human rights. R2P, as originating in the ICISS report, was designed to reconcile both the tension in principle between sovereignty and humanitarian intervention, and the opposing perspectives on intervention in the policy world.

R2P's depiction of sovereignty specifically emphasizes the durability of the state, and implies a very clear-cut dual responsibility: internally, toward one state's population; and externally, toward other states. The focus of the R2P report on relativism, independent statehood, and the equality of states had the double purpose of putting forward a workable balance between sovereignty and human rights, and of addressing the main objections to humanitarian intervention. With respect to cultural relativism-based objections that had been raised in the past in relation to defining thresholds for humanitarian emergencies, R2P emphasized that issues of cultural relativism cannot arise in instances of mass atrocities where the use of force might be necessary. While acknowledging the changes in how sovereignty is perceived on the international stage and in evolving customary law, R2P actually reinforced the importance of state sovereignty. R2P reaffirmed the nonintervention principle as default through its focus on independent statehood, and this was the primary way in which it met any objection to humanitarian intervention. One essential aspect of R2P that was kept unaltered in all variations of the framework emphasizes that the main responsibility to protect lies with the state, which is illustrative of its role as the primary level for action. To further highlight the enduring importance of states, the expectation to pick up the responsibility to protect civilians if their own government fails to do so falls on other states. Ultimately, states are the only actors capable of ensuring respect for international law and compliance with the human rights regime. That is, even if international organizations and NGOs push for compliance, it is individual states that have to put human rights norms into practice. For such reasons, I have described the relationship between sovereignty and human rights put forward by R2P as balanced. The R2P recipe clearly expresses deference to both state sovereignty and protection of human rights.

The question of authorization for the use of force is the second major controversial issue from the intervention debate that I have discussed in relation to the responsibility to protect framework, while emphasizing the differences in approaching this issue between successive R2P reformulations. One of the main motivations to set up ICISS revolved around developing a normative framework to ensure that no more Kosovos and Rwandas would result from the UN Security Council's own failure to act. Complete reliance on the Council for authorization has been problematic for moral and practical reasons. As seen more recently, for instance, the Security Council's dithering since early 2003 in spite of massive murder and displacement in Darfur resembles its inability to address the woes of the DRC. It was both logically and ethically imperative for the ICISS report to ask what happens when the Council cannot agree on collective action. Indeed, one of the major merits of the 2001 R2P report is precisely its recognition that the Council cannot be the sole authorizing body, in view of its past inability or unwillingness to fulfill this role. As such, the R2P report considered two alternative sources of authority to the Security Council, namely regional organizations and the "Uniting for Peace" General Assembly procedure, and proposed that the P5 concur to a code of conduct for the use of veto in Council deliberations. Chapter 3 of the book discusses the merits of these alternatives that seemed the most legitimate options after the Security Council. This discussion was framed in relation to a "legitimacy ladder" designed to verify the proposals on authorization advanced in the original R2P formulation.

These proposals were too controversial to be retained in any subsequent R2P formulations at the UN. As expected, the issue of an alternative authorizing body was left out of the negotiations leading up to the adoption of R2P in the 2005 Summit Outcome Document. Without doubt, this was a significant retreat from the ICISS report's advantageous proposal regarding the issue of authorization for the use of force. While paragraph 139 of the 2005 Outcome Document made no reference to the use of veto in the Council either, the Secretary-General in his 2009 report on R2P urged the P5 to refrain from employing or threatening to employ the veto in situations of manifest failure to meet obligations relating to R2P (United Nations 2009a: 27). Many states that spoke during the 2009 General Assembly debate on R2P criticized past Security Council failures to halt atrocities, and described the Council's inaction as the reason for failures to protect Rwandans, Bosnian Muslims, and Darfuris. Over thirty-five member states expressed frustrations about the conduct of the permanent five members in the Security Council, and called for them to refrain from using the veto in R2P situations. Alternatives to the Security Council as authorizing body were, predictably, also left out of the Secretary-General's 2009 report on R2P. There is, however, a brief acknowledgment in one of the report's paragraphs detailing the work of the General Assembly that suggests the Assembly "may exercise a range of related functions under Articles 10 to 14, as well as under the 'Uniting for peace' process" (United Nations 2009a: 9). And so, all formulations of R2P subsequent to the ICISS report fail to discuss what should happen if the Security Council is unable or unwilling to act. While certainly problematic in this regard, it is not the ICISS formulation that represents the reference point for responsibility to protect considerations and for what R2P currently stands for, but the version of R2P portrayed in paragraphs 138 and 139 of the 2005 Summit Outcome Document. And so, in light of the failure to consider the ICISS report's proposition to evade the firm procedural rules of the UN Charter, we are left with the 2005 Outcome Document representation of R2P and with contemplating ways to improve the work of the Council. Security Council reform is obviously necessary, but the difficulty of reaching an acceptable resolution in the short term is just as obvious, even if there is no lack of proposals for the UN on how to make the Council more representative. Even without alternatives to the Security Council and finalized proposals to make it work better, the 2005 agreement on R2P does recognize collective UN interventions for humanitarian purposes as one course of action, which was completely unthinkable during the Cold War.

Apart from the question of authorization, concerns related to finding those available, willing, and capable to carry out the intervention are just as important. The key question of "who conducts interventions?" is omnipresent in all debates on humanitarian intervention. The lack of operational readiness is one of the main challenges faced when reaction is required in cases of genocide, war crimes, crimes against humanity, and ethnic cleansing. And so, capacity is the third issue considered in this study's exploration of how R2P addresses the most contentious aspects of the intervention debate. In Chapter 4 of the book, I look at how the ICISS report and subsequent R2P reformulations have addressed the question of who actually has the capacity to put R2P into practice, and I also review the actors available to use force and their resources. While the ICISS report offered workable recommendations in regard to the previous two issues of sovereignty and authorization, it failed to provide similarly specific answers on this topic. The ICISS report did not consider operational principles in depth, mainly because R2P was designed as a political solution to the intervention debate, rather than as an instrument to address military concerns. Similarly, subsequent formulations of R2P in the UN setting avoid discussing capabilities for the use of force and focus instead on the need to enhance early warning. The 2005 Summit Outcome Document does not elaborate on the practical implications of the use of force, other than to reaffirm that missions should have "adequate capacity to counter hostilities and fulfill effectively their mandates" (UN 2005a: para. 92). Both paragraph 139 of the Summit Outcome Document and the Secretary-General's report on implementing R2P talk about the international community's commitment "to assist states in building their protection capacities" (United Nations 2009a: 1). A noteworthy point is the Secretary-General's portrayal of the issue of capacity as the most serious challenge of the three main gaps R2P faces before implementation (ibid.: 26). However, all representations of R2P to date assess the capacity question very broadly, and when they provide proposals, such as encouraging collaborations between the UN and regional actors, their recommendations lack any specificity. And yet, in those extreme situations when only the use of force will do, if the responsibility to protect is invoked it only seems natural also to have the capacity to protect.

To discuss R2P's coverage of the topic, I reviewed the capabilities of the few actors that can conduct military interventions, such as the UN, NATO, the EU, the AU, ECOWAS, and the so-called coalitions of the willing with powerful individual states at the helm. The overview of these actors' capacities has suggested that all face a shortage of trained troops for peace operations. Apart from the reluctance of the West to provide well-trained personnel, the slow progress of various regional capacity-building processes amplifies the current capacity crisis. In this context, I have also noted which actors come closest to being able to intervene in R2P-type scenarios, such as the EU and NATO, in light of their preparedness for the particular operational requirements R2P-type missions entail. Depending on the circumstances on the ground, such operations might necessitate uniformed personnel to apply deadly force in defensive attempts to protect civilians and the troops' own safety, which in turn involve capable air forces and ground forces, as well as a large logistical infrastructure to support them. Putting together the required number of troops in some last-resort situations remains one of the most challenging tasks in today's increasingly demanding environment to address humanitarian emergencies.

Taken together, the separate analyses of the three controversial questions on sovereignty versus human rights, authority, and capacity shows that the responsibility to protect framework provides a theoretical basis for consensus on what to do when faced with mass atrocities. R2P introduced new principles and concepts to reconcile sovereignty with the need to protect, which was previously unachievable given the focus on the "right" to intervene. Its theoretical framework is also evidence of changing security trends in the international system and the focus on those in need of help rather than the interveners' perceptions. If R2P, in its various reformulations, has addressed two concerns about humanitarian intervention – sovereignty and authorization – in enough detail to provide material for assessment, the same could not be said about the issue of the operational capacity to carry out military operations. Attempts to appease critical states – mostly NAM – that regard R2P as another way of phrasing the old humanitarian intervention enterprise, together with the efforts to make it broadly acceptable to UN member states, have translated into a move away from concrete proposals on capacity and direct guidelines pertaining exclusively to the use of force. On the whole, however, R2P is important as a theoretical proposition for a sound framework to replace the humanitarian intervention one, which proved conceptually unhelpful and politically unfeasible. Getting the responsibility to protect right at the theory level is a prerequisite for getting it right in practice and for applying it consistently. Without reconciling the main components and prescriptions of the responsibility to protect framework, the practice of R2P is certainly not going to be effective.

Practical considerations

After exploring the main theoretical tenets of the responsibility to protect in the first part of the book, Chapters 5 and 6 followed R2P's normative development up to the support it attracted in principle in the political realm, and focused on the more practical dimensions of R2P. R2P's normative progress is a good illustration of the need for new rules of the game. Debates following the 2003 invasion of Iraq showed that states prefer to have an agreed set of rules about the use of force, which would stop the powerful from intervening as they please. The fact that the responsibility to protect was adopted at the 2005 World Summit by heads of governments – two years after the norm's abuse in Iraq – suggests that member states sought to prevent future abuses by clarifying the conditions under which the use of force for human-protection purposes was permitted. The choice we are facing now is no longer between intervention and nonintervention, but between rules-based, multilateral, and consensual intervention and ad hoc, unilateral, and deeply divisive intervention. This is why advocates have pushed for embedding international intervention within the principles underlying R2P rather than risking "the inherently more volatile nature of unilateral interventions" (Thakur 2008b: 6).

In Chapter 5, I highlighted the most important steps along the progressive route that saw R2P moving from an "idea" in the 2001 ICISS report to the formulations linked to two key developments in 2009, namely the UN Secretary-General's report on implementing the responsibility to protect and the general Assembly's plenary debate on R2P. I have argued that R2P's trajectory is part of the broader normative evolution toward reshaping sovereignty and collective concerns. The key idea behind R2P is that egregious human rights abuses are no longer a matter of sovereign concern, but belong to the international domain. The framework is controversial not only because it touches upon very sensitive issues like sovereignty, nonintervention, and using force, but also because of its possible impact on the rules governing the use of force. In order to assess the stage R2P has reached on its normative path, I have discussed the key steps on its trajectory in relation to the early stages detailed in theoretical models for a norm's "life cycle." R2P's normative progress verifies the types of social interactions characteristic to the norm diffusion stage, namely instrumental adaptation and argumentative discourse. The most important normative advance of R2P to date – the 2005 endorsement in the World Summit Outcome Document – reflects a shared understanding among member states, albeit much debated, of what R2P entails and the four types of crimes it applies to. The developments between 2005 and the July 2009 General Assembly debate on the topic reflect how the September 2005 agreement on R2P was used as the platform for subsequent negotiations and compromises on the responsibility to protect. The efforts to advance R2P during this period indeed fit the description of the interactions from the early stages of a norm's formation, namely denial and tactical concessions, when bargaining among proponents and opponents is prevalent. By seeking affirmation and reaffirmation through the UN as the organizational platform to propel R2P further on its normative track, its supporters tried to create the possibility for R2P to eventually become institutionalized among states, but also within states, which is the final measurement of a new norm. Given these processes, I have argued that R2P's depiction as nascent norm best captures the stage R2P has reached and its current portrayal in the international discourse. I have also identified three major factors that, taken together, have contributed to R2P's emergence and progress. These include the demand-driven nature of the ICISS report, the "normative fit" context in which R2P emerged, namely a normative environment marked by greater concern for human rights and humanitarian law, and the various actors' efforts to promote R2P, which encompassed manifestations of effective individual entrepreneurial leadership, states acting as norm entrepreneurs, and civil society also promoting R2P.

Chapter 5 concluded with a discussion of whether the normative development of the responsibility to protect provides it with any legal force. A quick look at R2P as articulated in paragraphs 138 and 139 of the 2005 Summit Outcome Document suggests that the framework's possible legal content derives from references to existing legal obligations. The Genocide Convention was too narrow to address the need to protect civilians from mass atrocities, the UDHR was too broad, and so R2P emerged to fill the gap. By building upon established norms of international law with consequences for non-compliance, if R2P mobilizes action and actors pursue it to induce compliance, they also act toward consolidating the already- established norms. In this context, I have depicted a mutually reinforcing normative process between R2P and the established norms of international law it is tied to, which implies that implementing R2P could also strengthen existing legal obligations.

Although the preparedness "to take collective action … on a case-by-case basis" expressed in paragraph 139 of the Outcome Document resonates well with the concept of state responsibility, it also announces a potentially inconsistent application of R2P by the Security Council. An agreement on the principles of the use of force would surely establish a straightforward benchmark against which to verify the accuracy of states' humanitarian claims. The predicament, however, is that no agreement on a workable set of codified criteria for intervention is in sight, which leaves the parameters for recourse to force open to political determination. This is certainly problematic when considering the legal force of R2P. The responsibility to protect has not yet achieved the status of a legally binding norm and no new collective legal obligation has been created. However, R2P has already established its normative foothold through a platform that details how what used to be a state's internal business is now of international concern and could become, in extremis, appropriate terrain for the Security Council, thus shifting classical interpretations of the UN Charter on the issue. It is expected that the policy agenda proposed in the Secretary-General's report for implementation will inform the work of the UN, shape states' decision-making processes, and influence behavior in response to civilian protection. And so, rather than thinking about R2P as a legal tool, the framework available should be used as a political tool with the potential to create the much-needed agenda to set off the political option for actors to protect civilians from mass atrocity situations.

I have focused on the correlation between the normative and the operational dimensions of R2P in Chapter 6, where I have discussed ways in which practice and politics could catch up with R2P's normative development. The rhetoric of international institutions, states, civil society and, advocacy groups, invoking, or not, R2P in conflicts in Darfur, in the eastern region of the Democratic Republic of the Congo (DRC), in post-election Kenya, in the aftermath of Cyclone Nargis in Burma, and more recently in Sri Lanka and Guinea suggests that the R2P language is gaining increased recognition. I have looked in more detail at six conflict situations – in Iraq, Darfur, Kenya, Myanmar, South Ossetia and Zimbabwe – which are, at the time of writing, the most cited ones for the application of R2P by media commentators, diplomats, policy makers, and scholars. As seen in crises like Darfur, the protection of civilians represents the center of recent efforts to operationalize R2P. Each of the conflict situations addressed in Chapter 6 has illustrated important challenges that need to be addressed if R2P is to be implemented effectively. Taken together, they reveal a major gap between the rapid evolution of R2P on the normative side and the enduring problems on the operational side. I have divided the gaps between the normative and the operational dimensions of R2P into five categories, which are, inevitably, interlinked: conceptual, political, institutional, operational, and a significant divide between expectations and capacity. After examining what each of these five categories of challenges entail, I have concluded Chapter 6 with a discussion of potential structures, strategies, and policies that would diminish and eventually close these gaps. In this context, I have looked at what supporters could do to ensure that R2P is implemented properly and also to bring those ambivalent or opposed to R2P on board.

With respect to closing the conceptual gap, supporters of the responsibility to protect could increase the framework's conceptual clarity at four levels: within the UN, regional organizations, national governments, and through an effective advocacy network involving transnational civil society exchanges of information. Publicizing examples of successful R2P enterprises is another way to build more knowledge about R2P and the costs associated with its implementation. Drawing attention to misrepresentations of the responsibility to protect such as those seen in Myanmar, South Ossetia, and Iraq also helps to reduce the conceptual gap in two essential ways, by suggesting first that R2P should not be seen narrowly, and second, that R2P should not be viewed as covering the protection of everyone from everything. Decisions on how to protect civilians involve not only operational considerations, but also normative choices. Having a shared understanding of what the responsibility to protect entails increases the chances of generating the necessary political will when a potential R2P crisis arises. Mobilizing political will, however, is very challenging precisely because it requires long-term resource commitments and not too obvious, or substantial, political returns. I have discussed several ways to sustain political will, and have emphasized the role of civil society in this sense, which I have argued could play a more important role in regard to this particular challenge than in any of the other four gaps discussed in Chapter 6.

In turn, increased political commitment is more likely to provide international and regional actors with the necessary resources for implementation, which has the potential to translate into an improved protection agenda. Furthermore, I have argued there are two ways to diminish the institutional gap that hinders the effective implementation of R2P: the first one relates to reforming the existing structures within institutions at the national, regional, and international level – some of which might be already engaged in R2P-type activities, but without applying the responsibility to protect framework; and the second one relates to creating new structures that would facilitate the R2P decision-making process. As for diminishing the operational gap, I have emphasized how operationalizing the use-of-force dimension of R2P is directly dependent on the existence of political will and the necessary institutional structures in place. Concerns related to military capacity, training, equipment, rules of engagement, and doctrine, with a focus on detailed guidelines on how actually to protect, were addressed in this context.

I have argued that the most important gap from the five major gaps R2P is facing before implementation relates to closing the expectations–capacity gap.

This should definitely take priority over the other four in the long-term strategic thinking on R2P. Despite the complexity of the challenge, the solution is extremely straightforward, namely decreasing the inflated expectations about what R2P can achieve at the same time as increasing the level of commitment and capacities available to make R2P work. Decreasing expectations and increasing capacity would also narrow the gap between rhetoric and action. It is paramount to set modest expectations in terms of what R2P can achieve. As Darfur best illustrates, the "success" or "failure" of R2P on the operational side should be examined within reasonable expectations of success, and especially after giving careful consideration to circumstances on the ground. It is always important to define the scope of what is possible to achieve in particular situations where R2P is contemplated. Emphasizing that R2P is just one tool among others available to address conflict situations is equally important for minimizing the inflated expectations about the responsibility to protect. Very few exceptional cases of the Rwanda type are likely to emerge in the future. These aside, other responses are available in the international toolbox to address various types of conflicts or serious human rights violations around the world. Ultimately, closing the expectations–capacity gap would translate into getting R2P right in practice.

The R2P framework, in its various expressions culminating with the Secretary-General's "three pillar approach," represents a new way of thinking about mass atrocities, which proposes obligations owed to both persons and states, and is indicative of evolving international customary law. R2P's relevance is explained by the fact that it proposes a more viable way of engaging with protection issues than the humanitarian intervention framework. As a new approach to providing protection, R2P holds promise both as a theoretical and practical proposition. It is the best framework available to move the humanitarian intervention debate forward to date. In addition to its conceptual contribution, R2P's superiority over the humanitarian intervention framework resides in recognizing that what is needed to protect today is much more than just the use of force, as suggested by the broader spectrum of mechanisms to protect it puts forward, short of using force.

The normative and operational potential of R2P is significant. Because of R2P, it is now normal to expect that state sovereignty is no longer a shield behind which states can hide to commit mass atrocities. While this is a big realization in itself, further refinement of its implications and commitment by states are required for R2P to become an organizing code of conduct for the international community. Indeed, the discussion of the gaps between the normative and operational sides of the responsibility to protect confirms that R2P is still a nascent norm, which states need to internalize in order to speed up the very slow progress on implementation to date. After all, R2P was not designed as, and certainly cannot be, a panacea. Plus, actors actually still debate the practical mechanisms through which to implement it. But if we set off on the responsibility to protect journey with increased political commitment and modest expectations about what it can achieve, perhaps we will not have to wait so long for R2P to live up to its potential to deliver real protection.

Notes

1 Introduction: humanitarian intervention and the responsibility to protect

1 For an excellent coverage of the origins of humanitarian intervention, see Gary Bass (2008), *Freedom's Battle.*

2 The language of "humanitarian intervention" has always attracted criticism for the association of the word "humanitarian" with military activity, a reason why alternative terminologies are used, such as "military intervention for humanitarian purposes," "military force to support humanitarian objectives," "military coercion to protect civilians," etc. For ease of reference, the term "humanitarian intervention" will be used throughout this book. Whenever humanitarian intervention is referred to, the involvement of military force is implied.

3 After the release of the UN Secretary-General's 2009 report on the topic, the "R2P" abbreviation changed to "RtoP," at least in UN circles, and the two acronyms are now used interchangeably. However, I am using either the full formulation or the "R2P" acronym throughout the book because this was the initial portrayal by which the responsibility to protect, as a product of the report of the International Commission on Intervention and State Sovereignty (ICISS), got to be known and developed.

4 The balance in its composition is reflected, first, by the two co-chairs of ICISS, and, second, by the fact that it included commissioners, academics and politicians from the north and south, with opposing positions on the intervention–sovereignty debate. The Commission held roundtable meetings on all continents, with more than 200 representatives from all sectors and with different views on intervention, many of whose positions were considered in the elaboration of the ICISS report. Many have argued that the formulation of the "responsibility to protect" is as innovative as the "sustainable development" terminology of the Bruntdland Commission. For more details, see Thakur 2006: 248.

5 These are: the seriousness of the harm being threatened (the just cause criterion), the motivation or primary purpose of the proposed military intervention (the right intention requirement); the question of whether the peaceful alternatives were exhausted (the last resort condition); the proportionality of the response, at the minimum necessary to prevent of stop the suffering (the proportional means condition), and the requirement to balance consequences, so that more good than harm would be done (the reasonable prospects condition).

6 Some scholars have also added the "threat of using force" to the actual "use of force" (see, for example, Jackson 1993: 581; Holzgrefe and Keohane (eds) 2003: 1); however, this is not a universally accepted position.

7 The four categories include: cases in which the R2P terminology is correctly used, R2P thresholds have been met and R2P was invoked but international reactions have fallen short of protecting victims, as in Darfur; instances in which R2P thresholds are cor-

rectly identified and interventions succeed in halting extreme violence, as was the case in Kenya; cases where thresholds are close to being met but R2P has not yet been invoked, as in Zimbabwe or Somalia; and instances in which the R2P language is either misused or disingenuously abused, as was the case with post-Cyclone Nargis Myanmar and South Ossetia, respectively.

2 The responsibility to protect: sovereignty *and* human rights

1 The importance of moving beyond the sovereignty–intervention dichotomy was recognized by many of the ICISS commissioners and its two co-chairs. See, for example, Evans and Sahnoun 2002: 101; Thakur 2004: 1–16.

2 This is the response given by developing countries to the former UN Secretary-General's speech on humanitarian intervention before the General Assembly in 1999 (Meron 2006: 523).

3 *Jus cogens* is an absolute rule of general international law, and as defined by Article 53 of the 1969 *Vienna Convention on the Law of Treaties*, it is recognized by the international community of states as a norm from which no derogation is permitted and which can be modified only by a subsequent norm of general international law, with the same character.

4 In 1965, the General Assembly passed resolution 2131, which states: "No State has the right to intervene, directly or indirectly, for any reason … in the internal or external affairs of any other State. Consequently, armed intervention and all other forms of interference … are condemned." In 1970, resolution 2625, "The Declaration on Principles of International Law Concerning Friendly Relations and Cooperation Among States," reiterated the norm of nonintervention.

5 This is the view expressed in the ICISS report (2001), see pp. 3–9. For more details, see the ICISS supplementary volume (Weiss and Hubert 2001), pp. 5–12.

6 It was not until the 1878 Treaty of Berlin that minority protection became a normal condition placed on new states, despite earlier developments, such as Europe's great powers granting independence to Greece in 1830 on the condition that it protect the religious rights of Turks (for more details, see Philpott 1995: 353–368). Self-determination was first advocated during the French Revolution, but it is commonly thought that it finally triumphed in the settlement of World War I. However, no lasting norm of self-determination emerged or won overall acceptance until 1960, when the UN condemned colonialism as "alien subjugation … and exploitation … a denial of fundamental human rights" and pronounced colonies illegitimate (General Assembly resolution 1514 (XV), 14 December 1960).

7 For an excellent review of this approach, see Werner and de Wilde (2001).

8 This is what Stephen Krasner calls "international legal sovereignty" (1999, 2001, 2004).

9 The "descriptive fallacy" refers to the wrong assessment according to which there must be something in reality that corresponds to the meaning of the term "sovereignty," understood solely as denoting the actual capacity of a state to exercise full control internally while also enjoying external independence. It describes the illusion that sovereignty is a percentage of effective power or independence that can be measured (for more details, see Werner and de Wilde 2001).

10 For more details on quasi-states, see Jackson (1990, 1993, 2000, 2004); for a good discussion on EU integration and how it affects the sovereignty of its member states, see Werner and de Wilde (2001).

11 A treaty is defined by the 1969 Vienna Convention on the Law of Treaties, Article 2(1)(a), as "an international agreement concluded between states in written form and governed by international law, whether embodied in a single instrument or in two or more related instruments and whatever its particular designation."

12 This includes the requirement to create the former UN Commission on Human Rights, in Article 68.

13 There are also two Optional Protocols to the International Covenant on Civil and Political Rights of 1966 and 1989. The First Optional Protocol allows for individual complaints. A state party to the Covenant that becomes a party to the Optional Protocol recognizes the competence of the Human Rights Committee to consider communications from individuals subject to its jurisdiction who claim to be victims of a violation by the state of any of the rights set forth in the Covenant (Article I). The Second Optional Protocol to the International Covenant on Civil and Political Rights aims at the abolition of the death penalty, and is, thus, designed to put teeth into the ICCPR provisions limiting the death penalty practice.
14 This was the world's first international human rights instrument, preceding the 1948 UDHR by more than six months.
15 But not on other human rights violations, such as detention without trial, lack of freedom of the press, etc.
16 An often-cited example in point is that of Islamic societies that do not recognize certain rights essential to Western countries, such as the right to change one's religion. Saudi Arabia's abstention from the vote on the UDHR, based on their concerns with the liberty of changing one's religion and the position of women within the institution of marriage, is one illustration of the relevance of such differences.
17 See Office of the United Nations High Commissioner for Human Rights (OHCHR), "Status of Ratifications of the Principal International Human Rights Treaties as of 16 June 2006," available from: http://www2.ohchr.org/english/bodies/docs/RatificationStatus.pdf.
18 To further complicate matters, legal scholars argue there is no agreement about what "soft law" is, or indeed if it really exists (e.g. Aust 2005: 11).
19 The supplementary research volume of the report gives extensive details on the emerging challenges to the traditional concept of sovereignty, see Weiss and Hubert 2001.
20 Samuel Makinda (2004) argues that despite recognizing, on the surface, the role of NGOs, the R2P report actually marginalizes the role of other relevant actors in the international society, such as NGOs, by placing too much emphasis on the state.
21 There is a variety of positions within this one side of the argument about the demise of the state: for instance, what Kurt Mills (1998) understands by the transformation suffered by the sovereign state as a result of the focus on human rights is different from what another proponent of the demise of the state thesis, David Chandler (2002), understands by the end of sovereign equality.
22 France was the exception; it argued in favor of expanding the range of crimes triggering R2P to include natural disasters and considerations for the potential of any deliberate refusal of a state to provide assistance or accept aid from the international community to produce humanitarian tragedies.

3 Who authorizes interventions?

1 Assessing the conditions accounting for legitimate humanitarian interventions is the second one.
2 Two articles of the UN Charter discuss the responsibilities of the General Assembly: Article 10 gives the General Assembly a general responsibility regarding any matter related to UN authority, and Article 11 gives the General Assembly "a fallback responsibility" in regard to the maintenance of international peace and security, but only in terms of making recommendations, and not binding decisions. The responsibilities of regional arrangements are stated in Chapter VIII of the UN Charter, which acknowledges the existence of regional actors and their security role.
3 The Report of the Danish Institute of International Affairs (1999) described Security Council authorization as one component of the definition of intervention: "....humanitarian intervention is defined as a coercive action of states with the use of

armed forces in another state without the permission of the state government, with or without UN Security Council authorization..," p. 11.

4 Allen Buchanan (2004), for instance, proposes a coalition of democratic, human rights-respecting states, bound by a treaty comprising the criteria for permissible intervention in the absence of UN authorization. This would require the participation of rich European Union states; such a treaty-based coalition should aim at either minimizing or eliminating altogether the role of world's policeman's played by the US, pp. 450–453.

5 One such proposal details a potential arrangement in the shape of a treaty, open to, but unlikely to be signed by all states. Such a treaty would

> ...define rigorously the circumstances in which collective intervention for humanitarian purposes could be undertaken, for a limited period, by a group of states whose action would be authorized by a strong majority of the treaty's signers. The nations would act through a secretariat set up under the treaty and would report all plans for action to the UN...

See Hoffmann 1992: 41. Such an arrangement is considered more democratic, while the Security Council still has a say in ending any measures it regards as unreasonable.

6 Such ideas are seen, for instance, in a proposal by Tom Farer. Farer picks up Hoffman's idea of a pact, but adds a greater role for the UN Security Council, see Farer 1993: 333. For such proposals, however, major concerns related to the veto power of the P5 remain (especially those for whom state sovereignty is paramount) as such states might veto any agreement.

7 See, for example, the Report of the UN High-Level Panel on Threats, Challenges and Change (United Nations 2004a), which, despite rejecting the idea of unilateral action, recognized that "...in some urgent situations ... authorization may be sought after [regional peace] operations have commenced," p. 85.

8 This is, of course, a major concern for China, given its record of respect for human rights. The same concerns apply to another permanent member of the Security Council – Russia – with respect to the conflict in Chechnya and the ways in which this was addressed.

9 A minority of Council members have prioritized their economic interests over their moral and legal responsibilities to address the crisis in Darfur. China, with its substantial investments in Sudan's abundant oil supplies, was their leader. However, in June 2008, China commenced to use stronger-than-usual language to urge Khartoum to cooperate with the UN peacekeepers and enforce a ceasefire in Darfur.

10 The four interventions in the 1990s that did not receive Security Council blessing were: Liberia (1990), Northern Iraq (1991), Sierra Leone (1997), and Kosovo (1999).

11 According to Yevgeny Primakov, quoted in Bellamy 2006: 152.

12 Nor does the UN Charter define human rights. However, the Charter allows the Security Council to define threats to peace and security as it sees fit, so violations of human rights could be defined as such threats.

13 Article 2(7) states: "Nothing contained in the present Charter shall authorize the United Nations to intervene in matters which are essentially within the domestic jurisdiction of any state or shall require the Members to submit such matters to settlement under the present Charter; but this principle shall not prejudice the application of enforcement measures under Chapter VII."

14 The Security Council has broadly defined as threats to international peace and security, among others: 1) refugee flows (in relation to Iraq, 1991); 2) human suffering (as seen in Somalia, 1992); 3) the overthrow of democratically elected government (as in Haiti, 1994); 4) ethnic cleansing (as in Kosovo, 1999).

15 Examples of such cases are the OAS intervention in Guatemala in 1954; in the Dominican Republic, in 1960 and 1965; and in Cuba, between 1960 and 1962. Some argue that great powers such as the US prefer regional actors, as the OAS for instance,

because they can dominate such organizations more easily than the UN. In the above instances, the use of the OAS was regarded as a political victory for the US, as the Latin American states prefer going through the UN.

16 What might have helped in this direction was the fact that the Kosovo intervention was a multilateral one, conducted by a coalition of democratic states under the approval stamp of a formal, powerful multilateral organization, namely NATO.

17 Defining a "large-scale" or "extreme" emergency requiring the use of force is one difficult issue. Kosovo, in 1999, is one example in point: many have assessed as problematic the fact that Kosovo represented "extreme emergency" for some, though not for others (i.e. China, India, Russia), while Chechnya did not cross the threshold, when in fact the level of abuse of civilians there had been higher than in Kosovo.

18 They took place in Liberia (1990), Northern Iraq (1991), Bosnia and Herzegovina (1992–1995), Somalia (1992–1993), Rwanda (1994), Haiti (1994), Albania (1997), Sierra Leone (1997–2000), Kosovo (1999), and East Timor (1999).

19 Overall, the year 2006 represented an all-time high, with thirty-five peace operations in place, corresponding to more than one-fourth of all operations ever authorized, see Diehl 2008: 62–63.

20 This does not mean that regional actors have replaced the UN. In a table listing the total number of peace operations per agency, Paul Diehl (2008) suggests that up to now, the UN has conducted more than half of all peace operations (sixty-eight), whereas regional actors organized thirty-three, and twenty-four represented multinational initiatives (p. 66).

21 The four interventions that received the consent of the host state were: Bosnia, Rwanda, Albania, and East Timor. For more details, see Adam Roberts (2004: 84), but note that he also includes Sierra Leone in this category, although in this case, the UN offered its *retroactive* approval.

22 For complete accounts of these interventions, see for example Nicholas Wheeler (2000), Simon Chesterman (2001), and Thomas Weiss (2005a).

23 This terminology became extensively used after the Independent International Commission on Kosovo described the intervention as such in its 2000 report.

24 Only five years after the conflict erupted in Darfur in early 2003, did the UN–AU cooperative efforts materialize into UNAMID, a hybrid mission that took over from AMIS in Darfur on 1 January 2008.

25 The UN Charter does not forbid states to intervene upon invitation from the host state. The Australian-led interventions in the Solomon Islands in 2003 as the Regional Assistance Mission to Solomon Island (RAMSI), and in 2006 as Operation Astute in Timor Leste are two examples of interventions undertaken without Security Council authorization, but with the consent of the host state.

26 For a more thorough discussion on the new AU security architecture, see Cristina Badescu and Linnea Bergholm (2009, 2010).

27 Some legal scholars encourage the evolution of a common law for multilateral humanitarian interventions, "with principles and parameters," in instances of extreme humanitarian emergencies when the Security Council is deadlocked, see, for example, Meron 2006: 526.

4 Who conducts interventions?

1 For a comprehensive discussion of such considerations, see Holt and Berkman (2006) and Seybolt (2007).

2 For a few notable exceptions, see Holt and Berkman (2006), and Holt *et al.* (2009).

3 See UN DPKO, Fact Sheet: United Nations Peacekeeping, available from: www.un.org/en/peacekeeping/documents/factsheet.pdf.

4 Examples of UN peace operations include the missions in Sierra Leone (1999); the Democratic Republic of Congo (DRC) (2000), MONUC; Afghanistan (2002), UNAMA;

Liberia (2003), UNMIL; Côte d'Ivoire (2004), UNOCI; Haiti (2004), MINUSTAH; Burundi (2004) BINUB; Sudan (2005) UNMIS; Sierra Leone (2006) UNIOSIL; East Timor (2006), UNMIT, Darfur, Sudan (2008), UNAMID; and the Central African Republic/Chad (2007), MINURCAT. As for non-UN operations, examples include the French-led Operation Licorne and ECOWAS in Côte d'Ivoire (ECOMICI, 2003), under SC resolution 1464, and in Liberia (ECOMIL); the African Union in Darfur, under SC resolution 1564, (AMIS), and in Somalia (AMISOM); NATO's International Security Assistance Force (ISAF) in Afghanistan; and the European Union's (EU) Force in Bosnia-Herzegovina, the DRC and Chad/the Central African Republic.

5 Information from "Fact Sheet – UN Peacekeeping," for more details, see www.un.org/en/peacekeeping/documents/factsheet.pdf.

6 For such data, see UN DPKO, Background Note, for the different years, available at: www.un.org/Depts/dpko/dpko/bnote010101.pdf.

7 For more details, see Holt (2005), p. 13. Holt exemplifies this argument by referencing states that are constrained from providing troops to *any* Chapter VII mission, Japan being a case in point.

8 See UN DPKO, UN Mission's Summary detailed by Country, 31 January 2010, available from: www.un.org/en/peacekeeping/contributors/2010/jan10_3.pdf.

9 See UN DPKO, Ranking of Military and Police Contributions to UN Operations, 30 April 2010, available from: www.un.org/Depts/dpko/dpko/contributors/2010/apr10_2.pdf.

10 The best example in point is a global survey on the issue conducted in 2007 by the Chicago Council on Global Affairs and WorldPublicOpinion.org, which covered 56 percent of the population of the globe, and found strong support for the idea of a standing UN force on all continents, see "World Publics Favor New Powers for the UN," available at www.globalpolicy.org/security/peacekpg/reform/2007/0509newpowers.pdf.

11 SHIRBRIG was designed to provide the UN with a multinational force of 4,000–5,000 troops with units deployable for a maximum of six months, self-sufficient for up to sixty days, and with a reaction time of fifteen to thirty days. SHIRBRIG operated from 2000 to June 2009, but its dependence on the case-by-case decisions of the participating member states on whether to contribute troops did not make it a viable solution for the more robust peace operations required in mass-killing contexts.

12 NATO prefers to have a UN Security Council mandate to operate, but it does not require one.

13 Despite being under the EU flag, the IEMF operation is also discussed as an operation undertaken by a so-called coalition of the willing, since non-EU states, such as Canada, South Africa and Brazil also contributed troops under the French lead.

14 See the European Union Council Secretariat, "EU Battlegroups," Factsheet, February 2007, available from: www.consilium.europa.eu/uuedocs/cmsUpload/Battlegroups_February_07-factsheet.pdf.

15 The emphasis on stabilizing conflicts in Africa is also reflected in the UN peacekeeping budget, 77 percent of which is assigned for operations in Africa, with seven missions out of the total sixteen peace operations currently managed by the UN being in Africa, and six of the seven being large and very complex operations. In a typical year, 60 percent of the UN Security Council agenda also covers issues of concern to the African continent.

16 In Chapter V, Article 25, the Protocol suggests that:

> The Mechanism shall be applied in any of the following circumstances: In cases of aggression or conflict in any member state or threat thereof; In case of conflict between two or several member states; In case of internal conflict: a) that threatens to trigger a humanitarian disaster, or b) that poses a serious threat to peace and

security in the sub-region; In event of serious and massive violation of human rights and the rule of law; In the event of an overthrow or attempted overthrow of a democratically elected government; Any other situation as may be decided by the Mediation and Security Council.

17 For a more detailed account, see Alex Bellamy and Paul Williams 2005: 169.
18 For more operational details, see Bellamy and Williams 2005: 179–184. Bellamy and Williams also point out that the Security Council did not explicitly authorize the UK mission. However, both President Kabbah and the UN Secretary-General requested it, and so the operation was generally regarded as legitimate by the international community, see Bellamy and Williams 2005: 181, 184.
19 See UN Security Council resolutions 1527 and 1528, available www.un.org/Docs/sc/unsc_resolutions04.html.
20 In the case of Australia, the country decided to intervene in the Solomon Islands after the Australian Strategic Policy Institute (ASPI) – an institute set up by the Australian government, and funded mainly by the Department of Defence – released a report in July 2003 arguing that the collapse of the government in the Solomon Islands represented a serious threat for Australia as it made the country a potential haven for terrorists and international criminals.
21 For two excellent discussions on European countries' choices to act unilaterally rather than taking a multilateral approach through the UN, and the implications, see Gray 2005 and Bellamy and Williams 2005.
22 As Taylor Seybolt (2007: 22) gloomily suggests, rapid reaction in humanitarian emergencies is likely to be the exception rather than the rule in the near future.

5 From concept to norm

1 For a detailed examination of ICISS's work and the R2P report, see Chapter 2 in Alex Bellamy's book on the topic (2009).
2 This is no longer the case, as explained later in the chapter.
3 Alex Bellamy (2009: 83–91) and Ekkehard Strauss (2009b: 11–16) have carefully documented the details of these negotiations.
4 This is suggested by edits to the original language proposed for inclusion in the two paragraphs on R2P in the 2005 Summit Outcome Document, as was the case with suggestions coming from the United States delegation, which are underlined:

> In this context, we stand ready [instead of "recognize our shared responsibility"] to take collective action, in a timely and decisive manner, through the Security Council under Chapter VII of the UN Charter and, as appropriate, in co-operation with relevant regional organizations, should peaceful means be inadequate and national authorities be unwilling or unable to protect their populations
>
> (excerpt from a document prepared by the Representative of the US to the UN, dated 30 August 2005)

5 After two Security Council resolutions on the protection of civilians in armed conflict – resolutions 1265 (1999) and 1296 (2000) – there seemed to be a need to create precedent by referring specifically to R2P in connection to civilian protection. Fundamentally, the idea of including a reference to "responsibility" in a Security Council resolution on the protection of civilians would not be new: in the wake of the 1999 Kosovo intervention, the UK proposed the Security Council to adopt standards on the use of force in humanitarian situations, an attempt which was dismissed immediately, by the US in particular, who did not want their hands to be bound by such "responsibilities."
6 During a conversation I had with Gareth Evans shortly after the release of the Secretary-General's report, he used an interesting metaphor to depict this reformulation

of R2P, which also downplays the diminished attention to the use of force. Using a "cake" analogy, Evans described the Secretary General's reformulation of R2P as a different way of actually slicing the very same R2P cake that the ICISS proposed in 2001; that is, whereas the ICISS sliced it horizontally among prevention, reaction, and post-conflict rebuilding, the Secretary-General's report slices it vertically, but still keeps the initial categories of prevention, reaction, and rebuilding within each of the three vertical slices.

7 For one example, see the International Coalition for the Responsibility to Protect, "Open Letter to Governments in Advance of the General Assembly Debate," available at www.responsibilitytoprotect.org/index.php/civil_society_statements/2442?theme=alt1.

8 This was China's assessment of R2P. For all delegations' statements, see "More than 40 Delegates Express Strong Scepticism, Full Support as General Assembly Continues Debate on Responsibility to Protect," UN GA/10849, 24 July 2009, available from: www.un.org/News/Press/docs/2009/ga10849.doc.htm.

9 This was the terminology used since 2005 by The Responsibility to Protect–Engaging Civil Society (R2P–ECS). R2P–ECS was the WFM project working to advance R2P, before serving as the Secretariat of the International Coalition for the Responsibility to Protect, which was founded on 28 January 2009.

10 The term "norm cascade" is generally associated with Finnemore and Sikkink, but Cass R. Sunstein (1997) coined it in *Free Markets and Social Justice*.

11 This point came up during several of my interviews with UN officials involved in these consultations (July 2009, New York).

12 I refer here to India's invasion of East Pakistan (1971), Tanzania's invasion of Uganda (1979), and Vietnam's intervention in Cambodia (1979).

13 For a thorough discussion on the key position of human rights within this agenda, see A/59/565 (United Nations 2004a).

14 For a few important landmarks, see for example, Security Council resolutions 1265 (1999) and 1296 (2000); S/PRST/2002/41 (United Nations 2002); S/PRST/2003/27 (United Nations 2003a); and also the Report of the Secretary-General to the Security Council on the Protection of Civilians in Armed Conflict (United Nations 1999b); The Brahimi Report (United Nations 2000b); and Handbook on United Nations Multidimensional Peacekeeping Operations 2003; Report of the High-level Panel on Threats, Challenges and Change (United Nations 2004a); and the UN Secretary-General's Report, "In Larger Freedom" (Annan 2005a).

15 The "demand-driven" terminology came up in several interviews I conducted with Canadian foreign affairs officials involved in the early stages of the process; for a scholarly citation, see Thakur *et al.* (2005).

16 For more details on the power of ideas, see Thakur, Cooper and English 2005.

17 This point came up during two confidential interviews with senior officials from the Department of Foreign Affairs and International Trade Canada (DFAIT), Ottawa, August 2006.

18 For more details on the role of the UN Secretariat during the 2005 negotiations on the Summit Outcome Document, see Traub 2006.

19 Juan Mendez was the first to hold this position, but part time, while Francis Deng was appointed full time.

20 Despite understandable reservations about the usage of acronyms in general, it is hard to justify Luck's decision to change the "R2P" abbreviation used continuously since 2001 with "RtoP." As noted in the introduction, I see no value in this switch of acronyms, and have therefore used "R2P" throughout the book.

21 Information gathered during three confidential interviews I made with UN officials in New York, July 2009.

22 Information gathered during confidential interviews conducted with senior DFAIT officials involved in the process, Ottawa, 2–3 May and 1–2 August 2006.

23 The specific examples of Canadian efforts to promote R2P were collectively gathered from confidential interviews conducted with officials from various DFAIT divisions, in Ottawa, 2–3 May 2006, and 1–2 August 2006.
24 This information emerged from interviews with DFAIT officials, in New York, 26 April 2006, and in Ottawa, 2–3 May 2006.
25 After the Harper government came to power in 2006, R2P language was forbidden to Canadian Foreign Affairs officials until very recently. The foreign policy language constraints surfaced in the summer of 2009, through a leaked DFAIT memo published in *Embassy* magazine, which suggested that political staffers in Ottawa made significant changes to policy language to distance the current government from the foreign policy advanced by its Liberal predecessors, see e.g. Davis 2009.
26 Information and examples gathered from interviews conducted at WFM–IGP's R2P–CS, HRW, ICG, and Oxfam, New York, 22–28 April 2006.
27 One illustration of norm promotion by NGOs is the letter sent on 26 May 2006 by HRW, ICG and AI to members of the Security Council, reminding them of their Outcome Document commitment to R2P, and urging the Security Council to fulfill its responsibility to protect the population in Darfur. As a result, the Council called upon the parties to the Darfur Peace Agreement of 5 May 2006 to respect their commitments and to facilitate access and preparation for future deployment of UN troops.
28 Prior to the debate, for instance, the ICRtoP sent a letter to UN member states that was co-signed by forty-two NGOs, calling for constructive engagement in the debate.
29 Based on interviews conducted at the ICRtoP and GCR2P in New York, July 2009.
30 The prohibition of genocide is the only instance, to date, when the International Court of Justice (ICJ) assessed the peremptory character of a norm, and confirmed its *jus cogens* status (see United Nations 2001).
31 I am thankful to Charlotte Ku for pointing this out to me.
32 See, for instance, Gareth Evans (2008a) who has always been in favor of such criteria, versus Alex Bellamy (2009) who remains opposed because he perceives the utility of criteria as limited.
33 I am thankful to Jutta Brunnée for suggesting this approach to R2P's normative progress.
34 Soft law, however, can become hard law, and various customary norms can become *jus cogens*. See Shelton 2006: 322.
35 This point came up during a conversation with Don Hubert, Ottawa, May 2006.

6 From normative development to implementation

1 Tony Blair, the former UK prime minister, linked R2P and the war on terror in a speech to his Sedgefield constituency, see "Full text: Tony Blair's speech," *Guardian*, 5 March 2004. A more frequent citation is from a speech before the Chicago Economic Club on 22 April 1999 that outlined the circumstances warranting humanitarian intervention, available at www.pbs.org/newshour/bb/international/jan-june99/blair_doctrine4–23.html.
2 For an opposing view, see . Tesón 2005.
3 Before the post-election violence, Kenya used to be regarded as a "model" of stability in Africa.
4 Commentators refer to Burma and Myanmar interchangeably, as do I in this chapter. In 1989, the military government officially renamed the country the Union of Myanmar.
5 Based on a telephone interview I conducted with *Le Monde* correspondent, Natalie Nougayrède, 15 June 2009.
6 After the conflict, some commentators have compared Kosovo to Georgia, and argued that Russia used the "Kosovo precedent" to send tanks into Georgia, see e.g. Antonenko 2008. However, Russian Foreign Minister Sergei Lavrov described any

parallels between Kosovo and Georgia as "irrelevant," and suggested "the difference [was] … evident between Belgrade's policy towards Kosovo and how Saakashvili's regime behaved towards South Ossetia and Abkhazia," see Marguand 2008, *The Christian Science Monitor*. And yet, after Western recognition of Kosovar independence, Vladimir Putin suggested that Russian support for irredentism in South Ossetia would intensify, see Harding 2008.

7 The EU-sponsored report is also known as the "Tagliavini Report" because it was written by the Swiss diplomat Heidi Tagliavini.

8 When sector commanders learned of impending attacks, they had to request helicopter backup from El Fasher, and it could take up to two days for a helicopter to arrive. Such a delay was caused not only by distances, but also by the fact that civilian pilots could not be ordered to fly in dangerous circumstances. The helicopter had to be back in El Fasher before 6 p.m. because of the curfew that the government of Sudan imposed on AMIS in 2005, from 6 p.m. to 6 a.m. (Badescu and Bergholm 2009: 299).

9 Doctrine informs military institutions how to assess situations, and how to plan and implement operations (Giffen 2010: 12). As defined by NATO and the US Department of Defense, doctrine refers to "fundamental principles by which the military forces or elements thereof guide their actions in support of national objectives. It is authoritative but requires judgment in application." Training goals are developed from doctrine, which also leads to tactics, techniques and procedures. For more details, see Holt and Berkman (2006: 102–132).

10 The most widely used definition of protection is the International Committee of the Red Cross (ICRC) one. ICRC defines protection as "all activities aimed at ensuring full respect for the rights of the individual in accordance with the letter and the spirit of the relevant bodies of law, i.e. human rights law, international humanitarian law and refugee law" see http://www.icrc.org/eng. OCHA (UN) has also outlined aspects of civilian protection in its Aide Mémoire (UN 2002a).

11 Interview with a Senior UN Policy Adviser, DPKO, New York, August 2006.

12 The former implies providing protection to the citizens of another country whose own government put them at risk, while the latter was intertwined with the right of self-defense, thus referring to a state's prerogative to act when the state or its nationals are threatened.

13 An example in point is the much-delayed meeting the Group of Friends held to discuss the Secretary-General's report on R2P, which was released on 12 January 2009, with the meeting taking place two months after, on 10 March 2009.

14 The full report, entitled "World Public Opinion 2007," is available from: www.thechicagocouncil.org/UserFiles/File/POS_Topline%20Reports/POS%202007_Global%20Issues/WPO_07%20full%20report.pdf. The findings summarized in Chapter 3 of this report, on "Genocide and Darfur," are particularly relevant to this discussion.

15 Among other issues related to the US government's commitment to prevent genocide and mass atrocities, the 2010 National Security Strategy suggests that "in the event that prevention fails, the United States will work both multilaterally and bilaterally to mobilize diplomatic, humanitarian, financial, and – in certain instances – military means to prevent and respond to genocide and mass atrocities" (United States 2010: 48). This is a big step forward from the 2006 *National Security Strategy*, when the US declared that armed intervention may be required "…when perpetrators of mass killing defy all attempts at peaceful intervention" (United States 2006: 16–17).

16 Since these are extremely complex topics in themselves, doing them justice would require a separate study; here, however, I only introduce some of the key aspects related to potential reform for R2P implementation.

17 Phone interview with GCR2P staff in New York, 26 May 2010.

18 Phone interview with GCR2P staff in New York, 26 April 2010.

19 See the 2006 National Security Strategy, especially Chapter 4, "Working with Others to Defuse Regional Conflicts," (United States 2006: 16–17).

20 In the first five months of 2009, which were the last months of the thirty-year civil war between the Sri Lankan security forces and the Liberation Tigers of Tamil Eelam (LTTE) the scale and nature of violence against civilians in Sri Lanka worsened until the government's declared victory in May 2009.

Bibliography

Abbott, K. W. and Snidal, D. (2000) "Hard and Soft Law in International Governance," *International Organization*, vol. 54, no. 3: 421–456.

Acharya, A. (2002) "Redefining the Dilemmas of Humanitarian Intervention," *Australian Journal of International Affairs*, vol. 56, no. 3: 373–381.

——. (2004) "How Ideas Spread: Whose Norms Matter? Norm Localization and Institutional Change in Asian Regionalism," *International Organization*, vol. 58, no. 2: 239–275.

Adada, R. (2008) "The U.N. Is Making a Difference in Darfur," *The Wall Street Journal*, 25 June.

African Union (2002) The Constitutive Act of the African Union, Lome: African Union, 11 July.

——. (2005a) The Ezulwini Consensus: The Common African Position on the Proposed Reform of the United Nations, 7–8 March, AU Doc. Ext./EX.CL/2 (VIII).

——. (2005b) Roadmap for the Operationalization of the African Standby Force, Addis Ababa: African Union.

Akande, D. (2006) "The Application of International Law Immunities in Prosecutions for International Crimes," in J. Harrington, M. Milde and R. Vernon (eds) *Bringing Power to Justice: The Prospects of the International Criminal Court*, Montreal: McGill-Queen's University Press.

Alagappa, M. (1998) "Regional Arrangements, the UN, and International Security: A Framework for Analysis," in T. Weiss (ed.) *Beyond UN Subcontracting: Task-Sharing with Regional Security Arrangements and Service-Providing NGOs*, London: Macmillan Press Ltd.

Albright, M. and Cohen, W. S. (2008) *Preventing Genocide: The Report of the Genocide Prevention Task Force*, Washington, DC: USIP Press.

Alderson, K. (2000) "Beyond the Linguistic Analogy: Norm and Action in International Politics," Working Paper No. 3, Institute of International Relations, The University of British Columbia.

Amnus, D. (2006) "Swedish State Practice 2004–5: The Responsibility to Protect," *Nordic Journal of International Law*, vol. 75: 125–129.

Amstutz, M. R. (2005) *International Ethics: Concepts, Theories, and Cases in Global Politics*, 2nd edn, New York: Rowman & Littlefield Publishers.

Annan, K. (1999) "Two Concepts of Sovereignty," *The Economist*, 352, 18 September: 49–50.

——. (2000) "'We the Peoples': The Role of the UN in the 21st Century," A/54/2000, Millennium Report of the Secretary-General of the United Nations, 27 March.

——. (2002) "The Responsibility to Protect," Address of the UN Secretary-General to the International Peace Academy, 15 February.

——. (2005a) "In Larger Freedom: Towards Development, Security and Human Rights for All," Report of the Secretary General, United Nations: New York.

——. (2005b) "The UN Summit: A Glass At Least Half Full," *Jakarta Post*, 23 September.

——. (2006) "A Responsibility We All Share," 18 September.

——. (2009) "Opening Remarks to the Opening Plenary Session – Kenya National Dialogue: One Year Later," 30 March. Online. Available: http://allafrica.com/stories/200903301452.html (accessed 2 November 2009).

Antidze, M. (2008) "Georgia Says Sue Russia for Ethnic Cleansing," Reuters, 12 August.

Antonenko, O. (2008) "From Kosovo to South Ossetia: in Search of a Precedent," *The International Institute for Strategic Studies*, 19 August.

Applegarth, C. and Block, A. (2009) "Acting Against Atrocities: A Strategy for Supporters of the Responsibility to Protect," Discussion Paper #09–03, Belfer Center for Science and International Affairs, Harvard Kennedy School.

Asia-Pacific Centre for the Responsibility to Protect (2008) "Cyclone Nargis and the Responsibility to Protect: Myanmar/Burma," Briefing no. 2, 16 May.

Aust, A. (2005) *Handbook of International Law*, Cambridge: Cambridge University Press.

Ayoob, M. (2002) "Humanitarian Intervention and State Sovereignty," *The International Journal of Human Rights*, vol. 6, no. 1: 81–102.

——. (2004) "Third World Perspectives on Humanitarian Intervention and International Administration," *Global Governance*, vol. 10: 99–118.

Badescu, C. G. (2007) "Authorizing Humanitarian Intervention: Hard Choices in Saving Strangers," *Canadian Journal of Political Science*, vol. 40, no. 1: 51–78.

——. (2009) "'The Responsibility to Protect': Embracing Sovereignty *and* Human Rights," in N. Shawki and M. Cox (eds) *Negotiating Sovereignty and Human Rights: Actors and Issues in Contemporary Human Rights Politics*, Farnham: Ashgate.

Badescu, C. G. and Bergholm, L. (2009) "The Responsibility to Protect and the Conflict in Darfur: The Big Let-down," *Security Dialogue*, vol. 40, issue 3.

Badescu, C. G. and Bergholm, L. (2010) "The African Union," in D. Black and P. D. Williams (eds) *The International Politics of Mass Atrocities: The Case of Darfur*, London: Routledge.

Badescu, C. G. and Weiss, T. G. (2010) "Misrepresenting R2P and Advancing Norms: An Alternative Spiral?" *International Studies Perspectives*, vol. 11, issue 4.

Ban, K. (2008) "On Responsible Sovereignty: International Cooperation for a Changed World," speech, Berlin, SG/SM/11701, 15 July 2008.

Barkin, S. (1998) "The Evolution of the Constitution of Sovereignty and the Emergence of Human Rights Norms," *Millennium*, vol. 27, no. 2: 229–252.

Bass, G. (2008) *Freedom's Battle: the Origins of Humanitarian Intervention*, New York: Alfred A. Knopf.

BBC News (2004) "EU Approves Rapid Reaction Force," 23 November.

——. (2006) "Profile: Kofi Annan," 2 October. Available from: http://news.bbc.co.uk/2/hi/americas/1411047.stm (accessed 5 October 2009).

——. (2008a) "Fears Burma Storm Toll Could Soar," 7 May.

——. (2008b) "World Wrestles with Burma Aid Issue," 9 May.

——. (2008c) "Interview with Sergei Lavrov," 9 August.

——. (2009) "Regions and Territories: South Ossetia," 13 May.

Beitz, C. R. (2002) "Human Rights as A Common Concern," *American Political Science Review*, vol. 95, no. 2: 269–282.

Bellamy, A. (2005) "Responsibility to Protect or Trojan Horse? The Crisis in Darfur and Humanitarian Intervention after Iraq," *Ethics and International Affairs*, vol. 19, no. 2: 31–53.

——. (2006) "Whither the Responsibility to Protect? Humanitarian Intervention and the 2005 World Summit," *Ethics and International Affairs*, vol. 20, no. 2: 143–169.

——. (2009) *Responsibility to Protect: The Global Effort to End Mass Atrocities*, Cambridge: Polity.

Bellamy, A. and Williams, P. (2005) "Who's Keeping the Peace? Regionalization and Contemporary Peace Operations," *International Security*, vol. 29, issue 4: 157–195.

Beyrer, C. and Genser, J. (2008) "Burma's Next Wave of Dying," *Boston Globe*, 21 May.

Bielefeldt, H. (2000) " 'Western' versus 'Islamic' Human Rights Conceptions? A Critique of Cultural Essentialism in the Discussion on Human Rights," *Political Theory*, vol. 28, no. 1: 90–121.

Blanchfield, M. (2006) "Harper Leaps into the Foreign Policy Pond," *CanWest News Service*, 16 September.

Booth, K. (1999) "Three Tyrannies," in T. Dunne and Nicholas Wheeler (eds), *Human Rights in Global Politics*, Cambridge: Cambridge University Press.

Brahimi, L. (2006) "United Nations Peace Operations in the 21st Century: A Few Personal Thoughts," in H. Ojanen (ed.) *Peacekeeping – Peacebuilding: Preparing for the Future*, FIIA Report 14, Helsinki: The Finnish Institute of International Affairs.

Brock, G. (2006) "Humanitarian Intervention: Closing the Gap Between Theory and Practice, *Journal of Applied Philosophy*, vol. 23, no. 3: 277–291.

Brockmann, M. d'E. (2009) "Statement by the President of the General Assembly, Miguel d'Escoto Brockmann, at the Opening of the 97th Session of the General Assembly," 23 July.

Brown, C. (1999) "Universal Human Rights: A Critique," in T. Dunne and N. Wheeler (eds) *Human Rights in Global Politics*, Cambridge: Cambridge University Press.

——. (2002) *Sovereignty, Rights and Justice: International Political Theory Today*, Cambridge: Polity Press.

Brunnée, J. (2007) "International Law and Collective Concerns: Reflections on the Responsibility to Protect," in T. M. Ndiaye and R. Wolfrum (eds), *Law of the Sea, Environmental Law and Settlement of Disputes*: Leiden: Martinus Nijhoff: 35–51.

Brunnée, J. and Toope, S. J. (2006) "Norms, Institutions and UN Reform: The Responsibility to Protect," *Behind the Headlines*, vol. 63, no. 3.

——. (2010) "The Responsibility to Protect and the Use of Force: Building Legality?" *Global Responsibility to Protect*, vol. 2: 191–212.

Buchanan, A. (1999) "The Internal Legitimacy of Humanitarian Intervention," *Journal of Political Philosophy*, vol. 7, no. 1: 71–87.

——. (2003) "Reforming the International Law of Humanitarian Intervention," in J. L. Holzgrefe and R. Keohane (eds) *Humanitarian Intervention: Ethical, Legal and Political Dilemmas*, Cambridge: Cambridge University Press.

——. (2004) *Justice, Legitimacy, and Self-determination: Moral Foundations for International Law*, Oxford: Oxford University Press.

Bull, H. (1977) *The Anarchical Society: A Study of Order in World Politics*, London: Macmillan.

——. (1984) *Intervention in World Politics*, Oxford: Clarendon Press.

Byers, M. and Chesterman, S. (2003) "Changing the Rules about Rules," in J. L. Holzgrefe and R. Keohane (eds) *Humanitarian Intervention: Ethical, Legal and Political Dilemmas*, Cambridge: Cambridge University Press.

Byers, M. (2005) "High Ground Lost on UN's Responsibility to Protect," *Winnipeg Free Press*, 18 September.

Caney, S. (2005) *Justice Beyond Borders: A Global Political Theory*, Oxford: Oxford University Press.

Carr Center Project Report (2005) "Measurement and Human Rights: Tracking Progress, Assessing Impact," Proceedings of the Conference "Measuring Impact in Human Rights: How Far Have We Come, and How Far to Go?," Harvard University, 5–7 May.

Cassese, A. (1999) "Ex iniuria ius oritur: Are We Moving towards International Legitimation of Forcible Humanitarian Countermeasures in the World Community?" *European Journal of International* Law, vol. 10: 23–30.

Center for International Cooperation (2009) *Global Peace Operations 2009*, Boulder: Lynne Rienner.

Challenges Project, The (2005) *Meeting the Challenges of Peace Operations: Cooperation and Coordination*, Stockholm: Elanders Gotab.

Chandler, D. (2002) *From Kosovo to Kabul: Human Rights and International Intervention*, London: Pluto Press.

——. (2006) *From Kosovo to Kabul and Beyond: Human Rights and International Intervention*, London: Pluto Press.

——. (2010) "R2P or Not R2P? More Statebuilding, Less Responsibility," *Global Responsibility to Protect*, vol. 2, nos 1–2: 161–166.

Chatterjee, D. and Scheid D. (eds) (2003) *Ethics and Foreign Intervention*, Cambridge: Cambridge University Press.

Checkel, J. T. (2001) "Why Comply? Social Learning and European Identity Change," *International Organization*, vol. 55, no. 4: 553–588.

Chesterman, S. (2001) *Just Wars or Just Peace: Humanitarian Intervention and International Law*, Oxford: Oxford University Press.

——. (2003) "Hard Cases Make Bad Law: Law, Ethics and Politics in Humanitarian Intervention," in A. F. Lang Jr (ed.) *Just Intervention*, Washington DC: Georgetown University Press.

——. (2004) "Humanitarian Intervention and Afghanistan," in J. Welsh (ed.) *Humanitarian Intervention and International Relations*, Oxford: Oxford University Press.

——. (2006) "Kofi Annan's Legacy: UN Reform at the End of Kofi's Term," *Embassy*, 6 September.

Chimni, B. S. (2002) "A New Humanitarian Council for Humanitarian Interventions?," *The International Journal of Human Rights*, vol. 6, no. 1: 103–112.

Chopra, J. and Weiss T. G. (1992) "Sovereignty is no Longer Sacrosanct: Codifying Humanitarian Intervention," *Ethics and International Affairs*, vol. 6: 95–118.

Claude Jr, I. L. (1966) "Collective Legitimization as a Political Function of the United Nations," *International Organization*, vol. 20, no. 3: 367–379.

——. (1971) *Swords into Plowshares: The Problems and Progress of International Organizations*, New York: Random House.

Cohen, J. L. (2004) "Whose Sovereignty? Empire versus International Law," *Ethics & International Affairs*, vol. 18, no. 3: 1–24.

Cohen, R. (1991) *Human Rights Protection for Internally Displaced Persons*, Washington, DC: Refugee Policy Group.

——. (2009) "The Burma Cyclone and the Responsibility to Protect," *Global Responsibility to Protect*, vol. 1, no. 2: 253–257.

Cohen, R. and O'Neill, W. (2006) "Last Stand in Sudan?" *Bulletin of the Atomic Scientists*, March/April.
Collier, P. and Hoeffler, A. (2004) "The Challenge of Reducing the Global Incidence of Civil War," Centre for the Study of African Economies, Department of Economics, Oxford University, 26 March.
Cortell, A. and Davis, J. (1996) "How Do International Institutions Matter? The Domestic Impact of International Rules and Norms," *International Studies Quarterly*, vol. 40: 451–478.
Council on Foreign Relations (CFR) (2006) Transcript: Interview with Jean-Marie Guéhenno. "Key Challenges in Today's UN Peacekeeping Operations," Federal News Service, 18 May.
Crawford, N. (2002) *Argument and Change in World Politics: Ethics, Decolonization and Humanitarian Intervention*, Cambridge: Cambridge University Press.
Daalder, I. and Goldgeier, J. (2006) "Global NATO," *Foreign Affairs*, September/October.
Daalder, I. and Stares, P. (2008) "The UN's Responsibility to Protect," *International Herald Tribune*, 13 May.
Davis, J. (2009) "Liberal-Era Language Killed Off," *Embassy*, 1 July.
de Coning, C. (2006) "The Future of Peacekeeping in Africa," in H. Ojanen (ed.) *Peacekeeping – Peacebuilding: Preparing for the Future*, FIIA Report 14, Helsinki: The Finnish Institute of International Affairs (FIIA).
Deleroz, A. (2008) "Russia-Georgia: The International Crisis Group Aftermath," *International Crisis Group*, Parliamentary Brief, 10 November.
Deng, F. M. (1993) *Protecting the Dispossessed: A Challenge for the International Community*, Washington, DC: Brookings Institution.
——. (1995) "Frontiers of Sovereignty," *Leiden Journal of International Law*, vol. 8, no. 2: 249–286.
Deng, F. M. and Zartman, I. W. (eds) (1991) *Conflict Resolution in Africa*, Washington DC: Brookings Institution.
Deng, F. M., Kimaro, S., Lyons, T., Rothchild, D. and Zartman, I. W. (1996) *Sovereignty as Responsibility: Conflict Management in Africa*, Washington DC: Brookings Institution.
de Waal, A. (2004) "Counter-insurgency on the Cheap," *London Review of Books*, vol. 26.
——. (2007) "Darfur and the Failure of the Responsibility To Protect," *International Affairs*, vol. 83, no. 6: 1039–1054.
de Waal, A. and Flint, J. (2006) *Darfur: A Short History of a Long War*, London: Zed.
de Wet, E. (2004) *The Chapter VII Powers of the United Nations Security Council*, Oxford: Hart Publishing.
Diehl, P. (ed.) (1997) *Global Governance*, Boulder: Lynne Rienner Publishers.
——. (2008) *Peace Operations*, Cambridge: Polity.
Donnelly, J. (2003) *Universal Human Rights in Theory and Practice*, 2nd edn, Ithaca: Cornell University Press.
Durch, W. J. (ed.) (2006) *Twenty-first Century Peace Operations*, Washington, DC: United States Institute of Peace Press.
Durch, W., Holt, V., Earle, C. and Shanahan, M. (2003) *The Brahimi Report and the Future of Peace Operations*, Washington, DC: The Henry Stimson Center.
Earle, C. (2004) *European Capacities for Peace Operations: Taking Stock*, Washington, DC: The Henry Stimson Center, March.

Economic Community of West African States (ECOWAS) (1999) *Protocol Relating to the Mechanism for Conflict Prevention, Management, Resolution, Peacekeeping and Security*, Lome: ECOWAS.

Economist (2009) "An Idea whose Time Has Come—and Gone?" 23 July.

Etzioni, A. (2006) "Sovereignty as Responsibility," *Orbis*, vol. 50, no. 1: 71–85.

Evans, G. (2004) "When Is It Right to Fight? Legality, Legitimacy and the Use of Military Force," Cyril Foster Lecture, Oxford University.

——. (2006) "Crimes Against Humanity: Overcoming Global Indifference," B'Nai B'Rith Anti-Defamation Commission, University of New South Wales, Sydney, 30 April.

——. (2008a) *The Responsibility to Protect: Ending Mass Atrocity Crimes Once and For All*, Washington, DC: Brookings Institutions.

——. (2008b) "Facing Up to Our Responsibilities," *Guardian*, 12 May.

——. (2009) "Statement to United Nations General Assembly Informal Interactive Dialogue on the Responsibility to Protect," New York, 23 July. Online. Available at: www.un.org/ga/president/63/interactive/protect/evans.pdf (accessed 3 September 2009).

Evans, G. and Sahnoun, M. (2002) "The Responsibility to Protect," *Foreign Affairs*, vol. 81, no. 6: 99–110.

Falk, Richard A. (1993) "Intervention Revisited: Hard Choices and Tragic Dilemmas," *The Nation*, vol. 21, no. 257: 755–764.

——. (2000) *Human Rights Horizons: The Pursuit of Justice in a Globalizing World*, New York: Routledge.

Farer, T. J. (1993) "A Paradigm of Legitimate Intervention," in L. Fisler Damrosch (ed.) *Enforcing Restraint: Collective Intervention in Internal Conflict*, New York: Council on Foreign Relations Press.

——. (2002) "Beyond the Charter Frame: Unilateralism or Condominium?" *American Journal of International Law*, vol. 96, no. 2.

——. (2003) "Humanitarian Intervention Before and After 9/11: Legality and Legitimacy," in J. L. Holzgrefe and R. Keohane (eds) *Humanitarian Intervention: Ethical, Legal and Political Dilemmas*, Cambridge: Cambridge University Press.

Feinstein, L. (2007) "Darfur and Beyond: What is Needed to Prevent Mass Atrocities," Council on Foreign Relations, CFR Paper No. 22, January.

Feinstein, L. and Slaughter, A. (2004) "The Duty to Prevent," *Foreign Affairs*, vol. 83, no. 1: 136–150.

Feinstein, L., Ku, C. and Fischer, J. (2006) "Roundtable: Old Rules, New Threats," Council on Foreign Relations and The American Society of International Law, 4 May.

Finnemore, M. (1996) "Constructing Norms of Humanitarian Intervention," in P. Katzenstein (ed.) *The Culture of National Security: Norms and Identity in World Politics*, New York: Columbia University Press.

Finnemore, M. and Sikkink, K. (1998) "International Norm Dynamics and Political Change," *International Organization*, vol. 52, no. 4: 887–917.

Flinterman C. and Gutter J. (2000) *The United Nations and Human Rights: Achievements and Challenges*, United Nations Development Programme (UNDP), New York, Paper No. 48: 1–26.

Florini, A. (1996) "The Evolution of International Norms," *International Studies Quarterly*, vol. 40, no. 3: 363–389.

Franck, T. (1999) "Lessons of Kosovo," *American Journal of International Law*, vol. 93.

——. (2003) "Interpretation and Change in the Law of Humanitarian Intervention," in J.

L. Holzgrefe and R. Keohane (eds) *Humanitarian Intervention: Ethical, Legal and Political Dilemmas*, Cambridge: Cambridge University Press.

Gardam, J. (2004) *Necessity, Proportionality and the Use of Force by States*, Cambridge: Cambridge University Press.

Giffen, A. (2010) "Addressing the Doctrinal Deficit: Developing Guidance to Prevent and Respond to Widespread or Systematic Attacks Against Civilians," Report from the International Experts Workshop 21–24 September 2009, Washington, DC: The Stimson Center.

Global Centre for the Responsibility to Protect (GCR2P) (2009a) "Open Letter to the Security Council on the Situation in Sri Lanka," April.

——. (2009b) "Implementing the Responsibility to Protect, The 2009 General Assembly Debate: An Assessment," August.

——. (2009c) "The Responsibility to Protect: the Next Five Years," Themes from Ministerial Roundtable Discussion, September.

——. (2009d) "Reflections on the UN General Assembly Debate on Responsibility to Protect," Meeting Summary, October.

——. (2009e) "Summary of Statements on Adoption of Resolution RES A/63/L80 Rev 1 September 2009."

Goodman, R. and Jinks, D. (2003) "Measuring the Effects of Human Rights Treaties," *European Journal of International Law*, vol. 14, issue 1: 171–183.

Gray, C. (2004) *International Law and the Use of Force*, 2nd edn, Oxford: Oxford University Press.

——. (2005) "Peacekeeping and Enforcement Action in Africa: The Role of Europe and the Obligations of Multilateralism," *Review of International Studies*, vol. 31: 207–233.

Greenwood, C. (2005) "International Law and the NATO Intervention in Kosovo," *International and Comparative Law Quarterly*, vol. 49, no. 4: 926–934.

Grono, N. (2005) "Darfur: The International Community's Failure to Protect," International Crisis Group, 29 November.

Guardian (2004) "Full text: Tony Blair's Speech," 5 March.

Hamilton, R. J. (2006) "The Responsibility to Protect: From Document to Doctrine – But What of Implementation?," *Harvard Human Rights Journal*, vol. 19: 289–297.

Hanson, S. (2006) "The AU's Responsibility to Protect," *Council on Foreign Relations*, 6 October.

Harding, L. (2008) "Kosovo Breakaway Illegal, Says Putin," *Guardian*, 15 February.

Hathaway, O. (2002) "Do Human Rights Treaties Make a Difference?," *Yale Law Journal*, vol. 111: 1935–2042.

Hehir, B. (1998) "Military Intervention and National Sovereignty: Recasting the Relationship," in J. Moore (ed.) *Hard Choices: Moral Dilemmas in Humanitarian Intervention*, Oxford: Rowman & Littlefield Publishers.

Heinze, E. (2004a) "Reconciling Approaches to Enquiry in the Humanitarian Intervention Debate," *International Journal of Human Rights*, vol. 8, no. 3: 367–376.

——. (2004b) "The Moral Limits of Humanitarian Intervention: Reconciling Human Respect and Utility," *Polity*, vol. 36, no. 4: 543–559.

——. (2009) *Waging Humanitarian War: The Ethics, Law, and Politics of Humanitarian Intervention*, Albany: State University of New York Press.

Higgins, R. (1999) "The Continuing Universality of the Universal Declaration," in P. Baehr, C. Flinterman and M. Senders (eds) *Innovation and Inspiration: Fifty Years of the Universal Declaration of Human Rights*, Amsterdam: Royal Netherlands Academy of Arts and Science: 17–26.

Hoagland, J. (2008) "In Burma: A Price for 'Stability'," *Washington Post*, 18 May.

Hoffman, S. (1992) "Delusions of World Order," *The New York Review of Books*, vol. 39, no. 7, 9 April.

——. (1996) *The Ethics and Politics of Humanitarian Intervention*, Notre Dame: University of Notre Dame Press.

Hoffman, P. and Weiss, T. (2006) *Sword and Salve: Confronting New Wars and Humanitarian Crises*, New York: Rowman and Littlefield Publishers.

Holt, V. K. (2005) *The Responsibility to Protect: Considering the Operational Capacity for Civilian Protection*, Washington, DC: The Henry L. Stimson Center.

——. (2006) "The Military and Civilian Protection: Developing Roles and Capacities," Humanitarian Policy Group Briefing Paper, 22 March: 1–4.

——. (2008) *Halting Widespread or Systematic Attacks on Civilians: Military Strategies and Operational Concepts*, Washington, DC: The Henry L. Stimson Center.

Holt, V. K. and Berkman, T. (2006) *The Impossible Mandate? Military Preparedness, the Responsibility to Protect and Modern Peace Operations*, Washington, DC: The Henry L. Stimson Center.

Holt, V. K. and Shanahan, M. K. (2005) *African Capacity-Building for Peace Operations: UN Collaboration with the African Union and ECOWAS*, 2nd edn, Washington, DC: The Henry Stimson Center.

Holt, V. K., Taylor, G., with Kelly, M. (2009) *Protecting Civilians in the Context of UN Peacekeeping Operations: Successes, Setbacks, and Remaining Challenges*, New York: United Nations.

Holzgrefe, J. L. (2003) "The Humanitarian Intervention Debate," in J. L. Holzgrefe and R. Keohane (eds) *Humanitarian Intervention: Ethical, Legal and Political Dilemmas*, Cambridge: Cambridge University Press.

Howard, L. M. (2008) *UN Peacekeeping in Civil Wars*, Cambridge: Cambridge University Press.

Howard-Hassmann, R. (2005) "The Second Great Transformation: Human Rights Leapfrogging in the Era of Globalizations," *Human Rights Quarterly*, vol. 27, no. 1: 1–40.

Human Rights Watch (2008) *Ballots to Bullets: Organized Political Violence and Kenya's Crisis of Governance*, vol. 20, no. 1 (A), March.

Huntington, S. P. (1996) *The Clash of Civilizations and the Remaking of World Order*, New York: Simon & Schuster.

Independent International Commission on Kosovo (2000) *Kosovo Report: Conflict, International Response, Lessons Learned*, Oxford: Oxford University Press.

Independent International Fact-Finding Mission on the Conflict in Georgia (2009) Report of the Independent International Fact-Finding Mission on the Conflict in Georgia, September. Also known as the "Tagliavini Report," Volume I, II, and III. Online. Available: http://91.121.127.28/ceiig/Report.html (accessed 30 October 2009).

International Commission on Intervention and State Sovereignty (ICISS) (2001) "The Responsibility to Protect," Report of the International Commission on Intervention and State Sovereignty. Ottawa: International Development Research Centre.

International Crisis Group (ICG) (2009) "China's Growing Role in UN Peacekeeping," Asia Report No. 166, 17 April.

——. (2010) "War Crimes in Sri Lanka," Asia Report No. 191, 17 May.

International Herald Tribune, The (2008a) "Myanmar Faces Pressure to Allow Major Aid Effort," 7 May.

——. (2008b) "France Urges UN to Force Cyclone Aid on Myanmar," 7 May.

International Monetary Fund (IMF) (2005) "Zimbabwe: Selected Issues and Statistical Appendix," Staff Country Report No. 05/359, 4 August.

Jackson, R. (1990) *Quasi-states: Sovereignty, International Relations and the Third World*, Cambridge: Cambridge University Press.

——. (1993) "Armed Humanitarianism," *International Journal*, vol. XLVIII, no. 4: 580–606.

——. (2000) *The Global Covenant: Human Conduct in a World of States*, Oxford: Oxford University Press.

——. (2004) "Sovereignty as a Doctrine of Moderation," in C. J. Nolan (ed.) *Power and Responsibility in World Affairs: Reformation versus Transformation*, Westport: Praeger Publishers.

Job, B. (2004) "The UN, Regional Organizations, and Regional Conflict: Is There a Viable Role for the UN?" in R. Price and M. Zacher (eds) *The United Nations and Global Security*, New York: Palgrave Macmillan.

Johnstone, I. and Bah, A. (2007) "Peacekeeping in Sudan: The Dynamics of Protection, Partnerships and Inclusive Politics," Occasional Paper, New York: Center on International Cooperation.

Karns, M. P. and Mingst, K. A. (2004) *International Organizations: The Politics and Processes of Global Governance*, London: Lynne Rienner Publishers.

Kausikan, B. (1993) "Asia's Different Standard," *Foreign Policy*, vol. 92: 24–41.

Keck, M. and Sikkink, K. (1998) *Activists beyond Borders: Advocacy Networks in International Politics*, Ithaca: Cornell University Press.

Kendall, B. (2008) "Russia Actions Confound Allies," BBC News, 12 August.

Krasner, S. D. (1999) *Sovereignty: Organized Hypocrisy*, Princeton: Princeton University Press.

——. (2001) "Problematic Sovereignty," in S. D. Krasner (ed.) *Problematic Sovereignty: Contested Rules and Political Possibilities*, New York: Columbia University Press.

——. (2004) "Sharing Sovereignty: New Institutions for Collapsed and Failed States," *International Security*, vol. 29, no. 2: 85–120.

Kratochwil, F. (1989) *Rules, Norms, and Decisions: On the Conditions of Practical and Legal Reasoning in International Relations and Domestic Affairs*, New York: Cambridge University Press.

Ku, C. and Diehl, P. F. (2006) "Filling in the Gaps: Extrasystemic Mechanisms for Addressing Imbalances Between the International Legal Operating System and the Normative System," *Global Governance*, vol. 12, no. 2: 161–185.

Kuperman, A. (2004) "Humanitarian Hazard: Revisiting Doctrines of Intervention," *Harvard International Review*, vol. XXVI, no. 1.

——. (2008) "The Moral Hazard of Humanitarian Intervention: Lessons from the Balkans," *International Studies Quarterly*, vol. 52: 49–80.

Laberge, P. (1995) "Humanitarian Intervention: Three Ethical Positions," *Ethics & International Affairs*, vol. 9: 15–35.

Landman, T. (2005) *Protecting Human Rights: A Comparative Study*, Washington DC: Georgetown University Press.

Lang Jr, A. F. (ed.) (2003a) *Just Intervention*, Washington, DC: Georgetown University Press.

Luck, E. (2010) "A Response," *Global Responsibility to Protect*, vol. 2, nos 1–2: 178–183.

MacFarlane, N., Welsh J. and Thielking, C. (2002) "The Responsibility to Protect: Assessing the Report of the International Commission on Intervention and State Sovereignty," *International Journal*, vol. 57, no. 4: 489–502.

Mack, A. (2005) *The Human Security Report 2005*, Oxford: Oxford University Press.

Makinda, S. M. (1996) "Sovereignty and International Security: Challenges for the United Nations," *Global Governance*, vol. 2, no 2.

——. (2002) "The Global Covenant as an Evolving Institution," *The International Journal of Human Rights*, vol. 6, no. 1: 113–126.

Malone, D. (2003) "Humanitarian Intervention: Ethical, Legal and Political Dilemmas," *The American Journal of International Law*, vol. 97, no. 4 (October): 999–1002.

——. (2004) "Debating Sovereignty and Intervention," *The Australian Journal of Political Science*, vol. 39, no. 2 (July): 430–436.

Marguand, R. (2008) "Russia's Case on Georgia Territories: Like Kosovo or Not?," *The Christian Science Monitor*, 28 August.

Marshall, J. E. (2009) "Building an Effective African Standby Force to Promote African Stability, Conflict Resolution and Prosperity," Discussion Paper 16, London: Crisis States Research Centre, London School of Economics, April.

Mass Atrocity Response Operations (MARO) (2010) *Mass Atrocity Response Operations: A Military Planning Handbook*, The Harvard Kennedy School of Government Carr Center for Human Rights Policy and US Army Peacekeeping and Stability Operations Institute.

Melander, E. (2009) "Selected to Go Where Murderers Lurk? The Preventive Effect of Peacekeeping on Mass Killings of Civilians," *Conflict Management and Peace Science*, vol. 26, no. 4: 389–406.

Mepham, D. (2006) "Darfur and 'The Responsibility to Protect'," *Open Democracy*, 12 September.

Mepham, D. and Ramsbotham, A. (eds) (2006) *Darfur: The Responsibility to Protect*, London: IPPR.

Meron, T. (2006) *The Humanization of International Law*, Boston: Martinus Nijhoff Publishers.

Mills, K. (1998) *Human Rights in the Emerging Global Order: A New Sovereignty?*, London: Macmillan.

Montreal Institute for Genocide and Human Rights Studies (2009) *Mobilizing the Will to Intervene: Leadership and Action to Prevent Mass Atrocities*, Montreal: Montreal Institute for Genocide and Human Rights Studies, Concordia University.

Morgenthau, H. J. (1948) *Politics Among Nations: the Struggle for Power and Peace*, New York: Alfred Knopf (1973 edn).

Nagan, W. P. and Hammer, C. (2003) "The Changing Character of Sovereignty in International Law and International Relations," Levin College of Law, University of Florida, article based upon a public lecture given by W. Nagan at the University of Asmara, Eritrea, 8 March.

Nardin, T. (2003) "The Moral Basis for Humanitarian Intervention," in A. F. Lang Jr (ed.) *Just Intervention*, Washington, DC: Georgetown University Press.

——. (2005) "Response to Ending Tyranny in Iraq," *Ethics & International Affairs*, vol. 19, no. 2: 21–26.

Neumayer, E. (2005) "Do International Human Rights Treaties Improve Respect for Human Rights?" *Journal of Conflict Resolution*, vol. 49, no. 6: 925–953.

New York Times (2008a) "More Shame on the Junta," 21 May.

——. (2008b) "Myanmar Faces Pressure to Allow Major Aid Effort," 8 May.

Nougayrède, N., Bolopion P. and Ferenczi, T. (2008) "Birmanie: Vif Débat sur la 'Responsabilité de Protéger'," *Le Monde*, 15 May.

O'Hanlon, M. (2003) *Expanding Global Military Capacity for Humanitarian Intervention*, Washington, DC: Brookings Institution.

Olonisakin, F. and Ero, C. (2003) "Africa and the Regionalization of Peace Operations," in M. Pugh and W. P. S. Sidhu (eds) *The United Nations and Regional Security: Europe and Beyond*, London: Lynne Rienner Publishers.
Onuf, N. G. (1989) *World of Our Making: Rules and Rule in Social Theory and International Relations*, Columbia: University of South Carolina Press.
Oxfam International (2008) *For a Safer Tomorrow: Protecting Civilians in a Multipolar World*, Oxford: Oxfam International.
Pace, W. and Deller, N. (2005) "Preventing Future Genocides: An International Responsibility to Protect," *World Order*, vol. 36, no. 4: 15–32.
Page Fortna, V. (2004) "Does Peacekeeping Keep Peace? International Intervention and the Duration of Peace after Civil War," *International Studies Quarterly*, vol. 48: 269–292.
Pattison, J. (2008) "Legitimacy and Humanitarian Intervention: Who Should Intervene?" *The International Journal of Human Rights*, vol. 12, issue 3: 395–413.
Pawlowska, K. (2005) "Humanitarian Intervention: Transforming the Discourse," *International Peacekeeping*, vol. 12, no. 4: 487–502.
Philpott, D. (1995) "Sovereignty: An Introduction and Brief History (Transcending National Boundaries)," *Journal of International Affairs*, vol. 48, no. 2: 353–368.
——. (2001) *Revolutions in Sovereignty: How Ideas Shaped Modern International Relations*, Princeton: Princeton University Press.
Price, R. M. (2004) "The League of Nations Redux?" in R. Price and M. Zacher (eds) *The United Nations and Global Security*, New York: Palgrave Macmillan.
Prunier, G. (2007) *Darfur: The Ambiguous Genocide?*, revised edn, Ithaca: Cornell.
Raymond, G. (1997) "Problems and Prospects in the Study of International Norms," *Mershon International Studies Review*, vol. 41: 205–245.
Reus-Smit, C. (2001) "Human Rights and the Social Construction of Sovereignty," *Review of International Studies*, vol. 27: 519–538.
——. (2005) "Liberal Hierarchy and the License to Use Force," *Review of International Studies*, vol. 31: 71–92.
Reuters (2008) "Russian NATO Envoy sees 'Genocide' in South Ossetia," 9 August.
Riddell-Dixon, E. (2005) "Canada's Human Security Agenda: Walking the Talk?" *International Journal*, vol. LX, no. 4: 1067–1092.
Rieff, D. (2008) "A False Compatibility: Humanitarian Action and Human Rights," *Humanitarian Stakes Number 1*, MSF Switzerland, September.
Risse, T. (2000) "Let's Argue! Communicative Action in World Politics," *International Organization*, vol. 54, no. 1: 1–39.
Risse, T. and Sikkink, K. (1999) "The Socialization of International Human Rights Norms into Domestic Practices: Introduction," in T. Risse, S. Ropp and K. Sikkink (eds) *The Power of Human Rights: International Norms and Domestic Change*, Cambridge: Cambridge University Press: 1–38.
Risse, T., Ropp, S. and Sikkink, K. (eds) (1999) *The Power of Human Rights: International Norms and Domestic Change*, Cambridge: Cambridge University Press.
Roberts, A. (1999) "NATO's Humanitarian War Over Kosovo," *Survival*, vol. 41, no. 3.
——. (2004) "The United Nations and Humanitarian Intervention," in J. Welsh (ed.) *Humanitarian Intervention and International Relations*, Oxford: Oxford University Press.
Robertson, G. (2000) *Crimes Against Humanity: The Struggle for Global Justice*, London: Penguin.
Roche, D. (2003) *The Human Right to Peace*. Toronto: Novalis.

Rochester, M. (2006) *Between Peril and Promise: The Politics of International Law*, Washington DC: Congressional Quarterly Press.

Roth, K. (2004) "Setting the Standard: Justifying Humanitarian Intervention," *Harvard International Review*, vol. XXVI, no. 1: 58–62.

Saideman, S. M. (2001) *The Ties That Divide*, New York: Columbia University Press.

Security Council Report (2006) "Twenty Days in August: The Security Council Sets Massive New Challenges for UN Peacekeeping," September.

Security Council Report (2008) "September 2008 Sudan," August.

Sen, A. (1997) "Human Rights and Asian Values," Sixteenth Morgenthau Memorial Lecture on Ethnics and Foreign Policy, Carnegie Council on Ethics and International Affairs: 1–32.

Serrano, M. (2010) "Implementing the Responsibility to Protect: The Power of R2P Talk," *Global Responsibility to Protect*, vol. 2, nos 1–2: 167–177.

Seybolt, T. (2007) *Humanitarian Military Intervention: The Conditions for Success and Failure*, Oxford: Oxford University Press.

Sharma, S. K. (2010) "Review Essay: Toward a Global Responsibility to Protect: Setbacks on the Path to Implementation," *Global Governance*, vol. 16, no. 1:121–138.

Shelton, D. (2006) "Normative Hierarchy in International Law," *American Journal of International Law*, vol. 100, no. 2: 291–323.

Shue, H. (1996) *Basic Rights: Subsistence, Affluence, and US Foreign Policy*, 2nd edn, Princeton: Princeton University Press.

——. (1998) "Let Whatever is Smouldering Erupt? Conditional Sovereignty, Reviewable Intervention, and Rwanda 1994," in A. Paolini, A. P. Jarvis and C. Reus-Smit (eds) *Between Sovereignty and Global Governance: The United Nations, the State and Civil Society*, New York: Macmillan Press Ltd.

——. (2004) "Limiting Sovereignty," in J. Welsh (ed.) *Humanitarian Intervention and International Relations*, Oxford: Oxford University Press.

Slaughter, A-M. (2005) "Security, Solidarity and Sovereignty: The Grand Themes of UN Reform," *The American Journal of International Law*, vol. 99, no. 3: 619–631.

Slim, H. (2010) "Values versus Power: Responsible Sovereignty as Struggle in Zimbabwe," *Global Responsibility to Protect*, vol. 2, nos 1–2: 155–160.

Slomanson, W. R. (2007) *Fundamental Perspectives on International Law*, 5th edn, Belmont: Thomson Wadsworth.

Smith, E. and Weiss, T. G. (1998) "UN Task-Sharing: Toward or Away from Global Governance?" in T. G. Weiss (ed.) *Beyond UN Subcontracting: Task Sharing with Regional Security Arrangements and Service-Providing NGOs*, London: Macmillan Press Ltd.

Stahn, C. (2007) "Responsibility to Protect: Political Rhetoric or Emerging Legal Norm?" *The American Journal of International Law*, vol. 101, no. 1: 99–120.

Steinberg, D. (2009) "Responsibility to Protect: Coming of Age?" *Global Responsibility to Protect*, vol. 1, no. 4: 432–441.

Strauss, E. (2009a) "A Bird in Hand is Worth Two in the Bush – On the Assumed Legal Nature of the Responsibility to Protect," *Global Responsibility to Protect*, vol. 1, no. 3: 291–323.

——. (2009b) *The Emperor's New Clothes? The United Nations and the Implementation of the Responsibility to Protect*, Baden: Nomos.

Stromseth, J. (2003) "Rethinking Humanitarian Intervention: The Case for Incremental Change," in J. L. Holzgrefe and R. Keohane (eds) *Humanitarian Intervention: Ethical, Legal and Political Dilemmas*, Cambridge: Cambridge University Press.

Sunstein, C. R. (1997) *Free Markets and Social Justice*, New York: Oxford University Press.

Taft, P. and Ladnier, J. (2006) *Realizing 'Never Again': Regional Capacities to Protect Civilians in Violent Conflicts*, Washington, DC: The Fund for Peace.

Tardy, T. (2006) "The EU and NATO as Peacekeepers: Open Cooperation *versus* Implicit Competition," in H. Ojanen (ed.) *Peacekeeping – Peacebuilding: Preparing for the Future*, Helsinki: The Finnish Institute of International Affairs.

Tesón, F. R. (1997) *Humanitarian Intervention: An Inquiry into Law and Morality*, 2nd edn, Irvington-on-Hudson, NY: Transnational.

——. (2003) "The Liberal Case for Humanitarian Intervention," in J. L. Holzgrefe and R. Keohane (eds) *Humanitarian Intervention: Ethical, Legal and Political Dilemmas*, Cambridge: Cambridge University Press.

——. (2005) "Ending Tyranny in Iraq," *Ethics & International Affairs* vol. 19, no. 2: 1–20.

Thakur, R. (2003) "UN Peace Operations and US Unilateralism and Multilateralism," in D. Malone and Y. F. Khong (eds) *Unilateralism and US Foreign Policy: International Perspectives*, London: Lynne Rienner Publishers.

——. (2004) "Iraq and the Responsibility to Protect," *Behind the Headlines*, vol. 62, no. 1: 1–16.

——. (2005) "Freedom from Fear: Effective, Efficient, and Equitable Security," in P. Heinbecker and P. Goff (eds) *Irrelevant or Indispensable? The United Nations in the 21st Century*, Waterloo, ON: Wilfrid Laurier University Press.

——. (2006) *The United Nations, Peace and Security: From Collective Security to the Responsibility to Protect*, Cambridge: Cambridge University Press.

——. (2007) "Humanitarian Intervention," in T. Weiss and S. Daws (eds) *The Oxford Handbook on the United Nations*, Oxford: Oxford University Press: 387–403.

——. (2008a) "Should the UN Invoke the "Responsibility to Protect?" *Globe and Mail*, 8 May.

——. (2008b) "Towards a Less Imperfect State of the World: The Gulf Between North and South," Friedrich Ebert Stiftung Briefing Paper 4, Friedrich Ebert Stiftung (FES), April.

——. (2009) "Ban a Champion of UN's Role to Protect," *Asia News*, 10 March.

Thakur, R., Cooper, A. and English, J. (eds) (2005) *International Commissions and the Power of Ideas*, New York: United Nations University Press.

Thakur, R. and Weiss, T. G. (2009) "R2P: From Idea to Norm—and Action?" *Global Responsibility to Protect*, vol. 1, no. 1: 22–53.

Tharoor, S. and Daws, S. (2001) "Humanitarian Intervention: Getting Past the Reefs," *World Policy Journal*, vol. XVIII, no. 2.

Thompson, H. (2006) "The Case for External Sovereignty," *European Journal of International Relations*, vol. 12, no. 2: 251–274.

Traub, J. (2006) *The Best Intentions: Kofi Annan and the UN in the Era of American World Power* (New York: Picador).

Tuck, R. (1979) *Natural Rights Theories, their Origin and Development*, Cambridge: Cambridge University Press.

United Nations (1948) *Universal Declaration of Human Rights*, General Assembly resolution 217 A (III), 10 December.

——. (1992) "An Agenda for Peace: Preventative Diplomacy, Peacemaking, and Peacekeeping," A/24/277-S/2411, 17 June.

——. (1996) Office of the High Commissioner for Human Rights (OHCHR). Fact Sheet

No. 2 (Rev.1), The International Bill of Human Rights, "Worldwide influence of the International Bill of Human Rights," June.
——. (1998) "Report of the Secretary-General to the Security Council on the Situation in Africa," S/1998/318, 13 April.
——. (1999a) "Annual Report of the Secretary-General to the General Assembly," SG/SM/7136 GA/9596, 20 September.
——. (1999b) Security Council, Report of the Secretary-General to the Security Council on the Protection of Civilians in Armed Conflict, S/1999/957, 8 September.
——. (2000a) "'We the Peoples': The Role of the United Nations in the 21st Century," Millenium Report of the Secretary-General of the United Nations (A/54/2000), 27 March.
——. (2000b). "Report of the Panel on United Nations Peace Operations," (The Branimi Report) A/55/305-S/2000/809, 21 August.
——. (2001) "Draft Articles on Responsibility of States for Internationally Wrongful Acts," in International Law Commission, Report of the International Law Commission on the Work of Its Fifty-third Session, UN A/56/10.
——. (2002a) "Aide-Mémoire," Attached as Annex to UN Security Council Presidential Statement, S/PRST/2002/6.
——. (2002b) Security Council, "Statement by the President of the Security Council," S/PRST/2002/41, 20 December.
——. (2003a) Security Council, "Statement by the President of the Security Council," S/PRST/2003/27, 15 December.
——. (2003b) Department of Peacekeeping Operations, Handbook on United Nations Multidimensional Peacekeeping Operations.
——. (2004a) High-Level Panel on Threats, Challenges and Change, "A More Secure World: Our Shared Responsibility," A/59/565, 2 December.
——. (2004b) Office for the Coordination of Humanitarian Affairs (OCHA), "Sudan: A Future without War?," Report by Jan Egeland, April.
——. (2005a) General Assembly, "2005 World Summit Outcome Document: Resolution," A/RES/60/1, 24 October.
——. (2005b) "Report of the Secretary-General on U.N. Assistance to the A.U. Mission in the Sudan," General/S/2005/285, 3 May.
——. (2005c) UN Security Council resolution 1590, S/RES/1590, 24 March.
——. (2006a) UN General Assembly resolution A/RES/60/251, New York, 3 April.
——. (2008) Department of Peacekeeping Operations and Department of Field Support. "United Nations Peacekeeping Operations: Principles and Guidelines."
——. (2009a) "Implementing the Responsibility to Protect," Report of the UN Secretary-General, Ban Ki-moon, A/63/677, 12 January.
——. (2009b) General Assembly, Report of the Special Committee on Peacekeeping Operations and its Working Group, A/63/19, 24 March.
——. (2009c) "Secretary-General Welcomes Adoption of Text on Responsibility to Protect," SG/SM/12452, GA/10855, Press Release, 14 September.
——. (2010) General Assembly, Report of the Special Committee on Peacekeeping Operations A/64/19.
United Nations News (1999) "The Secretary-General Presents His Annual Report to the General Assembly," Press Release, UN Document SG/SM/7136-GA/9596, 20 September.
——. (2005) Press Release SG/SM/10000, SC/8444, 12 July.
——. (2006a) Jan Egeland, "UN's Top Humanitarian Official Warns of Looming Catastrophe in Darfur," 28 August.

——. (2006b) "Ban Ki-moon appointed next UN Secretary-General by Acclamation," 14 October.
——. (2008a) "Rwanda: Ban Ki-Moon Says World Must Protect Civilians from Genocide," 29 January.
——. (2008b) "Darfur: Stepped Up Attacks on Food Trucks Could Shut Down Deliveries, UN Warns," 7 September.
——. (2008c) "UN Genocide Adviser Urges End to Violence in Kenya, Sends Staffer There," 28 January.
——. (2009a) "Ban Calls for Three-Pronged Strategy to Implement the Responsibility to Protect," 21 July.
United States (2006) "The National Security Strategy of the United States of America," White House, March.
——. (2010) "The National Security Strategy of the United States of America," White House, May.
Urquhart, B. (2000) "In the Name of Humanity," *New York Review of Books*, vol. XLVII, no. 7, 27 April: 19–22.
Vernon, R. (2006) "Compatriot Preference: Is There a Case?" *Politics and Ethics Review*, vol. 2: 1–18.
Vincent, R. J. (1986) *Human Rights and International Relations*, Cambridge: Cambridge University Press.
Voon, T. (2004) "Legitimacy and Lawfulness of Humanitarian Intervention," in M. Davis, W. Dietrich, B. Scholdan and D. Sepp (eds) *International Intervention in the Post-Cold War World: Moral Responsibility and Power Politics*, London: M. E. Sharpe.
Ward, O. (2006) "Peace Operations on Crisis," *Toronto Star*, 25 September.
Warner, D. (2003) "The Responsibility to Protect and Irresponsible, Cynical Engagement," *Millennium: Journal of International Studies*, vol. 32, no. 1: 109–121.
Walzer, M. (1977) *Just and Unjust Wars: A Moral Argument with Historical Illustrations*, New York: Basic Books Inc.
——. (1993) *Interpretation and Social Criticism*, Cambridge: Harvard University Press.
——. (2000) *Just and Unjust Wars: A Moral Argument with Historical Illustrations*, 3rd edn, New York: Basic Books.
Weir, E. (2009) "Greater Expectations: UN Peacekeeping and Civilian Protection," Refugees International Report, July.
Weiss, T. G. (ed.) (1998) *Beyond UN Subcontracting: Task Sharing with Regional Security Arrangements and Service-Providing NGOs*, London: Macmillan Press.
——. (1999) "Principles, Politics, and Humanitarian Action," *Ethics and International Affairs*, vol. 13.
——. (2003) "Principles, Politics, and Humanitarian Action," in A. F. Lang, Jr (ed.) *Just Intervention*, Washington, DC: Georgetown University Press.
——. (2004a) "The Sunset of Humanitarian Intervention? The Responsibility to Protect in a Unipolar Era," *Security Dialogue*, vol. 35, no. 2: 135–153.
——. (2004b) "The Humanitarian Impulse," in D. Malone (ed.) *The UN Security Council: From the Cold War to the 21st Century*, Boulder, CO: Lynne Rienner.
——. (2005a) *Military–Civilian Interactions: Humanitarian Crises and the Responsibility to Protect*, Oxford: Rowman & Littlefield Publishers.
——. (2005b) "Cosmopolitan Force and the Responsibility to Protect," *International Relations*, Special Issue: Roundtable: Humanitarian Intervention after 9/11, vol. 19, no. 2: 211–250.

——. (2007) *Humanitarian Intervention: Ideas in Action*, Cambridge: Polity Press.

——. (2010) "Halting Atrocities in Kenya: Acting Sooner Rather than Later," *Great Decisions 2010*, New York: Foreign Policy Association.

Weiss, T. G. and Hubert, D. (2001) "The Responsibility to Protect: Research, Bibliography, Background," Supplementary Volume to the Report of the International Commission on Intervention and State Sovereignty, Ottawa: International Development Research Centre.

Weiss, T. G., Carayannis, T., Emmerij, L., and Jolly, R. (2005) *UN Voices: The Struggle for Development and Social Justice*, Bloomington: Indiana University Press.

Weiss, T. G. and Korn, D. A. (2006) *Internal Displacement: Conceptualization and Its Consequences*, London: Routledge.

Welsh, J. (2002) "From Right to Responsibility: Humanitarian Intervention and International Society," *Global Governance*, vol. 8: 503–519.

——. (2004a) "Authorizing Humanitarian Intervention," In R. Price and M. Zacher (eds) *The United Nations and Global Security*, New York: Palgrave Macmillan.

——. (2004b) "Taking Consequences Seriously: Objections to Humanitarian Intervention," in J. Welsh (ed.) *Humanitarian Intervention and International Relations*, Oxford: Oxford University Press.

——. (2004c) "Conclusion: Humanitarian Intervention after 11 September," in J. Welsh (ed.) *Humanitarian Intervention and International Relations*, Oxford: Oxford University Press.

Welsh, J. (2010) "Turning Words into Deeds? The Implementation of the 'Responsibility to Protect'," *Global Responsibility to Protect*, vol. 2, nos 1–2: 149–154.

Wendt, A. (1999) *Social Theory of International Politics*, Cambridge: Cambridge University Press.

Werner, W. G. and de Wilde, J. H. (2001) "The Endurance of Sovereignty," *The European Journal of International Relations*, vol. 7, no. 3: 283–313.

Wheeler, N. J. (2000) *Saving Strangers: Humanitarian Intervention in International Society*, Oxford: Oxford University Press.

——. (2003) "Humanitarian Intervention after September 11, 2001," in A. F. Lang, Jr (ed.) *Just Intervention*, Washington, DC: Georgetown University Press.

——. (2005a) "A Victory for Common Humanity? The Responsibility to Protect after the 2005 World Summit," Paper presented at the conference "The UN at Sixty: Celebration or Wake?," Faculty of Law, University of Toronto, 6–7 October.

——. (2005b) "Legitimating Humanitarian Intervention: A Reply to Farer's Five-part Test," *International Relations*, vol. 19, no. 2: 237–242.

Wheeler, V. and Harmer, A. (eds) (2006) *Resetting the Rules of Engagement: Trends and Issues in Military-Humanitarian Relations*, Humanitarian Policy Group, Overseas Development Institute Report 21, London: Humanitarian Policy Group.

Williams, P. D. (2006) "Military Responses to Mass Killing: The African Union Mission in Sudan," *International Peacekeeping*, vol. 13, no. 2: 168–183.

Williams, P. D. and Bellamy, A. (2005) "The Responsibility to Protect and the Crisis in Darfur," *Security Dialogue*, vol. 36, no. 1: 27–47.

Wills, S. (2009) *Protecting Civilians: The Obligations of* Peacekeepers, Oxford: Oxford University Press.

Zajadlo, J. (2005) "Legality and Legitimization of Humanitarian Intervention," *American Behavioral Scientist*, vol. 48, no. 6.

Index

For Product Safety Concerns and Information please contact our EU representative GPSR@taylorandfrancis.com
Taylor & Francis Verlag GmbH, Kaufingerstraße 24, 80331 München, Germany

www.ingramcontent.com/pod-product-compliance
Ingram Content Group UK Ltd.
Pitfield, Milton Keynes, MK11 3LW, UK
UKHW020155250926
475702UK00038B/1726
9780415532440